Macmillan Business Masters

Management

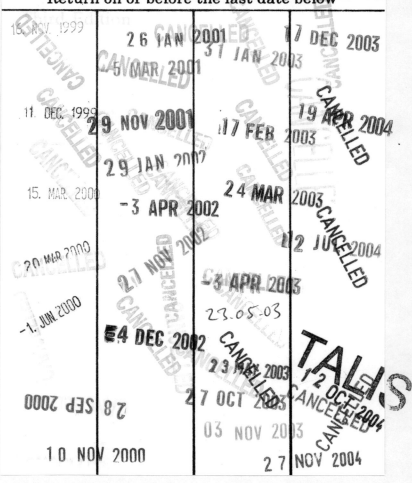

Macmillan Business Masters

Company Accounts   Roger Oldcorn
Management   Roger Oldcorn
Marketing   Geoff Lancaster and Paul Reynolds
Operations Management   Howard Barnett
Personnel Management   Margaret Attwood and Stuart Dimmock

Management

Third Edition

Roger Oldcorn

First published by Pan Books Ltd in 1982 as
Management: A Fresh Approach in the Breakthrough series
Second edition 1989
Third edition 1996

Published by
MACMILLAN PRESS LTD
Houndmills, Basingstoke, Hampshire RG21 6XS
and London
Companies and representatives
throughout the world

ISBN 0–333–59360–X

A catalogue record for this book is available
from the British Library.

10   9   8   7   6   5   4   3   2   1
05 04 03 02 01 00 99 98 97 96

Typeset in Great Britain by
Aarontype Limited
Easton, Bristol

Printed and bound in Great Britain by
TJ Press (Padstow) Ltd
Cornwall

Contents

Introduction

In that classic book *Mrs Beeton's Cookery and Household Management* the introduction to the first edition states: 'What moved me in the first instance to attempt a work like this was the discomfort and suffering which I have seen brought upon men and women by household mis-management.'

It is sad to have to report that, well over a hundred years later, mismanagement in all walks of life is still causing an excessive amount of discomfort and, sometimes, suffering. Fortunately the scene is not all bad; much good management can be found these days and a great deal of good thinking about it is taking place. The aim of this book is, therefore, to help along the process of improving the quality of management by introducing the reader to those aspects of management which have come to be regarded as good ideas or good practical advice.

This book is intended for use, first, as an introductory textbook by students who are just embarking on a course of study in management. Hopefully it will provide enough insights into the many aspects of the subject for them to be encouraged to develop their interest in it.

The book is also intended for use by practising managers (or would-be managers) who have not had the benefit of much formal management training outside their own areas of expertise. The book is offered with the message: You are not alone with your problems; others have faced similar problems and been successful. Here are ideas, thoughts and practices that can help.

To the teacher of management a special word or two needs to be said. First, the world of the practical manager is in danger of becoming too far removed from the world of management theory. Having seen management from both sides, I deplore this division. It seems to me to be very wrong for the practical manager to regard theory as a waste of time and energy. Yet the view is often expressed that 'when you are up to your waist in alligators, there isn't time to study a map of the swamp'.

The opposing end is the cynical view of the practical manager provided by the management theorist as 'out of date, out of touch, managing by the seat of the pants and gloriously inept'.

Both extreme points of view are untenable and this book tries to bridge the gap, showing how and where theory can help improve managerial effectiveness.

Two limitations have emerged in writing this book. First, although management is a universal activity, present in all organisations from the smallest shop to the largest corporation, and from the public service to the private sector, it is impossible to discuss in detail aspects of the management in all types of organisation. Second, space also limits the amount of text related to specific management techniques, and in this connection the use of 'information technology' and the management of information has had to be limited.

The scope of management as a subject is nowadays so wide that deciding what should be included and how much stress to put on each topic was a major issue in the early days of writing. No doubt there are some who would prefer more or less of this or that, but in the end the balance I have chosen is how I see it. This does not make any other opinion wrong; that is the good thing about management – there is always room for another view.

Introduction to the Professional Masters edition

In the six years since this book was first planned there has been a rash of books that have taken a look at the world of the manager from a different perspective than hitherto.

The emphasis now is on describing successful or 'winning' organisations and providing useful lessons to all managers who are striving for excellence. Unfortunately they make it sound easy, whereas the message that this book implies is this: that to be a successful manager today requires a great deal of effort – especially thinking! Therefore the temptation to go overboard with references to super-companies has been resisted except in the final chapter.

Other changes in this edition are either cosmetic or to bring the statistics up to date, and to incorporate the section of 'Policy' within the overall heading of 'Getting organised'.

Again, it is a matter of regret that insufficient space has been devoted to management in local and central government. However the principles are largely universal and I trust that managers outside the commercial sector – whose problems often dwarf those of business managers – will be able to relate most of the ideas in this book to their own environment.

Introduction to the third edition

A few months after the first edition of this book was published, I checked a university's microfiche catalogue to see if this book was on their shelves. Happily it was, but the next entry after OLDCORN, Roger was 'OLDE TALES NEWLY TAUGHT', which gave me pause for thought as well as some amusement. It is fair comment that this book contains masses of information on what others have written, said and researched about management. In some sense, therefore, the book is telling old tales again, but on closer inspection it becomes apparent that the stories I have related are themselves repeats and re-runs of even older tales. In management, there is very little that is genuinely new – what happens is that most of us miss some of what is, or has been, written on the subject. So a trawl from time to time is no bad thing.

Moreover, if we go back far enough and study the wisdom of the ages, management is about common sense and learning from the experience of others. These days, many of these conventional wisdoms cannot be taken at face value, but have to be researched and proved to have validity and there is no doubt that it is indeed comforting to know that one's beliefs and views can be supported by objective evidence.

So we find such gurus as Henry Mintzberg in his latest book, *The Rise and Fall of Strategic Planning*, making out that something is missing, that somehow we've got it wrong and that there is too much rationality in managerial activity. He believes that intuition should play a much greater role than it does. If he is right nobody would have made money during the 1991–2 recession, although maybe everyone would have made more. Agreed, intuition and gut-feel have a place in management, but unless these come out of knowledge and experience (of others as much as oneself) then you won't get good results in the long run.

I hope that this book is more than just a story-telling exercise, but a comprehensive, if superficial introduction to management. What managers should do, how they should behave, how they should operate – it's all well-documented – but making it happen still isn't easy. What is different from 1980 when this book was originally conceived is the world in which we live; no more cold war, global markets a real possibility, the opening up of Africa, China, India and Russia, information technology, global transferability of money, hands-off governments with less money to give away, to name just a few. So managers have to be more and more efficient to justify their existence. There are no guaranteed jobs any more – just as you cannot guarantee that yesterday's success story will be tomorrow's success as well, nor what you are selling today will be demanded tomorrow. Managers have to be multi-talented and the best will be those who have taken the trouble to learn. Here's a start.

How to use this book

Throughout the book you will find questions which you are encouraged to answer before reading on. There are three types of question:

Self-checks. Usually short questions requiring quick answers. They either help to prepare you for the text which follows, or they provide a means for you to test for yourself whether you have understood a particular principle or technique. Answers almost invariably follow directly after the questions.

It is obviously best for you to try to answer the question before reading on, but, whether you think you've got it right or wrong, read the answer before moving on to the next topic. If you have somehow made a mistake, the answer will usually tell you where you might have gone wrong.

You can, of course, 'cheat' and read the whole book from beginning to end without attempting to answer the questions at all. But if you do, there is only one person you are cheating. Guess who?

Reviews. Similar to the self-checks in purpose, but usually placed at the end of a chapter or at the end of a section, and intended to review your understanding of several principles or techniques.

Activities. Again, designed to test your understanding of the text, but they usually ask you to use some information which you will not find in the text. To answer these questions you have to use your own experience or discover some fresh facts for yourself. Sometimes an activity is simply an opportunity for you to stop and think about an important point raised in the text.

Acknowledgements

Many people have contributed to the writing of this book. First there are the many writers whose names have been quoted in the text; without these there would be no form to the subject. (Details of writers and books cited will be found in the section Further Reading on page 306). Second, and more important, are the many managers (good and bad) I have met over the years in large and small organisations. There have been very few really poor managers, and not all that many really good ones either. Most have been hard-working and conscientious, but it has been possible to learn from them all. Third, are the colleagues past and present who have provided many of the ideas in the book, verified or questioned many of the points mentioned and who have provided the stimulus to keep on writing. Those who have helped are too numerous to name; they know who they are. Fourth, the task would have been immensely difficult if it had not been for the efforts of Wendy Green in turning my scribble into meaningful text originally and to Margaret Bushill for putting this new edition on to disk. And finally, without the encouragement and enthusiastic support of my wife Dorothy there would have been no book at all.

ROGER OLDCORN

Note: The author and publishers wish to thank H. P. Bulmer plc for giving permission to reproduce its Company Objectives statement.

Part I

A Starting Point

1 Who Are the Managers and What Do They Do?

The aims of this chapter are to help you develop an understanding of what makes a manager different and how the job of management can cover many different tasks and responsibilities.

By the end of the chapter you will be able to define a 'manager', identify the main tasks and responsibilities of management, and classify the main functions of management.

Once upon a time, my Uncle James ran a shoe shop. It was a large shoe shop, situated in the main shopping street of a big town. The shop itself was a part of a chain of shoe shops which stretch across Britain. Uncle James did not own the shop, he was simply put in charge of it by the owners who gave him the title 'manager' so that he would be identified as the man in charge.

At first James thought that his job was to sell shoes, but he soon learned that selling shoes was merely a means to an end – the end being to make a profit. In fact he used to say that his job was exactly the same as the job of the top managers of the biggest firms in the country – the only differences were in size and in the number of people to help him do his job. Uncle James had only the sales assistants and an assistant manager working for him, whereas the top manager of a big company could afford to employ all kinds of people to do many of the tasks carried out by Uncle James himself. He used to describe himself as a very busy businessman whose job was to make sure that the shop made a profit – and more profit this year than in the previous year. 'It's all very well saying that your job is to make a profit,' I said to him one day, 'but that does not tell me anything about what you actually do all day in the shop. How do you make sure the shop makes money?'

Uncle James described his job like this: 'Every day I have to make sure the shop is open on time and that it is clean and tidy and that it looks inviting. I also have to ensure that the staff are clean and tidy too and are in a reasonably good mood. I have to answer the telephone and deal with customer complaints. I have to schedule the times when staff go on holiday and to lunch so there is always someone available to serve customers. Every day I take money to the bank and check the amount against the total in the tills' tally rolls.

'My assistant fills in all the forms under my guidance, sent in by head office. I supervise window-dressing weekly and make sure all repairs and maintenance are carried out quickly and properly. If I want to make major alterations to the shop I have to seek head-office approval – and to be sure of getting the approval I have to argue my case well and that means a bit of preparation. It's the same thing if I want to hire extra staff or even fire someone. I also have the task of deciding what styles to order from the warehouse and how many to order of each style and size. Finally, I have to read all the paper that comes in. A lot of it is from head office – telling me what I can and cannot do – and some of it is really important like the weekly accounting report that shows our turnover and profit; it tells me how I'm doing and keeps us all on our toes.'

Self-check

It is not difficult to see why Uncle James sees himself as a busy businessman. It is, however, a lot more difficult to see why he is called a manager. What is so special about his job that gives him the title 'manager'.?

Below, Uncle James's tasks are listed. Tick those jobs which seem to you to be 'management' jobs. As a clue, it is not a management task if it could be done by anybody. (Ten minutes.)

UNCLE JAMES'S TASKS

	√ *If a managerial job*
1 Open shop on time.	
2 Ensure shop clean and inviting.	
3 Ensure staff look good.	
4 Staff morale.	
5 Telephone.	
6 Customer complaints.	
7 Staff working times.	
8 Check cash in tills.	
9 Bank money.	
10 Guide assistant	
11 Supervise window-dressing.	
12 Shop repairs and maintenance	
13 Ideas for improvement.	
14 Decide on hire and fire of staff.	
15 Ordering supplies.	
16 Deciding quantities and styles to order.	
17 Read correspondence.	

18 Act on correspondence.
19 Look at weekly profit statement.
20 Do something if 19 not good enough.

If you put a tick against all these tasks, indicating that they are all managerial jobs, you would be right, but only in one sense, namely that as a manager Uncle James was responsible for seeing that all these things happened. However, quite a number of the jobs could have been carried out by any of the staff of the shop – Uncle James merely needed to delegate the tasks. In other words, get someone else to do it. On the other hand there were some jobs which only he could do and these are 3 and 4 (staff looks and morale), probably 8 and 9 (money), 10 (guide assistant), 13 (ideas), 14 (staff hire and fire decisions), 16 (decisions on ordering) and 20 (do something if profits too low).

Some of the jobs fall into the 'don't want to but no choice' category – like 5 (telephone), 17, 18 and 19 (correspondence). Others are in a category 'don't have to but like to' – like 6 (customer complaints), 11 (window-dressing).

The remaining jobs could be done by anybody, because they do not need any judgement. For instance, to ensure that the shop opens on time is a straightforward job; it is the manager's responsibility, but he can easily get someone else to do it for him because no decisions are involved. On the other hand the problems of ordering quantities, styles and sizes of shoes require judgement, and decisions have to be taken which significantly affect the profit of the shop. That area is the manager's own. Similarly staff matters are tasks the manager has to handle himself; Uncle James was paid to make sure the staff worked efficiently and with enthusiasm. Have you ever been in a shoe shop (or any other shop for that matter) and been faced with sullen assistants? Who is responsible? The manager.

It is fairly easy to see that Uncle James was a manager: his title was 'Manager' and the nature of his job indicates that he had responsibilities of a managerial nature. There are many thousands of people in Britain called manager and generally speaking they are given the title because they, like Uncle James, have these special responsibilities. Many people, though, are managers even though they do not carry the title.

Is your local butcher a manager?
Is the Prime Minister a manager?
Is an army colonel a manager?
Is a bishop a manager?
Is a senior customs officer a manager?
Is the secretary-general of a trade union a manager?

The answer to all of these questions is 'yes', even though the names do not include the word 'manager'. There are many other words that can be used instead – 'executive', 'administrator', 'director' and 'officer' being among the most common. But the title does not matter – what is important is the nature of the manager's job.

Self-check

Which of the following jobs deserves the title 'manager'?

(a) The man who reads the electricity meter
(b) The man who runs your local pub.
(c) The producer of a television programme.
(d) An actor.
(e) A head teacher.
(f) A chief constable.
(g) A farmer.
(h) A lorry driver.

So the managers in the list are:

(b) The publican
(c) The TV producer
(e) Head teacher
(f) Chief constable
(g) Farmer

If we add to the list Uncle James, the manager of your local newspaper shop, the managing directors of the ten biggest companies in Britain and the people we mentioned at the top of this page then you get some idea of the range of jobs covered by the word 'manager'. All the jobs described differ widely from the skill point of view – farming, running a shop, running a multimillion-pound international business, controlling a team of teachers. Yet all can be described as managers because they all have managerial responsibilities like those that Uncle James carried. So what are these responsibilities and how do you know if your job carries them? Indeed we can go a bit further and ask the question, Is it possible to identify whether someone is a manager simply by finding out what his job consists of? The answer becomes clearer if you look at the jobs pages in the paper.

Activity

If a copy of a newspaper is handy turn to the jobs column and look at the adverts for managers. Try to identify the common threads, using Uncle James's job as a reference. Alternatively consider the following extracts from real advertisements that have appeared in the paper. Read them all twice before answering the questions

1 *Managing Director*:...highly effective communicator...effective resource manager, able to generate maximum returns from finite resources...strategic thinker with drive and enthusiasm.

2 *Assistant General Manager*:...to manage and control the various service sections of head office. Major elements of the job are industrial relations and in-company communications. Will also deputise for the General Manager.

3 *Research & Development Manager*:...to take over an existing successful R & D section and build it up to a department of about twenty scientists, responsible for carrying out projects worldwide. Will have to be a talented leader with entrepreneurial skills.

4 *Production Planning Manager*:...involves the programming of current production and its control using computer systems to monitor and record production activity. Will also advise the Production Director on means of expanding the facilities to meet future growth.

5 *Marketing Manager*:...you will plan all marketing activities, liaise with sister overseas firms, plan new product launch, gather market intelligence, control all promotional activities, assist in the development of corporate plans.

6 *Marketing Manager*:...responsibility will encompass all aspects of business development from the creation of marketing and advertising plans to the motivation and control of distributors in the field.

7 *Distribution Manager*:...you will have responsibility for the overall control of the warehousing and distribution in the UK. You will manage the resources to ensure the efficient delivery of products into stock locations and distribution to retail outlets.

8 *Personnel Manager*:...will have overall responsibility for all personnel functions with particular emphasis on industrial relations. Negotiating skills are essential together with an ability to react quickly to changing circumstances.

9 *Manager Production Control*:...wide-ranging responsibilities including devising monthly production plans, coordinating regular checks on stock levels, maintaining first-class communications between production and sales.

Self-check

(Spend not more than fifteen minutes on this and put your answer (or guess) inside the boxes.)

1 How many of the managers described above have people working for them? □

2 How many of the managers have to make decisions? □

3 How many have to spend a fairly high proportion of their time making plans? □

4 Six of the jobs described include the word 'control', including here
the 'production control manager'. Do you think the other three
managers also will be involved in 'controlling'?   ☐
5 How many of the managers, do you think, do not have to spend some
of their time each day talking to other people inside the organisation
(besides their boss and their own staff)?   ☐
6 How many do you think will have some financial responsibility?   ☐

If these nine job descriptions are a realistic sample of what management is
all about, there are some features which seem to crop up time and again.
The six items selected occur in all nine situations, with the possible exception
of the first. Here is an analysis of the six questions:

1 *Staff responsibilities*: six managers in total. They are:
the managing director (No. 1) (implicit in the description)
the assistant general manager (No. 2) (implicit)
the research and development manager (No. 3)
the second marketing manager (No. 6)
the distribution manager (No. 7) (implicit)
the personnel manager (No. 8) (implicit)

From the job descriptions, it is not at all clear whether the production
planning manager (No. 4), the first marketing manager (No. 5) and the
manager of production control (No. 9) actually have the staff of their own to
manage. We might guess that the marketing manager (No. 5) has such a big
job that some assistance would be needed, but it is far from clear. The other
two jobs give no indication of staff responsibilities at all.

2 *Making decisions*: all nine managers in total.
This particular question is the hardest to answer partly because the words
'decision-making' do not appear anywhere, nor do we really know enough
about their jobs. However, we can come to some conclusions on this by
reading between the lines. For instance all the managers with staff
responsibilities will have to take decisions about their staff. All the managers
responsible for seeing that something is done will have to make decisions.
'Ensure the efficient delivery of products' is the kind of responsibility that can
only be effective if a decision-making power is included.

    The only manager who appears to have little decision-making to do is the
manager of production control (No. 9), even though the description talks
about wide-ranging responsibilities (which actually means very little). The
only bit of the description to imply any decision-making is the words
'devising monthly production plans'. The fact that a production plan is
necessary at all suggests that production is not straightforward: that there
may be more than one way of achieving production. If there is more than one
way, then the manager has a choice, and if there is a choice then in choosing a
decision must be made.

Finally the word 'control', as we shall see later in the book, also indicates that decisions have to be made. The extensive use of the word in these descriptions tends to confirm that all the managers take decisions.

3 *Making plans*: all nine of the managers in total.
Several explicitly have to make, create or 'devise' plans and in the case of the managing director (No. 1) the words 'Strategic Thinker' signify substantial planning work. The ones where it is not obvious are the assistant general manager (No. 2) and the personnel manager (No. 8). However, these managers are responsible for some area of activity within the business, and as soon as someone gets that kind of responsibility then they have to do some planning.

4 *Control*: yes, all nine managers have to exercise control.
The four managers who do not have the word 'control' in the description of their jobs are the managing director, the research director, the research and development manager and the personnel manager. Again the job description of each of these four managers suggests that they have to 'control' some aspects of their sphere of responsibility. The word 'responsibility' is contained in each of these four managers' job descriptions and that word alone is enough to suggest that control is an integral part of the job of being responsible for something.

5 *No need to talk to colleagues*: not one of the nine.
They all have to talk, to communicate with all kinds of people – subordinates, bosses, colleagues, as well as people in other parts of the organisation who have to be talked to. Some of the nine are much more involved with communications than others and this can be seen from the descriptions of their duties, but it is rare for any manager to have no regular need to communicate 'sideways'.

6 *Financial responsibility*: all nine of the managers in total.
This is another hard question because the word 'finance' is not specifically mentioned. Perhaps the easiest way of answering the question is to ask another one – namely, do any of the managers have responsibility for part of the business that spends money? The answer undoubtedly is 'yes' in most cases. We know that most have staff working for them and of the two we could not be certain about (the production planning and production control managers) both probably spend money. The production planning manager is involved with computers and the production control manager's job makes it unlikely there is no financial responsibility.

These nine job descriptions all portray different managerial jobs. Yet even though the work may differ greatly there are common elements running through most, if not all, of the descriptions – even to the extent that the same words crop up again and again.

Some of the words quoted need special mentions; one of them is '*leader*', a word which suggests an army officer going into battle first and getting the troops to rally round and attack. In that sense the word might not be all that suitable for a modern manager inside a big civil organisation, although all managers have to be 'out in front' some of the time. 'Leading' in another sense means 'direct the movements of', and where a manager has staff responsibilities the role of leader becomes meaningful in this context and indeed a manager with responsibilities for materials or services may have to direct their movement too.

Another word used that is directly related to leading is '*motivate*'. It is interesting that only one of the nine uses this word, yet at least six or seven have staff responsibilities. Why is it not mentioned? Is it because it is not thought to be important? Or is it because it is assumed that it is automatically part of the job?

'Industrial relations' are two words that also seem to crop up from time to time and suggest an area of concern for some organisations. This again is associated with motivation and leadership and revolves around the whole question of people at work – a question to which we will return frequently.

Finally, a phrase used once, but of some importance: '*entrepreneurial skills*'. Entrepreneur is a word used by economists to describe people who are in overall control of business; people who decide how the different parts of the business shall be run, which to push and which to leave alone. Technically they are also the ones who risk their own money and other people's money by putting it into a business venture. In effect, the use in the example of the research and development manager means, 'Here is a business within our big business. You get on and run it as though it was your own.' The manager is being told to be a mini-managing director.

What emerges, then, from the nine job descriptions, is a composite picture of a managers' job. It seems to be one which involves a fair proportion of planning the activities for which they are responsible. It also involves keeping these activities under control. Many managers have staff responsibilities, have to motivate staff and guide them and sometimes get involved in industrial relations matters. Many have a concern for the financial element in their area of responsibility. All managers do appear to have two more things in common – they all have to take decisions and they all have to communicate with others apart from their boss and the people below them.

In addition to all these specifically managerial skills and functions, managers must be experts in their own chosen field – in operations, marketing, sales, computers, or as a lawyer, accountant or headteacher.

The answer to the original question, 'Who are the managers?' is, then, all those people whose work gives them these kinds of responsibilities.

Review

Go back to page 6 and look at the list of people we decided had 'managerial responsibilities'. Do you think that what their jobs consist of could be described in the same way we have described the job of the manager generally? Refer to the key words we have found, like plan, control, communicate, motivate and lead staff, financial responsibility and taking decisions.

1.1 Henri Fayol and the Job of Management

One of the first persons to sit down and try to work out what managers do (and what they should do) was a Frenchman called Henri Fayol. Fayol was a mining engineer who became managing director of an ailing coal mining firm and turned it into a highly successful coal and steel business. All this took place between 1888 and 1918, when he retired. In 1916, after many years thinking about the job of the manager, he published a small book called *General and Industrial Management*. Oddly enough, it was years before a translation appeared in English, even though it contains a great deal of wisdom and sense. Part of the book deals with the 'elements' or 'functions' of management, and Fayol identifies five such functions. They are:

- Planning
- Organising
- Command
- Co-ordination
- Control

It is important to appreciate what Fayol meant by these five functions:

- *Planning* is looking ahead and making provision for the future. Failure to plan signifies managerial incompetence.
- *Organising* is providing the business with everything it needs to operate (equipment, materials, finance, people) and includes management training as a key part in it.
- *Command* is how organising gets achieved; in a nutshell, it is directing subordinates.
- *Co-ordination* is harmonising activities for successful results.
- *Control* is making sure things happen the way they were planned.

The first and last functions – planning and control – are immediately recognisable from the analysis that has just been carried out, and indeed there tends to be less argument generally about these two functions than about the others.

Organising is, of course, similar to planning in that it is concerned with preparation for some future events. But whereas planning is the more glamorous activity of deciding on the overall future direction of the business, organisation is that tough, demanding business of putting together the elements in such a way that the overall plans succeed.

Command is seen as the function that actually makes things happen. It is really derived from military practice, and no doubt in Fayol's time all employees in organisations responded to command. The very word suggests 'ordering about' and has been the subject of a great deal of debate and argument. Fayol did not really intend it to be taken in a very narrow sense, but rather in the sense of making sure that things get done – the actual operations of the organisation. As a result, all kinds of substitute words have been used in its place – like 'direction' and (horribly) 'actuating'. In this book we shall use the phrase 'getting the job done' instead.

The fifth function of the management, in Fayol's view, is that of co-ordination. It is concerned with harmony, with making sure that all the bits work together and, like an orchestra under its conductor, play the same tune. This is the only function that does not seem easily to stand on its own and will be found to be part of planning, of organising, of control and the key to successful operations themselves.

1.2 Scientific Management

Although the ideas of Henri Fayol have been taken on board by many writers and practitioners of management in the last twenty-five to thirty years, earlier management theory depended for its main prop on the writings of an American engineer called Frederick W. Taylor. In his work at the Midvale Steel Company in Philadelphia (from 1884 he was the chief engineer), he tried to apply scientific and engineering principles to the work of people (in those days steelmaking was highly labour intensive). He decided that there was one best way to do things and he sought to find it. In 1911 he published his book *The Principles of Scientific Management*, which is concerned mainly with explaining how a scientific approach to work could reduce stress and wear and tear on people, at the same time improving output. Taylor was the original 'time and motion' man. In addition he stressed such factors as planning work, getting work organised and training staff, all as part of the responsibilities of management.

Since those days a vast amount has been written about what management is, what it should be and what it does, both in business and in the public service sector. Some of these writers will be introduced as appropriate during the detailed discussions to follow. Suffice it to say that the broad functions of planning, organising, doing the job and control have all been studied, researched and analysed extensively.

1.3 What Should Managers Do?

Taking the four functions of management just described, one of the most fascinating games to play is to try to calculate how managers should spend their time and how they actually do spend their time. In theory the most senior managers in an organisation should spend most of their time planning, some time organising, some controlling and very little actually doing the work.

In contrast, middle management's job is mainly concerned with organising and control, a little on planning and some actual work. At least, it sounds right.

'First-line' managers, finally are mainly concerned with control and doing the job, and only a very small proportion of their time should be spent planning and organising.

Diagrammatically, total time spent by managers could look like Figure 1.1.

Self check

Do you think these 'pictures' truly reflect what managers do?

Research carried out during the last twenty years or so has revealed some very interesting things about what managers actually do. It appears to be accurate that lower levels of management spend most of their time actually 'doing the job'. Middle and senior managers, it seems, spend far more time 'doing' than planning, organising and controlling. Moreover a great deal of

Fig 1.1   How managers spend their time

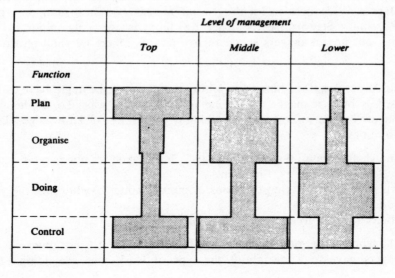

time is spent talking with people – at least three-quarters of it, by all accounts. The question is, what are they talking about? Let's return to Uncle James and his shoe shop for the answer.

Uncle James's job as manager could be classified in the terminology of Henri Fayol:

- Planning (ordering stock, dealing with staff leave and breaks).
- Organising (making sure the shop actually can work properly).
- Control (keeping his eye on things, people and money).
- Doing the job.

Another way of classifying his work would be in the way he does it, and Uncle James actually spends very little time reading and writing (in spite of what he says), and even less time thinking. The greatest part (over 80 per cent) is spent in verbal communication: talking!

A third way of classifying his work, and one which has gained some credibility lately, is based on the nature of the work being done. In Uncle James's case quite a chunk of his work is concerned with decision-making and gathering information to help him in that process (the decisions may be in the planning, organising, control or 'getting on with the job' stages).

More of his work is of a 'man in charge' status. All kinds of people (head office, customers and staff) talk to him because he is in charge – he is the boss of the outfit and, as far as the staff are concerned, the leader.

In addition his work involves a great deal of information-handling. He receives it, stores it in his head and passes it on. Some of it relates to decision-making, some may relate to his 'boss role', but a lot of it is just information which helps to get the job done better.

This kind of analysis has been developed by a number of people including Henry Mintzberg, whose book *The Nature of Managerial Work* (published by Harper, 1973) reveals a lot about what managers do. In Britain, the work of Rosemary Stewart (see 'Further Reading') is especially important in finding out how managers spend their time – a subject we shall return to later.

Uncle James described himself as a busy businessman; he might have called himself a busy manager, which he most certainly was. To do his job effectively he had to possess a remarkably wide range of knowledge, skills and abilities:

- Knowledge about the shoe industry, shoes, shoe retailing, retail shop matters, the company, the town.
- Skills relating to taking decisions, communicating, handling people and money, selling.
- Ability to plan, to control, to organise.

The whole range of activities seems formidable yet it is not unusual. All managers have to know about the type of work they are doing – the 'knowledge' aspects of the job. In addition there are all the skills and abilities. It does not seem possible that any one individual could be first-class at all these different activities – Uncle James certainly is not, nor is his boss, nor the managing director of his firm. Indeed out of all the hundreds of millions of managers in the world only a few could even be described as 'pretty good at most things'. These people are the heads, usually, of big and important organisations. For the rest, the aim must be to try to be as effective as possible in as many ways as possible. Ultimately it is the manager who is in charge, who is responsible for the success of the activities entrusted to him.

Review

Some of the words that have been used in this chapter to define what managers do are listed below. Read the list, then decide which of them are needed for success in the jobs listed on pages 6 and 7. (Fifteen minutes.)

communicate	keep things under control
plan	lead
make decisions	know about money
handle people	know about their trade or
organise	profession

It is fair to say that all nine characteristics listed above are needed for success in all the managerial jobs that were named. In fact all managers ought to have some skill in all (or most) of these features; sadly the average manager is well below this ideal.

Part II of this book looks at planning in some detail. Part III is about organising and contains something on money and other business functions. In Part IV you will find that the emphasis is on leadership, motivation and decision-making. Part V deals with control and Part VI looks at communications and other practical matters for improving the manager's effectiveness.

Part II

Preparing for the Future

The first task of managers is to make sure that the activities for which they are responsible are successful. This demands a lot of thinking about the future and action well in advance to make sure all goes well; in a word: PLANNING.

2 Setting Long-Term Aims and Objectives

By the end of this chapter you should be able to appreciate why it is important for every organisation to have aims and objectives, identify the main objectives to be found in organisations, and understand why different organisations have different aims and objectives.

Imagine what would happen if a visitor to London caught a bus which said on the front 'Piccadilly', but which said on the back 'Marble Arch'. Suppose that the conductor told you it was heading for Trafalgar Square and the passengers said they thought the bus was going to Euston Station. Obviously, sooner or later, the driver would have to be consulted, and he could do one of several things: stop the bus and tell everyone it was going to stay stopped until everyone agreed where it should go; or state 'I shall go where I want' – and go there, or set off on a trip round London dropping off passengers wherever they wanted to go.

Clearly none of the alternative courses of action is entirely satisfactory. In the end, whatever the driver did there would be a complaint from someone, and we have to ask ourselves the question, How could the situation have been avoided?

The keyword in the answer to the question is 'destination'.

The bus driver was placed in a rotten situation because the destination of the bus was not clearly defined at the outset. Before starting out the driver and conductor should have agreed the destination and put signs up on the bus to say so. It would also have helped if the conductor had stated where the bus was going before the passengers got on. The situation arose even though only one manager was involved (the driver of the bus). In many situations more than one manager is involved and so it takes even longer to arrive at a decision. It would be like two small boys in a rowing boat on a boating pond each with one oar; a lot of energy, noise and aggravation, but little progress of any significance.

These simple examples show that without some clear idea of destination things will not turn out well, and this is as true for any organisation as it is for a bus or a rowing boat. It should be possible to ask of any organisation,

Where is it going? Or, more accurately, What is the aim or purpose of this organisation? Unfortunately, the answer may not be as clearly stated as the question.

In one sense, however, all companies limited under the Companies Acts have their aims written down in what is usually referred to as the 'objects clause' in the firm's memorandum of association. The objects clause is a legal requirement and is constructed in such a way as to enable the company to do almost whatever it wants. Bearing in mind that the legal objectives of a company are established when the firm itself comes into being, it is quite likely that the words bear little relevance today for the company that is old-established.

Our concern here is with objectives that help the management of the organisation in its day-to-day running of the business. Clearly stated, objectives should provide the reference point around which all decisions affecting the future of the organisation can be taken. Without the objectives, the organisation is like the rowing boat full of little boys – except that nothing much is lost if the boys get nowhere, but an organisation which fails can be the cause of great hardship.

It is important to recognise that objectives may refer to something in the fairly near future or may be an expression of some wish that may take years to achieve (if ever). For instance, at the beginning of every football season the members, players and fans of every football club in the land will set out a whole series of objectives.

Self-check

What might the objectives of a football club be at the beginning of a new season? Think of a club near the top of the league on the one hand, and a school football team on the other. (Five minutes.)

The objectives will range from winning the first match of the season to winning the league title or some cup competition during the coming months. The more avid fans will dream of great success like winning the European Cup, and the manager will dream of being rich and famous because the club is rich and successful. For some clubs these dreams may be close at hand; for most, though, they are likely to be pipe-dreams only.

It is important to bear in mind that objectives can refer to the organisation as a whole. These are usually called 'corporate objectives'. However, each recognisable part of the organisation will also have its own objectives and these will be known as 'departmental', 'branch', 'project' or 'divisional' objectives, depending on how the organisation is split up. Finally, all the individuals in an organisation should have their own objectives (in relation to the organisation). Very often individuals' job descriptions are the only clues they get to their objectives, although some organisations provide each employee with a statement of 'duties and responsibilities' which is helpful and not just a vague statement to cover legal requirements. Objectives are often not clearly set out at any level in the organisation. It is, however, vital that all the objectives are explicitly set out and also that they all point in the same direction. For example, it is dangerous to have the buying department's objectives as 'to buy as cheaply as possible' while at the same time expecting the production department to have an objective which includes minimising waste. If this were the case the buyers would buy the cheapest materials on the market to satisfy their own objectives. In doing so they would possibly be buying materials at a quality too low for satisfactory production. This would lead to a high wastage level and the failure of production to meet its own objectives. Individual and departmental objectives have to be in line with each other and have to agree also with the overall objectives of the organisation.

What is needed therefore is a set of objectives for an organisation and its parts which are in harmony with each other: objectives which will guide the organisation's actions over a reasonable period of time. The key question to be answered is, What might reasonable corporate objectives be?

The answer to this question obviously depends on the organisation – its size and the nature of its activities. The more complex the organisation, the more difficult it is to come up with answers that have any real meaning. Even in the smallest, simplest organisation the answer to the question What are the objectives? is not necessarily as easy as it might seem. Take for instance the case of army officers retiring at the age of fifty who decide to go into business on their own. There will be a pension and a gratuity and they could afford to do nothing for the rest of their life if they invested the gratuity widely. Instead the gratuity is used to buy a small business – a pub, newsagent's shop or sub-post-office being among the favourites. Their reasons for going into business on their own usually start with a very strong desire not to rot quietly away in retirement. The second reason is an equally strong desire to be one's own master for a change, instead of living under strict rules, regulations and orders. From this point on the reasons tend to be financial, and while there are some who adopt a 'get rich quick' approach, the majority of people in these circumstances will have an aim that can be described like this:

> I want the business to be able to give me a lifestyle I should like to be accustomed to, and at the same time enable me to sell up in ten years' time having made my gratuity grow in real terms over the period (i.e. faster than inflation).

There is in this statement a potential conflict that all would-be small business owners have to guard against, namely that it is easy to take out of the business enough to give one a good living, but this may lead to starving the business of the funds it needs to grow and become of greater value.

It will be noticed that at this stage no mention has been made of the type of business the retiring officer wants to invest in. The reason appears to be that someone who goes through the rationalising process just described ends up choosing a business that is most likely to satisfy his requirements, irrespective of what the business might be. On the other hand there are some who enter a particular type of business because they have always had an ambition to do so. Many famous companies began in this way. Sainsbury's the supermarket chain began as a small grocer's shop in London's Drury Lane. The Beecham Group – world-famous for its pharmaceuticals as well as for Macleans toothpaste, Ribena and many other household products – began with Mr Beecham selling his pills in market places up and down the land.

So for the one-man operation there appears to be no problem; the owner/manager sets the objectives and these are fairly clear-cut and obvious. But what about in larger organisations? What are the objectives of a large company like ICI which has thousands of shareholders (who are legally the owners of the business)? The objectives we use for the small business cannot be suitable for the big firm, and in any case what about non-commercial organisations such as schools, hospitals, charities? What are their objectives?

Table 2.1 suggests some of the typical objectives that are quoted by organisations, and the ticks are intended to signify that the objective will be found in the type of organisation named across the top. The question-marks indicate 'possible' only, that may or may not be in the list depending on the organisation. Lines 8 to 10 can be used to insert any other objectives you may think of, and there is space in the right-hand column for noting those of your own organisation.

Table 2.1   Possible major objectives for different types of organisation

Objective	Charity	Hospital or school	Insurance company or building society	Paint manu- facturer	Your own organisation
1 Survive	✓	✓	✓	✓	
2 Provide a service	✓	✓	✓	✓	
3 Grow	✓		✓	✓	
4 Be big	?	?	?	?	
5 Be efficient	✓	✓	✓	✓	
6 Make a profit		?	✓	✓	
7 Be profitable		?	✓	✓	
8					
9					
10					

2.1 **Major Objectives Reviewed**

A brief comment on each of the objectives listed in the table above is worth making at this stage.

(1) Survive

Unless an organisation is set up with a specific task in mind, and is folded up on completion of that job, then it can fairly be assumed that all organisations (and indeed the parts of every organisation) want to survive. To be more specific, the individuals involved in the affairs of the unit or company do not want to see their jobs disappear (unless they are, Samson-like, deliberately planning self-destruction too). It is therefore a minimum requirement that organisations should survive, with no limits set on their lifespan. Generally, the threat of extinction concentrates management's mind, and that of all employees, more effectively than most other situations. It is worth reminding one's colleagues from time to time that, no matter how successfully everything is going now, something could be just around the corner to damage or destroy the set-up. This applies to departments or groups within organisations even more than it applies to whole outfits, and the event has to be avoided.

(2) Provide a service

This kind of objective is to be found mainly in non-commercial organisations, which do not have the yardstick of profit to consider but which are set up primarily for some social purpose. This is not to imply that they do not have to consider financial issues – indeed many social institutions are primarily concerned with money. However, money for such institutions is regarded as the means to the end – the end being effective performance of the service itself. In contrast, insurance companies and building societies all provide specific and valuable services to the community as a whole. The same is true of banks and many other organisations that provide professional or technical services, from estate agents to petrol stations. No doubt the services they provide are included in their objectives, but it is a matter of some debate as to whether they would regard 'provision of the service' as their primary objective.

Paint-makers, as a representative industry that is manufacturing useful products to many different end-users, are also providing a service by making available their products and satisfying certain requirements of the market. Again, the service provided can be an objective, but whether it is the main objective is the subject of a good deal of debate.

(3) Grow

Many organisations have an ambition to grow, but growth itself has little merit as an objective unless there is a clear idea of what it is that has to be grown. Many commercial organisations regard growth of the share of the market as a critically important objective. Others see a rise in market share as a means to achieving what they think are much more important objectives – growth in profits or profitability or in the size of the organisation.

For charities, growth in the amount of money available for distribution is a key objective, but the same cannot be said of the charity's own administration. Similarly the growth of the population of town halls and government departments should not be set down as an objective in such establishments – even though within them there are many managers engaged in 'empire-building'.

Growth is the objective of the ambitious and it can refer to the owner of a shop who wants to open another branch, or to the biggest firms in the world. Many large companies aim to make sales grow at least as fast as the growth in the economy of the country as a whole. The reasons for this kind of attitude are that real growth gives short-term tangible benefits in terms of profits. Everyone is kept busy and the psychological effect of being involved in a growing concern in a good feeling.

There is, however, a particular problem with growth which is contained in some ideas that have become popular since the first oil crisis of the 1973–4 period. The argument is known as 'zero growth' and makes the point that since natural resources are limited, it is important to conserve what is left and use it more efficiently. At the same time, deliberately preventing significant increases in wealth will help to slow down the arrival of the day when resources dry up. Although it is unlikely that many organisations are deliberately denying themselves the chance to grow, it is interesting to note that one survey (*Management Today*, June 1987) showed that over seventy of the 250 largest UK companies actually failed to achieve any real growth between 1977 and 1986. Also the losses sustained in the 1990–2 recession reduced the size of many firms.

It is also important to remember that many organisations have no desire to grow, particularly where ownership is in the hands of an individual family. There comes a point where to achieve any further growth in the business requires more money than can be raised or borrowed by the family. The only thing to do would be to offer outsiders shares in the firm and this would lead ultimately to the family not having a majority of the shares. Thus they would lose control of the firm. Effective control can also be lost if a business grows to the extent that the owner has to appoint, for the first time, managers and delegate some power and responsibility. Many owners do not want this to happen and prefer to stay small.

(4) Be big

To have an objective that includes being big automatically must also have growth in mind. Growth, then, becomes not an objective in itself, but a way in which the objective of size is to be achieved. There are several ways in which size can be measured.

- The value of external sales is popular since it does reflect the extent to which a company has penetrated the markets it is serving.
- The size of the firm's profits.
- The total value of the firm's assets (its land, buildings, machinery, stocks, investments, cash in the bank, and so on).
- The 'net worth' of the business (the value of assets less the amount borrowed; sometimes called equity capital).
- The 'market value' of the firm (only possible if the firm is quoted on the stock market. It is the value of the shares in total at a point in time).
- Other measures used are purely physical units – like the number of employees. Particular industries have their own favourite measures; the airlines use passenger miles, road haulage uses ton miles, and the paint industry will use gallons (or litres) of paint.

Finally, as regards being big, there are two major disadvantages. First, being large attracts a lot of attention, especially from groups who have legal, social or moral objections to such size. This includes the Monopolies Commission and from time to time (depending on the policies of the government in office) various prices control boards. Second, being large is no guarantee of survival or prosperity. Economists often write about 'economies of scale'. This means simply that if an operation is big, it can buy cheaper, make more efficiently and sell at lower cost than the smaller operator. These savings help the larger firm to make more profit and if this profit is used widely then the firm should have a better chance of survival than if it was small. Unfortunately the evidence does not always support this neat theory. Many large firms have failed to survive, many fail to make even modest levels of profit and many more will disappear before the end of the century. Size has a lot of disadvantages too.

(5) Be efficient

Efficiency is not usually regarded as the primary objective of organisations but rather as an ingredient used with other objectives. For instance, a charity may state that its primary objective is 'to collect and distribute money efficiently'; a building society's objective may also be 'to collect and distribute money efficiently'. Only two things need to be said about efficiency: first, no organisation, or part of an organisation, is 100 per cent efficient, and as there is always room for improvement, efficiency has to be built into objectives. Second, there is no point being efficient if nobody is interested in the results anyway. It is of no help to a maker of slide-rules that they are manufactured efficiently, when hardly anyone wants a slide-rule any more. The point was made vividly by Peter Drucker, the eminent American management consultant and author, in a talk he gave to the British Institute of Management in 1964. He said:

> I see 'efficiency' as being concerned to do things rightly – perhaps overlooking the fact that one is spending time and effort doing rightly and well things that ought not to be done at all! The people who spend considerable amounts of time and effort doing a little more efficiently what should not be done at all are the bane of my life.

If, however, efficiency is deliberately ignored then in effect *inefficiency* is being approved of and that cannot be good. It would appear that the requirement for a good objective is that it combined the need for efficiency with the need to do things right. Very often they are brought together under the specifically financial objectives of 'profit' and 'profitability'.

Activity

Take a few minutes off to consider this question: Do you know an efficient person or business that is doing something completely pointless?

(6) Make a profit

Profits can be made only when something is sold or hired out. Generally charities will not sell anything except maybe a little paper 'flag'. Similarly most hospitals and schools in Britain are not concerned with profits since they do not sell their services. The costs are met by the state, and if by chance they receive more than they spend, the surplus is not regarded as a profit but as a piece of good housekeeping. A private school and a private nursing home which charge fees are commercial undertakings and it is perfectly reasonable for them to have included the word 'profit' in their objectives. The important point about 'profit' is that failure to achieve it threatens the survival of any and every commercial undertaking.

The advantage of a financial objective, like profit, is that it can be turned into a number, and it is very easy to compare a number objective with the actual result – also expressed as a number. So if a company wants a profit of £1 million next year and only achieves £900 thousand, then it is easy for all to see that it has failed to achieve its objective. It should be noted here that when specific numbers are attached to objectives, as in this example, it is usual to refer to them as 'goals'. In other words they are specific targets to aim at.

Most companies include the word 'profit' in their statement of objectives. Unfortunately, on its own, profit is a meaningless statement because there are several different types of profit which can be very different in size, depending on whether such things as corporation tax have been included (for a more detailed explanation of this, see *Company Accounts* by Roger Oldcorn).

Profit measures are useful targets to aim at, but they do not lend themselves to comparison – mainly because inflation distorts the value of money over time. Moreover, to have as an objective 'to make a profit' is a bit simple: £1 would meet the objective. In the old days economists used to write that firms existed to maximise profit. The problems with this concept are that it is impossible to put a figure on it, it assumes a very short lifespan for the firm concerned and it fails to recognise that maximising profit one year could spoil the profits in the long run. To make an adequate profit is a better objective, but this leaves the problem of defining 'adequate', which is where the objective of profitability is helpful.

(7) Be profitable

If you put £100 into a building society for a year and receive interest of £10 at the end of the year, the return on your investment is 10 per cent. Similarly if you were a rich shipping magnate and spent £100 million on some new boats which brought in a profit of £10 million (after tax), your return on investment would be 10 per cent also. In both cases the equation can be called profitability; it is an expression of the successful use of the basic resources of the business – money and people. All businesses are the same in this respect: money is put in and used by people to obtain facilities, equipment and other resources which are used by people to produce and sell goods and services. The activities should yield a money surplus if the operation has been well run. If badly run, there is no surplus, no profit and ultimately the firm expires. To put £100 in and get £25 out each year is very different to only getting £2 out. Not only is the £2 result less profitable; the firm has been less efficient. The more we get out the more profitable we are. Precisely how to measure profitability is open to argument, and which is the best measure to use as an objective is also arguable. In America it is common to refer to 'earnings per share' (EPS) as the key criterion of a company ('earn-ings' being another word for profit after tax and interest payments have been deducted), and most companies will have this item quantified as a long-term objective. Many writers refer to 'return on investment' or 'return on capital employed' or 'return on equity' as the most suitable financial objective (usually abbreviated to ROI, ROCE or ROE). In Britain company accounts more often than not show earnings per share and often some other measure of profitability.

Activity

If a commercial organisation is very profitable, it can give the shareholders a good return on their investment and plough back a lot of money into the business. This enables it to grow and make more profits so it can give the shareholders an even better return on their investment, and so on.

The shareholders are therefore relatively well satisfied with the company. Is it enough just to have as a basic objective 'To satisfy the owners (shareholders)'?

The answer will depend on your own attitudes, beliefs and values, and in the same way the answer in an organisation depends on the attitudes, beliefs and values of the people setting the objectives. One expression which has grown in popularity during the 1990s is that the organisation's purpose is to add 'Shareholder Value' and all decisions have to be tested against that criterion.

So – organisations exist to satisfy whom?

Possibility 1 – the shareholders
This is the traditional view. The owners of the organisation invest (or really risk) their money in the business and, as long as they get a decent return, the company has fulfilled its purpose. This view is supported by reference to many clubs and societies – the local bowls club exists to satisfy its members and that is all.

Possibility 2 – the customers
As long as an organisation satisfies its customers then it has met its primary purpose. Certainly if it does not it will not survive for very long. Respectable organisations try to resist the image of the fly-by-night operator: the firm that sells a dud product and disappears. Moreover there is a tendency for firms to exercise a greater degree of responsibility in the goods and services they sell and the way they are sold.

Possibility 3 – the employees
Instead of regarding people as just another raw material to be exploited, many companies consider that trying to satisfy employees is a key aim. The equations are:

- Dissatisfied employees = low productivity, trouble, strikes.
- Satisfied employees = high productivity, peace, prosperity.

Contrast this with the Dickensian image of lower wages = higher profits for owners.

Possibility 4 – management
Managers are employees too, and also may be shareholders, and customers. The view is that because managers are the people with the power inside organisations (they make the decisions), they are the people who want to be

satisfied most. The organisation exists for them; not just 'top management' but all managers. John Kenneth Galbraith talks about the real control being in the hands of the 'technocrats' – those who have the skills and expertise within the organisation to be able to run it.

Possibility 5 – everyone involved

Why not try to satisfy everyone involved in the firm? Not just shareholders, managers, employees and customers, but the whole community whose lives are in one way or another affected by the organisation and its presence. The word 'stakeholder' has been used to describe all these different people, and there is a growing body of opinion to support the idea that organisations must seek to satisfy all the stakeholders.

Failure to keep any one group happy can lead to trouble. Avoiding trouble is a highly practical reason for trying to satisfy all the stakeholders, but there is a more powerful reason: that all organisations exist in society and must behave responsibly towards it. The suggestion is that they have a duty, beyond what is required by law or forced on them by pressure groups. To quote Peter Drucker again: 'the business enterprise has to add to its fundamental concern for the quantities of life (economic goods and services) a concern for the quality of life, for the physical, human and social environment of modern men and modern community'.

So there are two extremes:

- On one hand the objective is high profits to satisfy the shareholders – the other stakeholders and matters of social responsibility are factors which contribute to the main purpose.
- In contrast, the objective is to be socially responsible by satisfying all the stakeholders.

The argument is brilliantly set out as far as banks are concerned in the novel by Arthur Hailey, *The Money Changers* (Part 1, chapter 15). Two candidates for the presidency of an American bank each make a presentation to the board of directors of the bank in support of their claim. Both speak of the role of the bank, what it is and what it should be. However, one of the candidates states that profit is their principal objective, and they do not achieve maximum profit by becoming involved in various social issues such as loans to minority groups, housing projects, environmental matters. The other candidate, while reaffirming his own belief in profitability, goes on to assert that new standards are being demanded of industry and business so that the name of the game is 'corporate social responsibility'. In effect, the suggestion is that social responsibility is every bit as important as profit for the second speaker. Although this is a fictional debate, it is not untypical of the arguments that have been and are taking place in relation to commercial organisations generally.

Consider now three real comments.

2.2 **Three Views of Corporate Aims, Objectives and Responsibilities**

Three well-known British companies are quoted below. The statements have been made publicly in annual reports.

Tesco PLC

Tesco is committed to:

- offering customers the best value for money and the most competitive prices
- meeting the needs of customers by constantly seeking and acting on their opinions regarding product quality, choice, innovation, store facilities and service
- providing shareholders with outstanding returns on their investment
- improving profitability through investment in efficient stores and distribution depots, in productivity improvements and in new technology
- developing the talents of its people through sound management and training practices, while rewarding them fairly with equal opportunities for all
- working closely with suppliers to build long-term business relationships based on strict quality and price criteria
- participating in the formulation of national food industry policies on key issues such as health, nutrition, hygiene, safety and animal welfare
- supporting the well-being of the community and the protection of the environment.

(Statement of Corporate Objectives in Tesco's 1994 Annual Report and Accounts).

The Boots Company PLC

Our objective is to maximise the value of the company for the benefit of the shareholders. We will do so:

- by building on our position as one of the UK's leading retailers in our chosen markets.
- by investing in the research, development, manufacturing and marketing of innovative prescription pharmaceuticals, health and personal care products throughout the world.
- through enterprising development and management of our property assets.

While vigorously pursuing our commercial interests we will, at all times, seek to enhance our reputation as a well managed, ethical and socially responsible company.

Also in the Chairman's Statement:

Our decisions have fully reflected the principles of managing to maximise shareholder value which require us to evaluate every business and opportunity against the potential for long term shareholder return.

(Taken from Boots' Report and Accounts 1994).

H.P. Bulmer Holdings plc (Report and Accounts 1995)

Statement of Company Objectives

Our mission is to remain the world's most successful cider company. We will continue to measure our success in terms of market leadership, product quality, increasing shareholder value, and rewarding employment opportunities for our employees.

This will be achieved by attaining the following objectives:

1 Lead and grow the UK and International cider markets through meeting consumer needs by superior marketing and sustained high levels of customer service.

2 Maintain lowest industry costs and ensure the most economical supply of essential and quality raw materials.

3 Be dedicated to fulfilling the requirements of all our customers through achieving excellence in our products, operations and service.

4 Adopt best practice across all of our activities through an innovative approach to product, process development and information technology.

5 Foster a culture of continuous improvement through self-motivation, teamwork and acceptance of change.

6 Provide competitive pay, employee share ownership and single status employment while achieving a link between performance, reward and shareholder interests.

7 Give all employees the opportunity to develop skills and potential through actively improving their own and the company's performance. Promote from within whenever appropriate.

8 Keep employees informed of policy, plans and performance. Invite comments and feedback and, through employee involvement, show how individual and team efforts contribute towards the company's success.

9 Provide a high quality working environment taking all appropriate steps to ensure the health and safety of our employees, customers and the community.

10 Preserve the quality of life and environment in our everyday work and to benefit our local communities whenever an affordable opportunity arises.

Activity

- Do you think that the underlying purpose and aims of the three companies quoted above are similar?
- Does the list of objectives you drew up on page 22 bear any resemblance to the kind of words and phrases used in the three examples?

One question which remains to be answered is, Who sets the objectives? If we support the view that the shareholders (or owners) are the only beneficiary of a company then they set the objectives. If, however, we think that all the stakeholders have to be satisfied then presumably there has to be a consensus – everyone concerned has to agree on how the cake should be cut. This is really impossible; in practice it is top management that decides (whether 'top managers' are shareholders or not). Do you remember the bus without a destination at the start of the chapter? Who should decide where it goes – the driver, the owner, the passengers or everyone?

As we suggested, what top management sees as the objectives of the organisation depends on its values and beliefs. Non-commercial organisations often exist to be of service (as in a charity) or for the benefit of the members (as in a club or society).

Commercial concerns, especially if small, are often run for the benefit of the owner, with the other stakeholders and social responsibilities acting as constraints. Large firms these days recognise the need to look after many stakeholders, even though this can mean a lot of compromise. Also, social responsibility is increasingly being seen not as a constraint but as an aim in itself.

2.3 Final Words on Aims

Do not worry too much about the words which are being used when the talk is about aims and objectives, as long as you remember there are three levels:

- The general statement of aim – can be called purpose or mission.
- The precise things that are being aimed at – objectives themselves.
- The actual number being aimed at – the target or goal.

There is usually a major, or primary, objective and several supporting aims. Remember people have objectives too, and so should departments or parts of organisations, as well as organisations themselves.

Finally, aims and objectives, to have real meaning, must be specific, measurable, agreed, realistic, attainable, and be time-bound.

3 Analysing Strengths and Weaknesses

The aims of this chapter are to show why it is important to know what are the strong points and weak points in organisations. By the end of the chapter you should be able to identify the main areas in commercial and non-commercial organisations where weaknesses can lie and which can critically affect overall performance; you should also know how to go about finding them.

It is quite probable that within a mile or two of where you live a small business has closed down during the last year or so. The most likely small business to close is the corner grocery shop, but small cafés and restaurants, boutiques and petrol stations are all high on the list of failures these days.

Equally, it is probable that many other organisations near you – not only shops but clubs and societies too – may be teetering on the brink, and only the loyalty of the members or owners is keeping them going. How is the local Square Dance Society doing? History is full of examples of ventures of all kinds that have not been as successful as they should have been or as their founder members had hoped. In a sentence, they failed to meet their objectives.

On the other hand many ventures have been, or were, by any standards extremely successful. From Columbus to the Moon landings, from the East India Company to Shell Oil, all have managed to succeed, often against very high odds. Moreover there may well be a small business or society near you that is obviously successful.

The contrast between the successful and the unsuccessful is shown up in an interesting way if you have a look at the shops near you selling sweets, tobacco and papers, etc. There are hundreds of this type of shop often calling themselves newsagents but selling a huge range of products from ice cream to birthday cards and toys. Next time you go out play a game of 'spot the success story and spot the failure'. All you need to do is look at them and it becomes obvious: the success story is busy, the shelves are full, the window displays are interesting and you feel tempted to go in and look around. The failure is obvious too: quiet, dull and unappealing.

So what is it that makes some organisations successful and some unsuccessful? It may be that something has happened outside the organisation's control that has affected its activities adversely. For instance a shop could suddenly find that the goods it was selling had become illegal (or a tax increase doubled the price). Either way its prospects would be somewhat reduced through no fault of its own. These external influences on performance will be dealt with in Chapter 4. For now, our attention must be on factors within the organisation that are under its control and which have caused it to be successful or not. Usually these key factors are known as 'strengths and weaknesses', and it should be noted straight away that no organisation is entirely free of weaknesses, just as no organisation is entirely without any strong points. Even the biggest failure in the land has something to be said for it.

So the successful organisation is the one with a lot of strong points and only a few areas of weakness. If it wants to stay on top it has to concentrate on making sure it does not lose those areas of strength that are crucial to its success. Equally, the failure has many weaknesses and only a few strengths. If it wants to improve, it has to eliminate those areas of weakness. Moreover, looking into the future, if an organisation wants to develop, grow and prosper it has to build on its strong points; trying to build on weaknesses is reminiscent of the foolish man who built his house on the sand – he no doubt did very well until the rains came and washed the house away.

Strengths	*Weaknesses*
Maintain/build on	Cure/do not depend on

Activity

Think of a very successful organisation. It may be a company making well-known products or a shop that you use. It might be a football or cricket club or even an office within a firm. Having selected your success story try to think what its main *weakness* might be. (Five to ten minutes.)

Success stories usually do not have many weak points and often it is difficult to identify what these are. The following are among the most common.

Shortage of space or capacity

On the face of it, using space well is a strength. It is, though, a weakness because it limits the capacity of the business to grow. There are several successful football clubs who manage to have capacity attendances every time the first team plays at home. It is for them a real weakness that they cannot expand accommodation and so be even more successful. Similarly companies may also find themselves short of space, particularly if they want to expand sales in an area of the country. If they have only limited warehouse space, then it is useless having a super-efficient sales force because the sales could not get to the customer. The thoughtful manager will identify the weakness first and cure it before attempting to expand.

Another example of capacity being a weakness is where a firm's equipment is working flat-out. Clearly there is little point in having a huge advertising campaign designed to increase sales substantially if no more output could be obtained. First the weakness (i.e. not enough equipment) has to be cured.

Resources getting old

The main type of resources to be affected by age are people, buildings, and equipment. In any organisation, to have a very high proportion of old people is a weakness, not because they are old as such, but because if they all retire at once so much knowledge and experience will disappear overnight that the organisation is left considerably weaker. Ideally organisations have people of all ages in equal proportions at any one time or, some commentators think, a few young and a few old with most people in the middle.

A favourite exercise among personnel managers (if they ever get enough time) is to draw an 'age profile' chart of the organisation. Sometimes it is drawn for the managers only; this may produce a very different result to the general chart. An example of a chart of a company with a high proportion of younger people would look like Figure 3.1.

In terms of strengths and weaknesses it could be said that the 'age' of the organisation is a sign of reasonable strength. Its potential weakness would be if no new blood is brought in and that lump moves steadily towards the right-hand side.

Fig 3.1   Typical age distribution profile

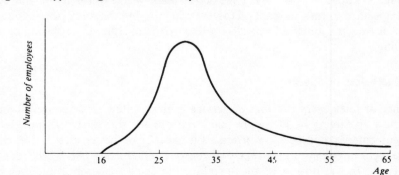

If the chart was that of a football club two weaknesses would be revealed: first, that no youngsters were coming along and, second, the bulk of the existing staff (roughly half about thirty years of age) were beginning to slow down.

Another way of looking at this is to ask yourself these questions:

- Would you fancy the English rugby XV's chances if the average age of the team was sixteen?
- Or if the average age was thirty-eight?
- Would you like to work in an office where everyone else was over sixty?
- Or everyone else was under twenty?

The factor of age is also important as far as buildings and equipment are concerned in assessing an organisation's strengths and weaknesses. An old building not only needs relatively high sums of money spent on it in repairs and maintenance, but it can also look poor. This is particularly relevant for establishments where the public in general have to go – shops, hospitals, public offices, pubs and restaurants – all are depressing places if they are not kept young (at least in appearance if nothing else). The only advantage in operating out of really old premises is that it is cheap (until it falls down, that is).

Old equipment is a weakness too. It is often less efficient, slower and the cost of fixing it rises continuously as its value diminishes with age. Possibly the biggest problem with old equipment, as anybody who has owned an old motorcar will agree, is that it gets unreliable and is likely to let you down at the worst possible moment.

Skill shortage

Even the most successful firms and organisations usually find that they do not possess people in all areas of the operation who have first-class skills. The easiest example to quote are football clubs: all of them would like to have eleven players with super skills, but nearly all of them have to put up with some good, some indifferent and some rather worse. Likewise, all managers would like to have a first-class team working for them, but the dream is hard to turn to reality. However, identifying the weak points is part of the manager's job and he has to try to cure them, either by replacing or by training.

Product's loss of appeal

Sooner or later every product or service ever invented loses its appeal and people stop buying it. There are many reasons for this: tastes change, new designs emerge, competition produces a cheaper or better alternative; but some seem to go on for ever (like strawberries and cream). This whole idea is embodied in the notion of the 'product life cycle', an important idea in assessing strengths and weaknesses. Many successful firms are in that position because their products are at their peak – in other words they are all highly popular. Unfortunately today's popular product (and personality) will be tomorrow's lame duck. So regard has to be paid to where products are in the cycle. Ideally they would all be at different stages of life, some just starting, some growing, some at maturity and some declining.

Money problems

Unfortunately, shortage of money seems to be a popular form of weakness these days in every kind of organisation, no matter how successful it might be. In fact it is surprising how short of money many companies are, which by all other criteria are doing extremely well. A shortage of money may arise in a successful firm if considerable investment has just been made in new facilities, equipment or stocks, or if a takeover has just been completed involving cash. It is, in this case, only a weakness to be short of money in the sense that the firm does not have the freedom to do what it would like for a while.

A shortage of money is far more serious if it is coupled with an inability to borrow or raise money in any other way, especially if the amount of money tied up in easily convertible resources is low (for example in stocks or in money owed by customers, i.e. debtors). In this case the weakness can be fatal, causing the business to fold up.

Wrong place

Once, Carlisle United Football Club were sitting on top of the First Division. To be there is undoubted success. Unfortunately the population in the area is not as big as around most of the other First Division clubs, so Carlisle could not get the support. They could not get the money they needed to stay at the top.

Companies too find themselves in the wrong place. A company in South London was selling its products throughout Britain with a great deal of success. It was distributing by road and the cost of shipping to the North was prohibitive. This company, unlike a football club, could at least move its premises or build a satellite depot nearer its markets.

Activity

Was there a business near you that closed down because it was in the wrong place?

The problem we posed back on page 34 was to identify a weakness in a successful organisation known to you. So far six have been suggested. They are:

- Shortage of space or capacity.
- Resources getting old (buildings, equipment or people).
- Shortage of skills.
- Products beginning to lose appeal.
- Money problems.
- In the wrong place.

If you identified a weakness not included in this list, then you may find it in the last part of this chapter, which is concerned with the sort of weakness more commonly found in unsuccessful organisations.

3.1 How to Identify Strengths and Weaknesses

Suppose that one Sunday morning you are chatting to your neighbour and you casually mention you have a touch of toothache. Before you know where you are, he has you tied to a chair in the kitchen and is pulling away on one of your teeth with a pair of pliers. Unless the neighbour happens to be a dentist who is completely up to date on the state of your teeth it is highly unlikely that such an event would actually take place. Why? For two reasons (at least). First, because no amateur would attempt to identify and remove another adult's tooth except in an emergency. Second, because before taking action so final as an extraction other ways would be examined to solve the problem.

It all seems obvious, yet when it comes to the problems of organisations, outsiders seem all too willing and ready to provide an instant diagnosis and an instant cure; especially for the 'favoured' targets of disdain like the National Health Service, British Rail, Woolworths, etc. 'The trouble with X (or the problem with Y) is that they... What they ought to do is...!

If the problem was *that* easy to identify and solve then there would be no problem! The first rule should therefore be obvious: no snap diagnosis, no instant cure. Instead a thorough analysis of all the factors is needed before any conclusions can be drawn, and this implies that it is every aspect of the organisation that has to be analysed.

A useful word here is 'audit', but not in the traditional sense of an examination of the accounts of a company to establish that the money side of the affairs is reflected correctly in them; rather, an audit in the wider sense, signifying a thorough examination of all the parts of the organisation.

It is, however, appropriate to begin with the accounting and statistical information of the organisation because using numbers helps to pinpoint more accurately relative strengths and weaknesses. For example, to say 'the managers are a bunch of old men' is not as believable as 'the average age of the managers is 63.2 years'. Similarly to say 'our distribution costs are too high' is only credible if the statement can be proved in numbers, like '25p per mile compared to the average for the industry of 18.5p per mile'.

To be really helpful, numbers need to be handled in a special way. It is of very little use to say, 'Last year the factory produced $2\frac{1}{2}$ million sausage rolls', because it is impossible to make any judgement about the number. It is better to compare the number with the previous year or with the competition: 'Last year we produced $2\frac{1}{2}$ million sausage rolls, almost 400 thousand more than in the previous year and more than any of our competitors.' Moreover if the object of the exercise is to assess such things as efficiency and productivity, it is even better to use percentages and other ratios like cost per hour and output per man: 'Last year we produced 52 thousand sausage rolls per man compared with only 42 thousand per man in the previous year.'

It is only when the numbers are used in this way that the manager can begin to make valid assessments of the strength or weakness of the different areas of the organisation. The above example is looking at productivity in a sausage-roll bakery and the conclusion that can be drawn from the data is that productivity has risen considerably – a sign of strength.

The important idea in all this is the need to compare and it is virtually impossible to draw any sensible conclusion about any bit of information unless it is compared.

Self-check

Read the following statements, then try to decide whether the information given signifies a strong point or a weak point for each organisation. (These questions are a bit tricky. Maximum ten minutes.)

1 My pub, the Fox and Hounds, has four weeks' supply of beer in the cellar at all times. *strong/weak/don't know*
2 The West Indies cricket team scored 328 runs in their first innings against England in the Second Test. *strong/weak/don't know*
3 Every time we recruit a manager it costs us £7,000. This is £1,000 less than it costs the firm across the road. *strong/weak/don't know*

If you had difficulty in answering any or all of the three questions, it is not surprising, since you were not given enough information to be able to form a sensible opinion. On the face of it a pub with four weeks' supply of beer in the cellars sounds like a position of strength. It certainly would be if you were expecting a siege or Arctic weather conditions, but ordinarily is it necessary to tie up so much money in stocks? It all depends on the frequency of delivery of beer from the brewery and how erratic is the demand for beer.

As far as cricket scores are concerned, if you think that 328 was a strong score you are probably drawing on your knowledge of cricket which tells you that on average over 300 runs in an innings is regarded as fairly good. However, comparing that figure against an average is of no help as regards one particular game: you can only make a judgement about that when you know England's score and the second innings totals.

The third question again seems easy on the face of it. To have your recruitment costs of managers £1,000 less than that of the company across the road seems to be a strong point – an efficient personnel department operation. But there is a catch: suppose that the saving is achieved by careless selection procedures, or only interviewing four candidates rather than five? This example indicates the danger of drawing a conclusion from an isolated example; at best it is merely a clue to be used with a lot of other evidence.

SCORING
Question 1 – *strong* 2; *weak* 2; *don't know* 3.
Question 2 – *strong* 2; *weak* 1; *don't know* 3.
Question 3 – *strong* 2; *weak* 2; *don't know* 3.

If you scored more than 9 or less than 5, there is something wrong with your addition. If you scored 5 you are probably not interested in cricket. A score of 8 or 9 indicates you are getting more cautious. 6 or 7? – You are OK too!

3.2 Standards for Making Comparisons

Having established the need to make comparisons if we are going to make sensible statements about parts of organisations, the next question to answer is, What can we compare our information with? There can be four such standards for comparison. They are:

- *the past*
- *other units in the same organisation*
- *other organisations*
- *internal targets or standards*

The past

The main value in comparing what is going on now with what happened in earlier months or years is that it enables the analyst to identify trends. If he can then state whether the trend is favourable or unfavourable then he has identified strong or weak points in the organisation. For instance, if the management of a furniture works found that the quantity of waste wood was increasing (relative to the total amount used) then they would have a good indication of a weakness within the business.

Other units within the organisation

This kind of comparison is easily made in such organisations as multiple shop companies like Boots or Tesco. Remember Uncle James and his shoe shop?

Well, every month he used to receive a whole pile of statistics from head office relating his shop's performance to that of other shops in the group. The information told him if he and his staff were operating as efficiently as others and gave clues as to where weaknesses and strengths might be. One of Uncle James's shop's biggest weaknesses was the very high rent that had to be paid per square foot. He knew it was a problem, but he made sure that there was more than adequate compensation by having the highest sales per square foot figure in the company – the big strength.

Other organisations

At the beginning of this chapter, success was discussed and it was noted that organisations that are very successful have many strong points. However there is in every type of activity only one 'best'; all the others are less successful. This is why in sport there are league tables, why there is a hit parade for pop music, why there are 'pub of the year' and 'horse of the year' competitions. All are an attempt to find the best in that particular area of activity – the one which has minimised its weaknesses and has many strengths. For the rest of the competitors, if they want to improve they must seriously compare themselves against the best both to see how far behind they are and, more important, what it is that makes the best so successful. In soccer the question is, Why is the team at the top successful? Not just that it gets more points or has a better goal difference, but because of the way it goes about its job.

League tables in the world of business are not as common as in football, but they do exist in one form or another, and it is interesting keeping a lookout for them. Products themselves are analysed in such magazines as *Which?* but the information about companies is much less detailed. Current research in this area is carried out under the general heading of 'Benchmarking' and is particularly important in public sector organisations where internal functions or departments need to be able to judge if they are operating as efficiently as outside agencies.

Internal targets or standards

If performance is compared against a target set earlier then any failure to reach that target can be regarded as a weak point, assuming of course that the target was realistic and sensible in the first place. A good example of this is the target set for salesmen of taking orders each week of at least £10,000. So long as the target is reached, everyone is happy, but persistent failure by only one salesman signifies a problem. This type of comparison is limited to identifying current operational weaknesses and is more appropriate for keeping things under control, as we will see in Chapter 14.

Table 3.1   Some comparative statistics

Situation	This year's result	Last year's result	Average of the others in the group	Best of the competition	Own target
1 Profitability of a bread-pudding maker	14%	13%	15%	21%	14%
2 Miles per gallon in my car at 56 m.p.h.	34.0	32.0	31.0	32.8	35.0
3 Sales turnover in a village post office	£75,000	£64,000	£74,000	not relevant	£70,000

Review

Which yardstick of comparison is most appropriate in the situations shown in Table 3.1?
(Circle whichever number you think should be compared with this year's result.)

To compare this year's result, in all three situations, with any of the four yardsticks shown in Table 3.1 is useful. But the most helpful are:

1 Profitability: compare yourself against the best.
2 Miles per gallon: once you are ahead of the rest, or if you are unique, compare against your own target.
3 Sales turnover: comparing one village post office against another village post office as far as sales is concerned does not tell you very much. The most interesting comparison to be made is this year against last year, giving you an indication of the rate of growth.

3.3 What to Look At to Find Strengths and Weaknesses

It was suggested earlier that the whole organisation has to be analysed to make sure that all the significant areas of weakness and strength are identified. There are a number of ways of going about it, but one way is to look at the key areas of the organisation in turn. But first, the question that has to be asked is, Overall how is the organisation getting on? This implies that it must know what its primary objective is, so that it can measure how far off its actual performance was.

The objective will have been set with some regard to the best experience in the field, so ideally there is a three-way comparison:

actual *v.* objective
actual *v.* the best
objective *v.* the best

These give a good indication of overall weakness and strength: the greater the gap between actual and the best or objectives then (assuming the best is higher) many specific areas of weakness need to be identified.

Some of the key areas to look at were highlighted earlier in this chapter (see page 38) and the six examples chosen naturally fall into categories. These are:

- Physical resource factors, e.g. location, space, capacity, and age of equipment and buildings.
- Human resource factors, e.g. age composition of the work force, skills profile of the work force.
- Financial resources, especially ability to raise money.
- Products, e.g. stages in the life cycle.

The examples quoted related to situations where successful organisations might have a weakness. If the list is extended to include unsuccessful organisations the list of possible weaknesses is endless. A brief reminder of the first four areas to look at follows and then some other aspects of an organisation to study are discussed (pages 44–5).

Physical resources
Organisations need adequate physical facilities in terms of age and capacity to keep costs down, provide for additional business (e.g. in storage or production) and, where customers are concerned, give a quick, and pleasant service.

Human resources
A personnel audit should reveal the age composition of the staff and a profile of their skills. Many organisations have failed to make new ventures succeed because they did not recognise that their staff did not have sufficient skills in the new areas.

Financial resources
Two issues are of major concern in this respect: the financial strength of the business and the extent of risk. Financial strength is related to an organisation's ability to generate or raise money, borrow it and pay interest on its debts. Risk is the question of getting involved in activities that may fail (or may do extremely well). Risk is also a question of how much finance is tied up in foreign currencies which may be subject to

adverse exchange rate changes. Financial strength makes most things possible; financial weakness makes only one thing possible if not cured – the close-down.

Products

A well-developed range of products or services is one of an organisation's greatest strengths. Conversely, a company with weak products seems to struggle to keep afloat. Among the key factors to examine are: stages in the life cycle, price levels (higher or lower than the competition) and share of the market in total.

For organisations not providing products but services these factors may also apply, except where the service is essential, e.g. hospitals, schools or various government departments. Here the concern is with levels of service and the extent to which 'customers' are pleased or disgruntled with that service.

Other key areas of the organisation to be examined include:

Buying

The buying problem has already been mentioned (page 21). In many organisations, strength in the buying area is critical if the business is to survive. The big retail grocery chains operate on such tiny profit margins that a 2 per cent increase in the price of purchases can halve profits. In nearly all firms that handle products (except the most labour intensive) the cost of purchases by far outweighs the cost of labour, hence the importance of strong buying.

Selling and promotion

It is important to make sure that selling and promotion are strong if growth of sales is envisaged. Questions such as the extent to which the sales force covers the territory and how well it penetrates the outlets for the products of the company have to be answered. So has the extent to which promoting the organisation's goods or services is carried out, compared to the competition.

Research and development

An area that must not be forgotten, because strength in this facility can be the key to a prosperous future. A weak research and development team helps nobody.

Management

As well as an audit of all employees, special regard has to be given to an audit of management. because it is not just the age profile of these people, nor their technical and professional skills, that are important, it is the ability to manage that determines whether the future will be bright or not. Issues such as leadership skill, business appreciation, vision and decision-making ability are all essential ingredients in the strong management profile.

The organisation

In looking at the individual trees it is easy to lose sight of the shape of the forest, and in terms of organisations the whole must be studied as well as its components parts. In particular there are four aspects to which attention should be paid:

- *Structure* – the actual organisational set-up as set out in an organisation chart. Who reports to whom? Who is responsible for what?
- *Systems* – the methods used to make sure things get done (or to prevent things going wrong).
- *Policies* – the rules which govern many of the decisions of the organisation (how to sell; where to buy; where to sell; who not to employ, etc.).

If these three are operating properly nobody is aware of them, but if they are wrong they can strangle the life out of an organisation. This will be discussed later, in Chapter 6.

The fourth and last part of the overall organisation question is:

- *Atmosphere and morale*

Have you ever been into an office, a club or a meeting and been aware of a depressing atmosphere? Conversely, you may have been somewhere (or even worked in a place) which seemed to hum with a sense of purpose. Pubs and restaurants carry atmospheres strongly and so do football clubs near the end of the season, especially where promotion or relegation is concerned.

To try to build up an organisation if there is poor morale or atmosphere is pointless. You have to rebuild morale first – that is a subject for much later (see Chapter 11).

Some of the key audit questions discussed are set out below in the form of a checklist. You may like to use it to assess the overall strength and weakness rating of the organisation you work for or know best.

If any of the questions are irrelevant substitute for them areas important in your own context. Remember that the list is not comprehensive and there may be more factors of importance.

You may not be able to get hold of suitable comparative information, so you have to use your own judgement to decide whether a particular factor suggests strength or weakness.

3.4 Twenty Key Corporate Audit Questions

Area of the business	Question
Buying	• Are we buying cheapest and best without too high stock levels?
Physical	• Are our physical resources modern and efficient?
	• Do we have adequate extra space for, and capacity in, both production and stores?

	• Is our distribution system quick and low cost?
	• Are we located in the right places?
Products	• Where are they in the product life cycle?
	• What share of the market do they have?
	• Are prices too high, too low or about right?
Sales and promotion	• Do the sales force sell to enough customers?
	• Do we advertise and promote as much as the competition?
Research and development	• Are we putting enough effort into it?
	• How good is the age and skills structure of our employees?
Managers	• Included in previous question; and are they providing good leadership?
Finance	• How much extra money could we raise either by borrowing or in share capital?
	• Are we at risk financially (e.g. because of foreign exchange fluctuations or because of high interest payments)?
Organisations	• Is the structure appropriate?
	• Are the systems a millstone?
	• Are the policies adopted by the firm sensible?
	• Atmosphere and morale, how good?
Overall	• How profitable are we?

Finally, the extent to which an internal appraisal is carried out depends on the size and complexity of the organisation and also on the degree of success it is enjoying. It is easy to ignore the exercise when things are going well – only to wake up and discover you are in difficulties. The wise manager is continuously evaluating performance to nip malaise in the bud and to push home the advantages that stem from strength.

How to cure weaknesses? Sometimes it is obvious, sometimes it requires considerable expertise. Some indications are given later in this book, but for particular complex problems it would be wiser to turn to books or experts on the area of concern itself.

4 Analysing Trends in the Outside World

This chapter is all about the way external factors affect the performance of the organisation. In particular you will see how an organisation is affected by outside events and why it is important to try to anticipate them. By the end of the chapter you should be able to identify the major areas of influence in the outside world and know what to look for in preparing for the future.

One warm and sunny week last summer my family decided to have a day out at the seaside. We got up early, made a picnic lunch, loaded up the car and set off. It was a beautiful morning, but the weather gradually deteriorated and it started to rain just as we got within sight and sound of the sea. We had our picnic lunch huddled together in a shelter on the deserted promenade and it was so cold and windy and wet that even the seagulls had given up. It was a thoroughly miserable experience – we spent a lot of time and money getting there and we got nothing at all out of it; the return on our investment was zero.

Compare that story with the case of the vanishing newspaper shop. This particular shop was situated on a busy main road midway between the town centre and the railway station (and an easy walk to either). It picked up a lot of passing trade, as well as people walking to and from the station. In addition, nearby was a popular sports ground and a lot of business was done on match days. The business was very prosperous and was always well stocked with a wide range of goods.

Then one day something happened. The owner was the same, the products were the same, the assistants were the same and the owner had done nothing different. Yet business simply disappeared, and within a few weeks the shop closed and the owner opened up another shop elsewhere in a much less suitable location.

Self-check

What do you think happened that caused the business to fall so dramatically?

The answer simply was that double yellow lines were painted along both sides of the road passing the shop and there was nowhere to park. So motorists no longer stopped there, and locals found it inconvenient: you could no longer just jump in the car and pop round for a birthday card or some ice-cream. The business depended on that kind of trade for its prosperity and, without it, it became just another 'average' shop.

My trip to the seaside and the sad tale of the newspaper shop are similar in that things happened completely outside my, or the newsagent's, control. There was nothing I could do about the weather and there was little the shop-owner could do about double yellow lines in the road. This kind of unplanned, unforeseen, unexpected event has been recognised for many years and has become popularly known as Sod's Law or Murphy's Law; no matter how carefully things are planned the most unlikely event will occur to thwart you. The things outside one's control are the events that take place in the outside world or, to give it the smart name, the 'environment'. There would be no problem if the environment was stable and never changed; unfortunately it does change and (just to make things even more interesting) the rate of change is not consistent.

To illustrate this idea, look outside at the weather. Most of us live in places where the weather is changeable, and the weather you are experiencing now will not go on for ever. You know it is going to change but what you do not know is:

- *when* it is going to change; and
- *what* it is going to change to.

It is probably easier to look at the problem in a different way by asking the questions, For how long is the present weather likely to continue? And, When it changes is it likely to change for the better or the worse?

Climate is, of course, one of the most unpredictable environments, although fortunately the range of possible types of weather that any one place at any one time can experience is fairly limited. Moreover there is an annual cycle which can fairly safely be predicted a long time ahead even though actual daily conditions may not be accurately forecast – for example, that on 2 January 2010 the weather in Liverpool will be fairly cold.

Future events are, therefore, of two kinds: the predictable (the weather is unlikely to be very hot; the National Westminster Bank is unlikely to go broke) and the unpredictable (the precise temperature in Liverpool; the precise profits of the National Westminster Bank in 2010).

Climate is just one environmental factor in hundreds that affect organisations to a greater or lesser extent, and many of these factors are highly unpredictable. Consider Liverpool on 2 January 2010. What will be the demand for digital watches on the day? How many people will want to travel on the buses? How many people will need hospital services? How many bottles of tomato sauce will be sold? There is no way of answering these questions with any degree of precision. Indeed in some instances the product or service may have disappeared completely (imagine a world without tomato sauce). It may be argued that there is no need to worry about what things are going to be like so far into the future – the 'let's cross that bridge when we come to it' argument. That kind of argument has a great deal of appeal; unfortunately it can lead to disaster. For instance, suppose you are in charge of the hospital services in Liverpool and you know that in 2010 the total number of people requiring hospital treatment on any one day was going to be five times as great as it is today; what would you do? You would set about making sure that the facilities were available that could cope with such a huge demand: new hospitals fully equipped with enough doctors, surgeons, nurses and all the hundreds of support staff needed to ensure their smooth running. How long do you think it would take to set it all up and get running (bearing in mind that the amount of available money is limited in any one year)? The answer lies anywhere between four and eight years, depending on the total size of the project, so it would be literally fatal to leave the decision until the last minute.

A small shop may be able to adapt fairly quickly to most changes, although even in that case, as we saw at the beginning of the chapter, there is always an exception. It would appear that as organisations grow and get more complicated so it takes longer and longer to change their set-up to meet changes in the environment. A small boat can change direction quickly, but it takes a giant supertanker a lot of miles and quite a time to change its course. Many new developments can take over ten years from start to full operation – aircraft and nuclear power stations are good examples – simply because they are so complicated and expensive to design, develop and build.

The questions which need to be considered regarding the environment, and to which we now turn, are:

- What aspects of the environment have to be taken into account in planning and what can safely be ignored?
- Is there any way of anticipating what is going to happen?
- How far ahead should organisations try to estimate what is going to happen?
- How can an organisation minimise the threats from the environment that lie ahead and take advantage of the opportunities that may exist?

4.1 What Aspects of the Environment (Outside World) Have to be Taken into Account?

A case for thinking about

A large company owned a nice hotel in the middle of a pleasant prosperous town. During the week the forty bedrooms were usually fully occupied, mainly by businessmen, and the restaurant and bars were always busy. At weekends in summer the hotel was popular with tourists breaking their journeys.

A proposal was made to increase the number of bedrooms by twenty, each with bath, shower and toilet. It was calculated that to make a reasonable return on the cost of the project all the extra rooms would have to be occupied at least every other night on average. This meant that because of the slack winter weekend trade, during the week an extra twenty guests would have to turn up each night.

The question was, if they built the bedrooms could they be sure of getting the extra business? Inquiries showed that people liked the hotel, the prices were reasonable and the only competition was a similar sized hotel on the outskirts of town.

The question was put by the managing director like this: 'If we start now we could open the new bedrooms in three years' time. Will the demand for bedrooms be so much higher then that all twenty rooms will be filled on three nights a week and just a few let the rest of the time?' There was no good answer to that question because nobody had the ability to see into the future, but the manager of the hotel said: 'Demand has been growing over the last few years and I can see no good reason for it to stop.' To this the chief accountant, who tended to get a bit unhappy if people wanted to spend money, responded: 'Well, I can think of at least half a dozen reasons why demand could stop growing...'

Self-check

Can you think of any reasons why the demand for hotel bedrooms could stop growing?
(Try to think of at least three, but take no more than five minutes.)

Among the reasons that the accountant gave for his belief that the demand for rooms in their hotel would not grow were:

- The next government would be the present opposition and they would clamp down on expense accounts for businessmen.
- The next government would also not spend so much money helping industry (by not giving research grants, etc.).
- The rising cost of fuel was going to put more and more people on to trains, planes and buses or coaches. There would be much more attempt to get 'there and back in a day', especially as trains were getting faster.
- There was likely to be an economic recession soon and organisations would be less likely to give their staff a free hand about travelling around. There would be less money to spend generally.
- The increase in demand had been associated with a growth in the number of organisations based in the town. That growth 'might well come to an end'.

- The competitor would not stand idly by to let us cream off the demand. They would build too, and *they* had space for a swimming pool.
- Social pressure was building up (as in Sweden) against businesspeople spending even a couple of nights away from home. Increasingly they would be expected not to be away overnight.

It is quite possible that you thought of other answers to the question, simply because of the enormous range of possibilities that do exist. It is, however, possible to group the answers into a number of different types of environment and this helps to make the analysis more effective.

Self-check

Can you see, in the examples quoted above (or in your own examples), how several different environments are being quoted?

The first two answers relate to government and could be called the 'political and legal' environment. The second example was also dealing with money matters and this, along with the third, could be described as the 'economic' environment. The third is also dealing with a technological issue and so we could refer to a 'technological' environment. Fourth and fifth are also economic (but at different levels). Sixth is the 'competitive' environment, and the last example is suggesting a social trend and is a 'social' environment.

These six different environments (including natural phenomena like the weather) are a convenient way of classifying the world around the organisation, and each one needs a closer look.

The political and legal environment

All organisations have to exist within the political and legal system wherever they operate. At home, politics can be national or local and both can have a significant effect on the life and well-being of the organisation. If the political party in power never changed, or if its policies never changed, then life would be very simple. But it is the way of political life, in Britain at any rate, that it changes frequently; sometimes organisations feel themselves blown to and fro as the political power base changes, to the extent that they do not know what attitudes to adopt themselves.

Some political parties are prepared to spend money, others are not. Some will have free trade policies and encourage organisations to set up in different countries and export and import their goods and services. Others do not welcome that kind of activity. As far as an organisation is concerned that operates across national frontiers, the worst type of country to deal with is the one with political instability, because you never know if the next group to come to power will favour you.

It is not only in relation to trade and business that the political environment is important, but in many other respects. Some governments seem to delight in creating laws that increase the number of forms that have to be filled in. Others, both at a local and national level, have an attitude of letting organisations get on with it and do not interfere. On the other hand there are those which pass many laws of a restrictive nature effectively making it illegal for organisations to do certain things.

All organisations have to live within an active political environment and have to be aware that what they do could be the object of some political action. Some organisations are actually owned and managed by political groups – hospitals, the nationalised industries, central and local government offices, the armed forces – all recognise that their success or failure depends on how well they cope with political decisions, and how well they anticipate changes in political attitudes and policies. In this sense senior civil servants and local government officers especially have to be very able managers.

Activity

Take today's newspaper and look for the *biggest story involving a political decision* (e.g. the passing of a new law, or a statement by the Prime Minister). Ask yourself how much does that decision affect:

1 the organisation you know best?
2 a car manufacturer?
3 your local grocery store?
   (You may take a political decision of a foreign government if you wish, but it may be harder to see the connection in numbers 1 and 3.)

The economic environment

Probably no organisation can avoid being affected by the economic environment. Again the state of the economy is continuously changing and the organisation that succeeds is the one that identifies rising and falling trends faster and takes action soonest, or which has sufficient flexibility to adapt to a new economic situation. The fastest responses to changing economic environment are seen on Budget Day when the Chancellor of the Exchequer announces an increase in the tax on petrol and alcoholic drink. Instantly queues form up at petrol stations and all the off-licences to a roaring trade. Some individuals are a bit slow off the mark and arrive just as stocks run out, but others – the ones who have taken a chance – made their purchases a day or two before because they felt the probability of increased duty was very high.

The economic environment has many aspects and the main ones that affect organisations are:

The prosperity of the market

Using the word 'market' in its widest possible sense to mean all the possible customers for the organisation's goods or services, it is not hard to see that if customers are not feeling well off they are not likely to spend much. For example, the amount of business a public house does reflects fairly well how prosperous the market is. The story is virtually the same for all organisations that sell products or services, but some are much more sensitive to the ups and downs of the economy than others. Firms in the motor trade are very vulnerable, because the sale of new cars falls off rapidly when times are not so good; the problem for motor dealers especially is that they buy from the manufacturer in anticipation of being able to sell the cars. If, however, the customers do not come into the showrooms and buy, the dealer is left with a heap of new cars, little money in the bank and the problem of paying next week's wages.

Inflation

Inflation is known to everyone as increases in the price we have to pay for goods in the shops. All organisations, in inflationary times, find that they have to pay out more for the goods and services they are using than they were before. Raw materials' costs rise, wages rise, electricity and petrol prices increase and so on. For a time organisations can overcome this by increasing the prices of their own goods and services to compensate. For example, a local council providing the usual services – street lighting, cleaning, refuse collection, schools, etc. – finds that the costs of providing the services have risen by 10 per cent from £500,000 to £550,000. The only ways the council can deal with the extra £50,000 are by making the ratepayers pay more or by cutting the services. (They could also borrow the money – then the ratepayers would pay the interest.)

Similarly companies get customers to pay increased costs if they can. But people have a habit of resisting and there comes a point when the price increase causes a big drop in demand. Some organisations try to beat inflation by anticipating increases in commodities and buy before the price goes up. The hard part is guessing which products are going to go up in price and when.

Exchange rates

Organisations that are involved in buying from other countries or which sell into other countries, as well as those that are set up in more than one state, are particularly concerned about the way exchange rates fluctuate, because a great deal of money can be lost if the wrong currency is being held at the wrong time. Moreover, buying goods from overseas at the wrong time can cost a great deal of profit, just as selling into an overseas market at the wrong time can also bring in less income.

Interest rates
Interest is the cost of borrowing as well as the reward of lending, and these days there are very few organisations that manage without at some time having to borrow money. There are many advantages in borrowing (and there are risks too), but the timing of that borrowing can be critical. For instance, a company wanted to borrow £$\frac{1}{2}$ million to equip a new factory with modern machinery. They were offered the money at 10 per cent interest, but they failed to take action fast enough and by the time they got round to it the cheapest offer they could get was 11$\frac{1}{2}$ per cent interest. The delay cost the firm £7,500 a year in extra interest.

The technological environment

Is there much demand these days for gas lights, slide-rules or mangles? It is fairly plain that gas is no longer used for lighting, calculators have replaced slide-rules and the washing machine's spin-dry facility has finished off the mangle. All these are simple examples of products that are no longer any use because something better has come along to do the job (or in some cases make the job obsolete).

The changes in the technological environment (using technology here in a very wide sense) that have been seen over the last thirty years are immense, particularly in such areas as chemicals, drugs and electronics. Space-age technology is the advertising man's way of describing many of the products in our homes or for sale in the shops – from cameras to ceramic cooker tops. Whether the speed of technological change is accelerating or not, does not really matter (some people say it is, some say it is not). What is important is that there is a lot of change about, and organisations have to be aware of the possibilities in three ways.

First, there is the problem that competitors may achieve a technological development which may bite into your own market. What is worse is an entirely new form of opposition from a different type of competitor. For instance, the electrically driven motorcar is being developed by the existing car-makers, and also by a battery-maker.

Second, organisations have to be aware of general technological advances in the broad area which they can build into their own products.

Third, all organisations use equipment of one kind or another, even if it is only the normal range of office equipment – typewriter, photocopier, telephones. Technology is updating all the equipment used by organisations at a very fast rate. The managing director of the British side of a multi-national organisation manufacturing heavy equipment said that the hardest part of his job was nothing to do with unions, pay or products, but whether to spend the money on the latest technologically improved equipment (like the latest telephone switchboard, computer system or even 'robotics' – the silicon-chip-based machines that copy human movement.

The point is that the organisation that fails to keep up to date will die (how many dentists still use a foot-powered drill?), but the organisation that kicks off the development of a new piece of technology very often succeeds. Xerox photocopiers and Polaroid cameras are both examples of being first and staying winners.

Activity

Identify the most up-to-date piece of technology you know about – at home or work. How soon do you think it will be out of date?

Competition

Possibly the best-known element in the environment as far as commercial organisations are concerned is competition. 'Know your enemy' is an old military saying and it applies to business just as much, because firms that are in competition with each other are trying to do each other down. Even within organisations there may be rivalries, by no means an uncommon occurrence. The first problem for a commercial organisation is often to define exactly who the competition is. For instance, in recent years there has been an advertising campaign for tea using the slogan 'best drink of the day'.

Activity

What products are in competition with tea? (List four in five minutes.)

Coffee is the obvious competitor, being called a beverage like tea; but tea is, more broadly, a drink, and once we start listing the different types of drink it seems that the whole world is lined up to compete with tea – even water is a competitor.

It is the job of the marketing managers to study the market in which the product competes to establish not just what are the competitors but, more important, which are the relevant competitors. A relevant competitor is a product which could be a replacement for your product – or which could lose out to your product. If tea is seen as something to wake you up in the morning then its obvious competitors are coffee, milk and fruit juice. Gin and brandy are not relevant competitors in that context (at least not to most people). Each of the products tries to take away customers from the other, and if one product fails to secure for itself an identifiable niche with a steady body of support then sooner or later it gets too weak to exist.

This situation applies to commercial organisations of every kind, not just those making products. Shops, hotels, road transport firms, advertising agencies and so on all have to recognise and deal with competition.

Commercial organisations, therefore, spend a good deal of time and effort finding out about the competition, through market research, market intelligence and business analysis. It is not difficult to find out something about one's competitors and their products; the hard part is finding out about those firms who are going to compete against you *next year* – the firm that is not in your market, but is looking at it as a possible new venture. Various Japanese companies have entered into world markets over the last twenty-five to thirty years, quite unexpectedly in many cases: motorcycles, watches and motorcars being the best-known examples. Recently the lawnmower industry has demonstrated that it is possible to anticipate such an event and has taken early steps to combat the entrance of a new competitor.

Social environment

The social environment of an organisation can change as much as any of the other types of environment. Often the changes are not so dramatic as a new technology, for instance, and this makes them less easy to identify until their impact cannot be avoided. An obvious social change is the way in which the number going to the cinema declined, slowly and steadily, year after year.

Another example is the way in which smoking has become less sociably acceptable and is continuing to be less and less popular. In fact there are strong social pressures against tobacco products, and these have led to specific political moves such as the abolition of cigarette advertising on television. Very often this tide of opinion, of changing social values, is impossible to reverse once it has gained some standing. If an organisation fails to recognise the trend – or tries to fight back – sooner or later it will lose out. The tobacco companies have recognised the trend in society's attitude to smoking and have adopted, deliberately, programmes for investing in other, more acceptable products. Imperial Tobacco Company was heavily involved in the food and drink industries before being taken over by Hanson, for instance.

Self-check

There is a trend, which seems to be growing in strength, for a shorter working week. On the assumption that it is an irreversible trend, what kind of organisations could benefit from it and what kind of organisations might well be harmed?

(There is no specific answer to this, so try to think of two examples of winners and two of losers from the trend in about ten minutes.)

Examples of organisations that would benefit from shorter working hours would possibly be the leisure industries – companies that cater for people's part-time activities, everything from sport to bingo.

On the other hand an organisation where labour costs are a high proportion of total costs might well find that shorter hours (for the same pay) mean higher prices. So the examples you have chosen are possibly labour-intensive organisations, and government offices (both local and national) will be hard hit. The significance of *that* is higher rates and taxes for you and me.

Natural environment

One of the most important parts of the natural environment is the weather, as we have already seen. It is obviously relevant in farming, building and cricket, and of importance to the makers of such products as ice-cream and soft drinks. These companies find that as the temperature rises sales increase and as the temperature falls sales decline. Have you ever heard the expression 'we didn't do as well as we'd hoped because of the bad winter (or spring, or summer)'? It is the most plausible and understandable excuse in the world for poor performance. Yet in reality it is simply saying 'we failed to consider the possibility that the weather may be no good for us'. It is quite astonishing how many people and organisations are surprised and unprepared when it snows in January.

Another key climatic factor is that relating to crop yields; the famous example of Brazilian coffee is a case in point. In Brazil, frost strikes occasionally, and if it is severe enough the coffee crop can be reduced substantially. A company in Europe using coffee can be in difficulties if it fails to get its supplies on time at the right prices; these firms have to be on their guard against the possibility of such an event.

Another important natural aspect of the environment is population and its structure – not in general but in the area where the organisation operates. Put simply, if you think there are going to be more youngsters you build schools. If you think there are going to be more old people you build hospitals.

4.2 Is There Any Way of Anticipating What is Going to Happen?

On page 49 four questions were posed and the subsequent discussion has been on finding a way of classifying the environment to help us minimise the threats that the future may bring and to help us grab the opportunities that may present themselves.

To the next question – can we anticipate what might happen? – the short answer is 'no, not precisely'; if the future were easy to predict there would be no gambling. Nevertheless there has to be an attempt, and several specific aids are available to try to reduce the lack of uncertainty about the future.

'Futurology' is the name given to the business of trying to assess what the environment might look like in a number of years ahead. Anyone can produce these 'scenarios' as they are called, by identifying current trends and extending the idea into the future as far as you want.

The technique of scenario planning goes further. The idea is to produce two or three views about the long-term future which are radically different and then ask what the organisation has to do now to ensure survival if either 'future' occurs.

Activity

Suppose you run a small bakery. What would you do today, if you knew that the demand for bread would increase threefold in the next five years? What would you do if you knew that the price of flour was going to rise threefold in the next five years?

It's not easy to see how to reconcile these two . . . yet both are possible.

Activity

Consider a sporting place you know – a tennis or football club, golf course or cricket ground for instance. Imagine the year 2010. Will the club be there? If not, why not? If it is, how will it look? This is good for an hour's discussion.

The Delphi technique

This is named after the ancient oracle at Delphi in Greece, which was famous from the eighth to the fifth century BC for the forecasts it made. Nowadays the forecasts are made by consulting experts in the subject under review rather than by the priestess of Apollo. In outline, the technique is to see if a number of experts in a subject agree on some future event. If thirty experts in vehicle engineering agree that the electric motorcar will be commonplace by 2010, you may decide to sell your petrol station on the basis of their opinion. They could, of course, be totally wrong, but this is unlikely.

Economic models

A popular way of looking ahead in the economic world is to set up an imaginary economy on a computer and feed it with a lot of information. Hopefully the results that come out will give an indication of the state of the economy from one year to five or six years ahead. The only problem is that there has to be an assumption that people, organisations and governments will behave in certain ways. So often the conclusions are qualified with statements like 'assuming no change in government policy'. Even so, they are useful indicators, especially in the short term, of the way the economy is going.

4.3 How Far Ahead Should Organisations Try to Estimate What is Going to Happen?

The answer depends on the problem. If you want to do an hour's gardening now you do not need tomorrow's weather forecast. What you do want is some way of being able to have enough time to plan your own response to some future event. To use an example from defence strategy, if it takes your airforce three minutes to get to a combat level, there is little point in having a radar system that tells you when a missile is two minutes from your territory. You need more time and this is only obtainable if you can pick up signals on your radar at least four minutes' equivalent distance away. One writer in this area, Igor Ansoff, talks about picking up weak signals from the environment (H. Igor Ansoff, *Strategic Management*, Macmillan, 1979). In other words, the organisation has got to try to look far enough into the future so that it has time to prepare (if it picks up that weak signal). One successful British company habitually makes economic forecasts three years ahead. It saw the recession of 1990 early in 1989 and made its plans accordingly (cutting its capital expenditure plans). On the other hand one organisation only realised the problem in the autumn of 1990 and found that it had to continue with its projects because it would have been more expensive to stop. It had, therefore, to cut expenditure in other, more sensitive, areas – including considerable staff redundancies.

The distance to look into the future is called the 'planning horizon' – a time in the future that the organisation can 'see' with a reasonable degree of confidence. At one extreme most small shops will have a planning horizon for most things of a few days (a greengrocer has a 24-hour horizon). The larger and more sophisticated the firm the longer the horizon.

Some organisations do not need to worry about long-term effects because their environment is relatively stable or their activities are not especially sensitive to most happenings. Shoe shops are a good example of organisations that come into this category. There are, in contrast, some whose activities are very sensitive to the changes in the environment, which may itself be very unstable. An excellent example of that is the 'rag trade', the business of garment manufacture, especially ladies' fashions. It is subject to many environmental changes, some of which are very volatile and sudden, yet it has to plan new designs well ahead of the season; this year's autumn collection was being planned at least eighteen months ago in successful firms and negotiations were taking place with the buyers from the shops.

Fig 4.1   Assessing the stability of a firm's environment

Name and type of the organisation:............

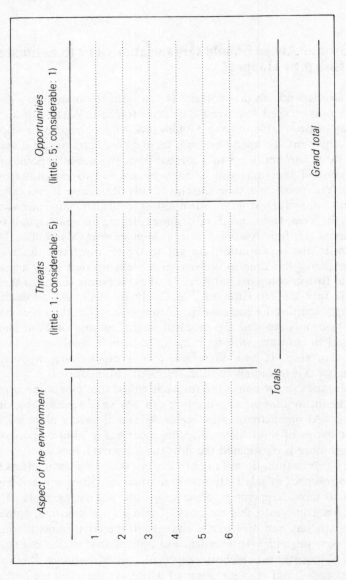

4.4 How Can an Organisation Minimise the Threats/Take Advantage of the Opportunities?

The fourth question posed on page 49 recognises that every organisation's environment changes: sometimes the change is favourable and the wind blows the right way; other times the storm clouds gather and steps have to be taken to make sure the organisation is not blown off course. The course itself is, in management terms, the 'strategy', and this will be looked at in the next chapter. Changes in the environment that can be seen a long way off can be built into one's strategy, but other changes – the sudden ones – have to be handled differently. The way these can be dealt with has to wait until Chapter 13, which is all about managing change.

Review

On Figure 4.1, p. 60, list the six parts of the environment we have looked at and try to think how each might affect an organisation you know well. Then rank each from the point of view of a threat and an opportunity. If you think the aspect of the environment is a big threat, write down 5 in the space; if it is a threat but not so much, write 3; if no threat, write 1.

Rank opportunities the other way round; a big opportunity scores 1 and no opportunity scores 5.

Complete the quiz before reading the scoring system.

SCORING

A score of 12 indicates an unbelievably stable organisation – 'roses all the way'. At the other extreme a score of 60 belongs to an organisation under siege. A score of more than 42 indicates considerable sensitivity to the environment. A score of less than 24 would be a happy position for any organisation – plenty of opportunities and/or few threats. Between 24 and 42 should be considered normal.

Note finally the scores in each of the two columns. The extreme results are:

1 *Threats, 30, opportunities 6*; this kind of organisation is one that is involved in, for example, new consumer products with a lot of fierce competition, like pocket calculators.

2 *Threats 6, opportunities 30*, an organisation like this has few opportunities but is not exposed to any major threats, living in a stable, predictable – even boring – world. Pin-making, for example. Normally the two sides of the equation tend to be more in balance.

5 Choosing a Strategy: How to Get to the Long-Term Objective

The aims of this chapter are to examine the meaning and importance of strategy in the job of management. By the end of the chapter you will be able to appreciate why organisations have chosen certain strategies, what the basic alternatives could be, and how to select a suitable strategy for any organisation.

A popular activity in summer is climbing up to the top of mountains and hills. One of the favourite mountains is Snowdon in North Wales, which on a sunny day in August is crowded with walkers and climbers. Part of its attraction is the fact that it is the highest mountain in England and Wales, but in addition it has spectacular views from the summit (if you are lucky) and there is a restaurant just below the summit to quench the thirst.

The interesting thing about Snowdon is that there are no less than nine or ten recognised normal routes up to the summit, seven different starting points and countless uncommon routes frequented only by rock climbers. Some of the ways up are easy – there is a railway to within a few yards of the top – some are long and laborious. Others are short but need special rock-climbing equipment and skills – otherwise they are virtually impossible and exceedingly dangerous.

If you choose to climb Snowdon, the most important decision to make is the route itself, and we can refer to this decision as the 'strategic decision'. Of course, the word 'strategy' is not normally used in relation to a mountain in Britain, but it certainly is used in describing the broad way of tackling peaks in the Himalayas or Andes. This is neatly illustrated in the book *Everest the Hard Way* by Chris Bonington (Hodder & Stoughton, 1976). In the foreword, Lord Hunt, who led the successful Everest expedition of 1952, writes 'Upon no one was the stress so great and so prolonged as on the leader of the expedition. His was the original decision to make the bid; his the choice of companions, the general strategy, the supervision of the whole complex plan and its unfolding on Everest.'

Later in the book Bonington refers to himself as a 'frustrated field-marshal', which is apt because strategy actually refers to 'leading an army'. Today the word is used extensively and has become quite common in management literature over the last fifteen to twenty years, although its use is not restricted to leading people. Strategy is not concerned with details; rather it is concerned with basic directions, broad intentions and the general approach to the problem. Our decision to climb Snowdon comes first; then we decide the general strategy which may be expressed like this: 'We will ascend by the route known as the Watkin Path and return the same way, leaving the car in the car park at the bottom. We will climb it on the first fine day we get next week.'

It is easy to see what strategy means if we are referring to a journal, an expedition or a war. It is not so obvious how it relates to the problem of organisations reaching their objectives. Fortunately a good example of a business strategic problem is provided by Uncle James, whom we met in Chapter 1, and his shoe shop.

His shoe shop had a natural growth rate of 4 to 5 per cent a year in terms of the number of shoes sold, but when the shop rental was doubled it was clear that something had to be done of significance to restore the shop to its former position at the head of the profitability league.

Self-check

To raise sales revenues enough Uncle James calculated that he could not rely on the natural growth of the market; something else was needed. Which of the following decisions do you think could be described as strategic decisions?

- Paint the front of the shop.
- Close half an hour later each day.
- Sell socks and stockings.
- Advertise in the local paper.
- Get the lady sales assistant to sell men's shoes.

(Five minutes.)

The only decision which can really be described as a strategic decision is the third one, because this is the only one that is concerned with a major shift in the emphasis of the business. The others, to a greater or lesser extent, are merely tinkering with the existing system. The problem was to get more sales £s into the tills, and painting the place, opening longer and getting ladies to sell men's shoes would not solve the problem. A big change was needed, even bigger than an advertising campaign could produce in the circumstances (although advertising might have formed the marketing strategy to support the general strategy).

5.1 Steps in Choosing Strategies

Generally speaking the need to develop strategy is of particular importance in organisations with commercial activities, rather than in government departments, schools and hospitals where services are being provided. Even so all organisations have to achieve long-term objectives and it is *always* worth asking the question, Do we need to review the way we go about achieving our aims?

What follows relates mainly to business, but up to page 69 it is applicable to non-commercial organisations as well.

Step 1: where are we?

It may seem obvious, but you would not choose to climb Snowdon tomorrow if today you are in Paris. You would probably not choose to climb it tomorrow if you climbed it yesterday. Similarly a company would not try to double its sales of a particular product if it already held 85 per cent of the market. Unless it knows where it stands, however, it could waste a lot of time and energy pursuing the impossible.

Step 2: where do we want to be?

Again it seems obvious, and as far as organisations are concerned all that needs adding is the answer to the question, When do we want to get there?

In terms of corporate objectives these two steps can be described like this: 'Our primary objective is a return on capital of 25 per cent in five years' time. Currently our actual return is only 12 per cent – the difference to be made up by selecting some suitable strategy.'

It is simple enough to draw this idea on a graph – see Figure 5.1.

The line connecting the current return on capital with the target figure in five years' time is important only because the steepness of the slope indicates the size of the problem to be tackled. If your company is highly profitable now then the target may not be much higher – so the line is almost horizontal. But if the firm has only a 1 or 2 per cent return and wants to be at 25 per cent, its line is so steep it looks 'unclimbable' – see Figure 5.2.

Fig 5.1   The planning gap (1): where we are and where we want to be

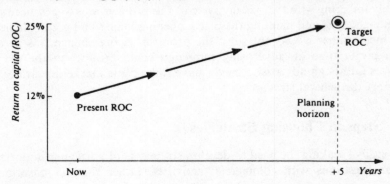

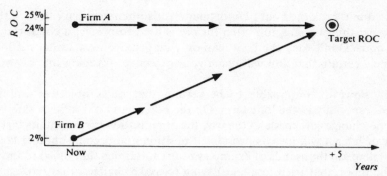

Fig 5.2   The planning gap (2): an easy target and a hard target

Self-check

Which of the two firms illustrated in Figure 5.2 has the best chance of reaching its five-year target ROC?

There is not much doubt that firm *A*, already earning 24 per cent has a much better chance of achieving a return of 25 per cent than firm *B* down near the bottom which is only barely profitable. Firm *B* is not generating as much profit as needed to finance the climb up the chart, whereas all *A* has to do is use its resources to hang on.

These two examples represent firms near the extremes of the results typically found. Many firms obviously enjoy returns in excess of 25 per cent and many fail to make any money at all. The danger for the firm at the bottom of the league is obvious: its weak points make it so vulnerable it could easily fade away. Its strength is probably fear of extinction, which can do wonders for the ailing organisation.

On the other hand the danger for the organisation currently high in the league is complacency – letting things go on and assuming they will be OK. To identify this danger properly is the next step.

Step 3: where will we be if we do nothing different?

Self-check

What would happen to a car or a plane if it was never serviced?

Some people regard the 'do nowt' attitude as a strategy in itself and it is probably fair to say that sometimes it is best not to change things too much – don't 'rock the boat'. Unfortunately it's often necessary to rock the boat to get things going; too often the cry is used to protect a comfortable status quo. 'Don't rock the boat' can only be justified as a strategy if it is absolutely certain that you will reach your objective travelling the way you are.

It is, however, impossible to be certain that one's objective will be reached, especially in the long term. On the other hand it is a fairly safe bet that if no changes are made to the way the organisation carries out its tasks, sooner or later it will lose its prominent position and become another lame duck. There are thousands of examples of organisations that failed to move with the times, that tried to avoid having to make changes, that refused to adapt and innovate. The French Revolution is one of the most devastating examples of what happens if the 'do nowt' strategy is pursued to the bitter end. At the other end of the scale there is the corner shop that closed down because it never had a coat of paint, a new look or a new range of products.

Again the idea can be put on to our simple chart, Figure 5.3.

Activity

Bert's Buses was a small coach operator, running advertised tours from a small town in Staffordshire to the coast and to places of interest all around Britain. Occasionally Bert would hire out one of his coaches to a private party, but he did not really enjoy that kind of business – it was too unpredictable.

He decided to pursue a strategy of changing nothing from year to year except his prices, which he increased to keep pace with inflation. He kept his coaches, his drivers and his tours, but from a position of reasonable prosperity the business declined; within four years the inevitable headline appeared in the local paper, 'BERT'S BUSES BUSTS'.

List four reasons why the performance line might have fallen. (Ten minutes.)

Fig 5.3   The planning gap (3): what happens if no action is taken

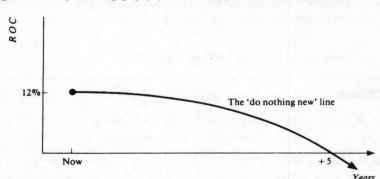

There are in fact many dozens of reasons why a 'no change' strategy could lead to failure, but, in a nutshell, either its internal operations have become inefficient, or some environmental threat has become a reality. In other words if you do nothing different your strengths evaporate, your weaknesses grow, the threats materialise and you cannot seize (or even see) any opportunities. In the case of Bert's Buses some of the main causes of decline could have been:

Internal	External
1 Wasteful spending.	1 New competition with super de-luxe coaches.
2 Coaches old and breaking down.	2 New competition with new tours.
3 Drivers often sick.	3 Social change – no demand.
4 Lack of efficient booking arrangements	4 Economic change – no money.
5 Poor financial control over money borrowed from the bank.	5 New legislation takes coaches off the road because of smoke emission.

It should be unnecessary to study these twin aspects again since they were adequately discussed in Chapters 3 and 4.

As far as strategy is concerned the 'do nothing new' line has to be calculated using information from the internal appraisal and the environment evaluation. This kind of projection into the future is normally called a 'forecast' – a simple statement of what will happen if present trends continue – and it is a very common activity especially in marketing.

There is little point in spending a lot of money advertising a product if it is going to sell like hot cakes anyway. Nor is there much point in redesigning the packaging of another product if it is clearly at the end of its life cycle.

Forecasts, then, assume that the organisation does nothing to meet the threat and opportunities coming up in the environment, and these reveal the downward slope sooner or later. Perhaps it should be noted here that for many years long-range planning as a management technique simply projected present trends into the future – 'extrapolation' is the word to use – and decisions about the future were taken on the basis of these lines alone.

It is a simple matter to superimpose the 'do nothing new' line on to the 'what we would like' line – see Figure 5.4.

Three things have to be noted about this chart. First, each organisation's chart is different, depending on where it is at the present time and how fast its decline is projected.

Second, the two lines are together at first and may continue to be close for several years ahead. It would be a lucky organisation to be able to say with confidence that within five years nothing will happen to blow the firm off course.

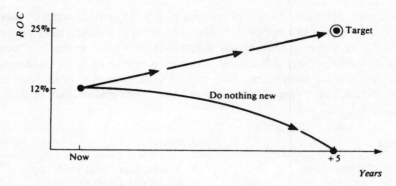

Fig 5.4   The planning gap (4): measuring the size of the problem

The third point is that the gap between the two lines is gradually getting wider, and the size of the gap is of vital interest to the planner because it shows the size of the problem. It is known, quite simply, as the 'planning gap' – the difference between what will happen and what you would like to happen: forecast *v.* target.

Having identified the size of the planning gap the problem is the difficult one of choosing suitable strategies that will fill the gap. Before that can be done it is worth making a list of the main constraints that exist to prevent you doing what you want.

Step 4: what can we not do?

Activity

Suppose you decided to open a newspaper shop. List five things you could not do, either because you would not want to trade in that particular way, or because the law says you cannot. (Ten minutes.)

A detailed, complete list of things you cannot do would be endless. Instead a 'top twenty' list of constraints can be constructed, some of which are the result of internal decisions and others which are imposed on the organisation from outside.

Internally generated constraints
All organisations deliberately make laws that stop them doing the most sensible thing in terms of efficiency or effectiveness. For instance, there is the manager of the pub who refuses to sell tobacco (or permit smoking inside). There is the company which logically should be situated in Central London but is located in Devon because the managing director runs a small orchard

down there 'on the side'. Another example is the business that refuses to buy materials and components from a particular supplier or country, and which refuses to sell its products to particular customers or countries.

There can be many reasons for these kind of internal laws – religion, ethics, politics, personal preference or just plain bigotry being among the most common. They are important and must be kept separately from weaknesses, because weaknesses have to be dealt with, but constraints have to be lived with.

External constraints

The most obvious external constraints on organisations are those that come out of the laws of the land where the organisation is based. Of particular interest and importance are those laws and regulations which constrain the organisation in its day-to-day operations. Such things as hours of opening for shops, building regulations, rules about the use of certain chemicals including artificial flavourings and colourings in food products, and import and export regulations all limit the organisation's choice of ways of making progress (while hopefully protecting the public from the unscrupulous).

The difference between external threats and external constraints should be noted; a threat is something in the future but a constraint is something here and now imposed on the organisation.

Step 5: how do we fill the gap?

On the face of it there is not much difference between this question and the question that all business organisations have always asked, namely, How do we make more money? However, referring to the 'planning gap' is much less vague and it is a question that can be applied to any organisation since it is not limited to money.

The search for a suitable strategy can be undertaken in a number of ways; every management textbook that discusses strategic planning seems to have its own system. In general, however, strategies can be grouped into three. They are:

- *improve*
- *expand*
- *diversify*

Each has distinct advantages and disadvantages.

Improvement strategies

Simply to have a strategy which concentrates on improving the efficiency or the effectiveness of the organisation seems to be rather dull and uninspiring. Improving means being better at doing existing things, and as we saw earlier there is no such thing as being 100 per cent efficient; there is always scope for being better. Of course it is not as easy to be more efficient when you are already top of the league, but it should be easy if your organisation is near the bottom.

In manufacturing organisations, improving means taking existing products and existing markets and finding ways of producing, distributing and selling that are more cost-effective. It means tapping the existing market harder to get more 'market penetration' and it means greater productivity and better utilisation of assets.

Sometimes improvement is the only strategy a firm can pursue in the short run since expansion and diversification demand greater resources than the very weak firm can get hold of. Until it improves, it cannot afford to expand or diversify, and no one will lend it money.

In organisations that are not business oriented, improvement still means being more cost-effective and being faster in providing the service.

The key to improvement lies in the internal strengths and weaknesses appraisal which has already been looked at in Chapter 3. The biggest advantages of pursuing such a strategy are that it can be set under way quickly, it is cheap, it is easily quantified and is within the complete control of management. Unfortunately it has a weakness which makes it unsuitable in the long run as the only strategy to pursue. The weakness is that improving existing operations will not prevent the ultimate downward curve of performance because it is doing nothing to adapt products or services to meet the changing environment. All that improvement does is partly fill the gap. (See Figure 5.5.)

The importance of improvement as a strategy can be seen in three different situations:

- The very poor firm has to improve before anything else just to survive.
- The middle-of-the-road organisation needs to improve so that its weak points do not hamper its other strategies.
- The good organisation needs to improve to stay on top.

In the first two cases the strategy is predominant for two or three years until performance is at a suitable level to support expansion.

Fig 5.5   The planning gap (5): impact of improved efficiency

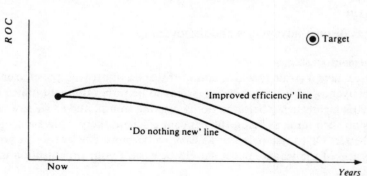

Review

There was once a bicycle shop called Daisy Cycles. It had been around as long as anyone could remember but it had become dingy and unexciting. Very few customers came in to buy cycles – most sales were of accessories like bells and lamps, and repair work which was cheap. Cash was never plentiful, so the stock of bikes was never very high, so few customers came in. One day the owner retired and his son gave the shop a coat of paint and turned a corner of it to fishing equipment, using every penny he could lay his hands on. The business closed down just over a year later.

Why did it fail and what should the son have done?

Take five minutes to picture the scene in your mind's eye, try to work out what might have happened and think of a better course of action.

Every new venture takes time to get off the ground. The trouble with Daisy Cycles was the lack of customers: not enough people knew about the diversification into fishing tackle. Moreover there was insufficient money for an adequate stock in that area. What cash there was from the cycle side of the business was diverted to fishing, leaving the cycle side even weaker. They borrowed to pay the bills, but little cash came in. In the end, the bank manager would not allow any more overdraft. The son should have concentrated his efforts, time and money on improving existing operations.

Expansion strategies

Expansion is a popular strategy to follow because it is fairly easy to get going and it keeps everyone busy. Strictly speaking, expansion means one of two things in a business organisation: either it is taking the existing range of products and services and moving into a new market to try to increase their sales, or it is developing new products or services and trying to sell them in the existing market. Expansion is *not* a new product in a new market – that is diversification, which will be looked at in a moment. For now let's take a close look at these two types of expansion strategy.

Market expansion

Market expansion means the process of extending the area in which your business operates, so that more potential customers are aware of the products or services you are providing. The most obvious example of this kind of activity are in the high street of your nearest town. There you will find several organisations represented that are also in every other high street in the country. The banks, for instance, are nearly always all to be found, as are various well-known shops like Boots, W. H. Smith and Marks & Spencer. Inside the shops the same products will be found over and over again. This repetition across the land stretches to insurance companies, building societies, garages dealing with a particular motorcar manufacturer and many more. This market spread has not occurred accidentally, nor simultaneously; it is the result of a deliberate decision on the part of the management of the company concerned to seek growth by this method.

Very often organisations cannot operate at full efficiency unless they are covering the whole of a region or country; it is not very effective to advertise your product on television if half your audience cannot buy your product. (A tiny proportion is probably acceptable, but half *is* wasteful.)

This kind of strategy has a number of advantages. First, it is fairly easy to implement. All you need is a team to go into the market and set the operation up. Second, the products or services being sold can easily be transferred from the existing locations, and the additional volume going through the system is a strong lever for more favourable prices from the suppliers: economies of scale again (see page 25). Third, the possibility of something going wrong is not very high because the services or products that are being offered are known to be acceptable in the market. Unfortunately this can sometimes backfire on a firm: just because your product is popular in Devon does not guarantee that it will be popular in Yorkshire. Moreover trying to expand across national frontiers can be very risky, as Marks & Spencer discovered when they opened up a store in Paris: the way M & S operate in Britain in clothing (i.e. try it on at home, bring it back if it does not fit) was not in line with the custom in Paris. The whole operation nearly collapsed. A further problem with expansion geographically is that it becomes more difficult to keep an eye on what is happening. This is a particular problem for the independent retailer who opens his first branch. This issue will be examined again later.

A more subtle form of market expansion occurs not geographically but where it is realised that only a proportion of the population who could buy the product in fact do buy it. For instance, in America research was carried out seeking ways of increasing the consumption of prunes. It was discovered that most people regarded the product as something to be eaten only as a mild laxative. The product was subsequently promoted as an alternative dessert to more usual fruit, in an attempt to capture a different market segment.

Product/service expansion

Some organisations prefer to expand by adding to the list of products or services they are selling rather than to expand the territory in which they operate. The underlying idea is that by offering customers a wider range of products there is a better chance of them buying your products rather than your competitors'. Good examples of this are to be found in the food industry, especially in confectionery where new chocolate products arrive on the scene regularly, and in the frozen food business, with new frozen meals being introduced.

The advantages of this kind of expansion are that the new products can easily be added on to the firm's list of products; no separate sales force is needed, nor special distribution facilities, and no different paperwork. The chances of success should be high, since the company should know its market.

Unfortunately, new products are often expensive to develop. The collapse of Rolls-Royce in the early 1970s can be largely attributed to the huge cost of developing a new aero-engine, the RB211. Even developing an attractive new bar of chocolate costs money.

Moreover set-up costs can be high if extra plant and machinery is required, and the cost of launching the product, in terms of advertising and sales promotion, can be very high. To recoup the heavy outlay in getting the new product off the ground it has to sell extremely well, but there is no guarantee of success, no way of being certain the new baby will thrive. In fact the 'death rate' of new products in the consumer goods industries is very high. Estimates suggest that as many as eight out of every ten new products are abandoned soon after their introduction, and large numbers never reach the shops.

Activity

Most people from time to time try something new and find it unacceptable, either because it is far too expensive, because it does not do the job it should or because it breaks down and cannot be repaired. Possibly the worst is the product which (through colour, smell or taste) makes you throw it away instantly. My own favourite disaster was a blueberry-flavoured breakfast cereal, which not only turned the milk blue but actually turned the children off cereals for a while.

Look out for other disastrous products.

Diversification

To diversify is the only way to fill up the gap available to organisations which are efficient and which have expanded their markets and products as far as possible. This is because there is no limit to the amount of diversification that can be undertaken in the long run. Diagrammatically the alternative basic strategies look like Figure 5.6.

Put simply, diversification is doing something different – not in place of existing products and markets, but in addition.

There are several reasons why organisations choose to diversify:

- It may be the only reasonable way of filling the 'planning gap'. If your market is the world, your product range comprehensive and you are efficient, then you have to diversify.
- It may be a better alternative than expansion. There are situations when to expand a market or the range of products is so expensive and the potential benefits are so small that it would not help much to expand in either direction; to achieve the required increase in performance needs diversification. For example, a company selling its products throughout

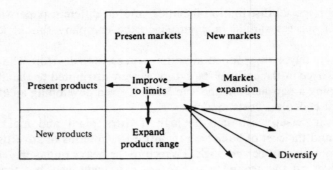

Fig 5.6   The product/market matrix

Europe may look at North America as a potential market. The cost of getting into that market would be very high and the risk of failure very great.

- Diversification can be an insurance policy. If an organisation thinks that its existing operations are subject to an unacceptable level of threat from the environment, then it may put some effort into another type of activity which will keep the business going if the old activity dies. This is known as 'spreading the risk' or simply not putting your eggs into one basket.
- Sometimes organisations find that their current operations are generating so much money that the only way they can use it is in buying or starting up a new venture: not so much a strategy as opportunism.
- Finally some organisations diversify for some whimsical reason, such as being offered a company which had some appeal to the management. This is diversifying 'just for the hell of it'.

Types of diversification
At one extreme, diversification can appear to be a logical extension of an organisation's current activities. *Reader's Digest* magazine also publishes books – the market is similar (but not the same), the product is similar (but not the same), and the techniques used in all stages are similar.

Then there is the kind of diversification seen in the case of Ford, manufacturing motorcars and tractors. The products and markets are different; the similarity is in the technology.

At the extreme there is the sort of diversification where everything is different; no similarities exist at all. This is normally called 'conglomerate' diversification, and an excellent example of this is the British company Tomkins PLC, which had a turnover of some £3.2 billion in 1994 and owns over 70 different businesses, worldwide, including the manufacture of:

- lawnmowers
- handguns (Smith and Wesson)

- safety footwear
- bicycles
- fluid control equipment
- flour (Hovis)
- food products, including famous brands like Bisto, Paxo and Robertson's jams

and many others.

A further type of diversification is what is known as 'vertical integration', meaning getting involved in a business commercially connected with your own. For example, a book-publishing house may buy a printing firm, or even an ink works; and it may also open up bookshops to sell its products. The great advantage of this kind of arrangement is the control of supplies and the fact that profits stay inside the business all along the line.

Review

In the example of Daisy Cycles (page 71), the bold venture into fishing tackle failed because the organisation was too weak.

It was suggested that if an improvement strategy had been followed the firm would not have collapsed.

- Which of the following strategies were they actually following?
  (a) Product expansion
  (b) Market expansion
  (c) Diversification: (i) similar technology, similar market; (ii) different technology, similar market; (iii) similar technology, different market; (iv) different technology, different market (i.e. a conglomerate move).
- If they had succeeded in making the cycle business successful, do you think that it would have been a good idea to go into fishing tackle then?

By moving into fishing tackle from bicycles, the shop was following a strategy of conglomerate diversification (c) (iv) because the product technology is completely different and the market (although geographically the same) is completely different too. There might be a little overlap (i.e. cycling fishermen) but there is no other natural connection.

Would such a move make sense later? If you decided 'yes' you were possibly thinking of such factors as: fishing is an increasingly popular leisure activity; it can be a very profitable venture; it would spread the risk; it would utilise space effectively and spread the shop overheads costs.

If you decided it would not be a good idea your reasons would include: the high cost of getting into the business; the lack of knowledge of the business (different from a knowledge of fishing itself); the uncertainty: will it be a success?

There is no clear-cut answer to this; a great deal depends on whether you would be prepared to take a chance. If money is too precious to risk then it goes into the bank. If any risk is acceptable then the money can be put on a 100-to-1 racehorse in the Grand National. Between these two extremes lies the level of acceptable risk each organisation is prepared to tolerate. (More on this in Chapter 10.)

One further element that helps to make the decision easier is known as 'synergy'. Sometimes this is called the '2 + 2 = 5 effect', and it has been developed in a management sense by Igor Ansoff (in his book *Corporate Strategy* – see Further Reading). It is the idea that if two activities are put together, the outcome is a much better result than if they had been working apart. With conglomerate diversification there is usually very little synergy, whereas most synergy is experienced in expansion strategies. For instance, when two organisations merge, the combined research function has far better results than the independent units.

However, there can also be a negative synergy (2 + 2 = 3). This can happen in any strategy, but particularly where the new activity is bought (through a takeover for instance) rather than developed from within. The merger of the British car firms to form British Leyland resulted in negative synergy, and there have been many more.

Synergy can only come from strengths within the business; it cannot cure a weakness. It is like the effect of yeast on flour and water – without it the compound is not very palatable, but add it and good bread can result. The only difficulty is that synergy cannot be purchased on its own.

Competitive strategy and competitive advantage

Another way of looking at strategy is provided by the work of Michael Porter, whose first two books take as titles the two phrases used above. Porter argues that five forces affect the degree of competition within an industry. These are:

- barriers to entry
- threat of substitute products
- buyer power
- supplier (including labour) power
- existing competition (rivalry)

Once a firm knows where its relative strengths and weaknesses are vis-à-vis the five forces, it can plan its strategy accordingly. Firms have three kinds of competitive advantage – *low cost* (buying most efficiently), *differentiation* (do something to add more value so that premium prices can be obtained) and *focus* (concentrate on a particular segment or geographic market and excel in it). Moreover he stresses the need to create *sustainable* competitive advantage by creating barriers of its own or by being a 'moving target' and by creating value for its buyers. He uses the concept of the *Value Chain* – those activities in a firm upon which competitive advantage is determined.

Making strategy happen

Once chosen, a strategy can be implemented by growth from within the firm, or by taking over or buying up another company. A third option is a merger, where both firms in effect create a completely new organisation, ceasing to exist themselves. British Aerospace and the National Westminster Bank are two such (successful) examples, but there are many failures.

Two increasingly popular methods of achieving one's strategic ambition are those of the Joint Venture and the Strategic Alliance. If your organisation lacks a particular skill or resource necessary to achieve a strategic objective, then invite another party to work with you which has those skills but which does not possess your strengths. These forms of co-operation are to be found in, for instance, the construction industry, in electronics, heavy engineering and anywhere where a single company will lack either adequate finance or expertise to go it alone.

Joint ventures are often designed to achieve a particular task and have a finite life – building the Channel Tunnel, for example. A strategic alliance can continue for years – such as that between Honda and Rover cars, which lasted for fifteen years until BMW made a takeover bid for Rover in 1994. In either type of activity, there are risks – not least that you may fall out with the other party. Another risk is that the venture may take on a life of its own and both 'parents' find they are unable to control it (just like family life, at times).

The choice as to which method to use is governed by time, cost and the resources at one's disposal. The home-grown system is slower, but cheaper, and depends on the ability and willingness of staff to change (as we will see in Chapter 13). Acquisition is quicker, more expensive and can be much riskier.

Last words on strategy

The choice of strategy depends partly on the size of the planning gap and the strengths and weaknesses of the organisation. It also depends on the threats and opportunities seen to be in the environment and the strength of competitive forces. This evaluation is commonly referred to as SWOT and, coupled with an understanding of the constraints placed on it, forms the basis of the search for a strategy to secure the long-term objectives of the organisation.

There is a lot to be said for the approach known as 'widening the search', i.e. looking for an opportunity close to one's existing operations that builds on a strength and offers some synergy. If there is nothing suitable, look further afield, and so on until the requirements of the gap have been met.

An alternative approach, popular some years ago, was to ask the question, What business are we in? The answer provides the clue to where to look for new opportunities. The difficulty with the question is that too broad an answer (e.g. We are in the money-making business) is useless; too narrow an answer (We sell bicycles) provides no ideas at all, and a middle answer (We are in the transport equipment business) can lead to odd diversification moves with no synergy (the bicycle shop starting a taxi service).

What about strategies for departmental managers? Normally improvement is the only option to consider, but there are times when it is appropriate to seek to expand the department's activities and even diversify. This might be thought of as empire-building, but if the new activity could make a contribution to the overall objectives of the organisation, then it must be considered.

Finally, most of the discussion in this chapter has been focused on commercial organisations, but what about the non-business sector? Here the constraints are often much greater and there is less freedom to choose alternative ways of achieving goals. Hospitals can improve, they can expand their services and their facilities, but it is not their role to diversify. Managers in local government and in the civil service have comparatively little room for manoeuvre. However, their responsibility is to provide a particular service efficiently. The strategy to be pursued has to be one of improvement, but again there are times when it is appropriate to consider expansion of the service. The important idea to bear in mind is the principle that strategy is the path chosen to the objective. All organisations should have objectives; it follows that they should all have a strategy too.

Strategy in action: a recent case

In July 1992 Imperial Chemical Industries (ICI), one of Britain's biggest industrial corporations, announced that it was going to demerge, making its pharmaceuticals business a separate company called Zeneca, with shares quoted on the stockmarket.

At the time ICI employed some 130,000 people all over the world and consisted of some 500 subsidiary companies. A strategic move such as this is rare at any level, but the scale of this demerger must constitute one of the boldest strategic decisions ever taken.

Why was this option taken? In an interview with the *Financial Times*, the Chairman, Sir Denys Henderson, stated:

> the world of the 1990s differs from anything that has gone before. Economic growth is going to be slow and painful. The classical chemicals industry has largely run out of ideas. It faces competition from new parts of the world, such as the Asia Pacific region, and is obliged to spend more on the environment than it can readily afford. The collapse of communism has created chaos in the markets of eastern Europe, and has harmed a valuable customer in the form of the defence industry. (Quoted in the *Financial Times*, 9 March 1994)

The demerger option was taken to 'release shareholder value', a thought which was brought home forcibly to ICI's managers when Hanson PLC seemed to be about to attempt a takeover...and the outcome of that, it is believed, would have been a large-scale 'unbundling' of ICI.

The logistics involved in the exercise were incredibly complex and expensive in both time and money. At a personal level everyone in the company felt the effects of an even more uncertain future than hitherto.

So has it worked? In Sir Denys' words: 'It will be quite a while before each company proves how it can grow. None of us saw this as a magic wand. It's the opening of a door, and it's saying to each company "you have a new start, but you've got to get on and deliver".' The merger took place in mid-1993 and a year later the prospects for both companies looked good.

Review

If you were appointed manager of your nearest garage and given a free hand and plenty of money, what would your strategy be for the next four years?

Part III

Getting Organised

Getting organised follows directly from planning. It is concerned with the way the parts of the institution fit together – what is often called 'structure' – and also with the internal rules and agreed ways of working – normally referred to as 'policies'. Structure and policy are vital for the successful achievement of the strategy of the organisation. They embrace all aspects of it, keep it running smoothly and save time, effort and money.

6 How Organisations Develop and Grow

By the end of this chapter you should be able to identify the main stages of growth of an organisation and understand how (and why) its structure changes as it develops and grows.

At the start of Chapter 3 you were invited to try to identify the successful and the unsuccessful small shops in your neighbourhood. The successful shop was described in terms of activity as well as appeal, and the failure (or pending failure) was described as 'quiet, dull and unappealing'. Moreover it has also been mentioned that some of our biggest companies began as small shops – not even as big as that sometimes – more like street traders than retailers. Nowadays, just as always, some very small firms grow and become big, others fade away and die. This chapter is concerned with what actually happens inside an organisation when it grows.

6.1 The New Organisation

Consider first of all the situation of an organisation that has just come into being as an independent concern; maybe where someone has decided to go it alone and start out in business on his own, or it could be where a relative takes over an old business, as in the case of Daisy Cycles (page 71). Even at the start it is highly unlikely that the owner will be operating on his own; he will be using the advice and help of several others, not necessarily paying them a wage or a salary but possibly paying them fees.

Self-check

Who might a small shopkeeper, just starting out, refer to for advice and help?

The obvious source of advice is not Uncle Joe or Cousin Bert, but the bank manager, and indeed any small firm that starts up without doing so is asking for early trouble.

The second obvious source of advice is a solicitor, who will advise on a number of legal matters such as drawing up a rental or lease agreement on the property.

Very soon a third piece of help will be required, namely that of a firm of accountants. Their role, for the small businessman, is usually preparing the accounts at the end of the year and getting them approved by the tax and VAT people. Again an essential function.

These three types of advice and assistance can be called 'professional services'. They are services which organisations can never do without, although many firms do not employ accountants of their own until they have reached a considerable size, and are quite big before they have their own legal experts.

The owner of the very small business has to be a jack-of-all-trades at first, in the sense that he has to be able to turn his hand to any and every aspect of the business. Soon, in a small shop, it is likely that he will employ one or two sales assistants, often part-timers, and a small practical businessman such as a plumber or jobbing builder will often employ a 'mate' – someone to do the general, unskilled work. The owner's own job is a mixture of tasks, including buying, selling, pricing, housekeeping, display and carrying out the basic book-keeping activities that are needed to keep the money side of the business in order. Very often this last job is not considered sufficiently important to warrant the owner spending his time on it, and it is therefore common to find in such firms a part-time book-keeper employed too. The organisation chart of a small independent shop may look like that in Figure 6.1 once it has got going.

Other small organisations will have a similar appearance, although instead of assistants on the selling side there will be assistants in other functions. For instance, in the case of a small firm of solicitors or estate agents, the first employee to be taken on will probably have general clerical or secretarial skills. Similarly, a small engineering workshop might usefully have a skilled welder or a general labourer.

Fig 6.1   A simple organisation's structure

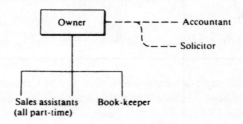

Activity

The need to take on staff comes about for any number of reasons. In the organisation chart shown in Figure 6.1, what reasons could there be for employing two part-time sales assistants and a book-keeper? Name three possibilities and then try to think of a good reason why they should not be employed.

(Fifteen minutes.)

Similarly there are several good reasons for not taking on staff, including the obvious point that nobody hires assistance if the business is not making any money. Moreover some small businessmen prefer not to be responsible for staff in any way, preferring a complete do-it-yourself approach. This in turn can come about for several reasons, such as difficulty in getting on with people, unwillingness to get involved in all the legal matters that are needed when people are employed, and also an inability or fear of delegating work to someone else.

Paying more wages and making more profit

Consider a greengrocer's shop on a Saturday morning. Nearly always there is a queue of people waiting to be served; some potential customers, seeing the queue, will not wait but will go elsewhere to buy their goods. If the shopkeeper had employed another sales assistant, the queue would have been shorter and he would have got the business that did not wait. The questions he has to resolve are, How many extra customers will I get if I hire another sales assistant? and, Will the extra profit pay the extra wages and leave some over for me?

Fortunately there is a useful, simple technique for solving this kind of problem; it is called 'queuing theory' (surprise, surprise). (More information on queuing theory is to be found in any book on operational research. See Further Reading on page 306.)

Another similar situation crops up where the owner feels his time would be more profitably spent in some other activity. For example he may, like the owner of Daisy Cycles, be both selling cycles and repairing them. If he does both, then every time a customer comes into the shop, the repair work stops and gradually less and less work gets done. The owner has to decide which activity he himself can most profitably carry out, and employ someone else to do the other work. Then he has to answer the question, Will I pick up enough extra work to pay for the extra wages and make me more money? If he does not feel happy trying to solve this problem, then he should ask his accountant.

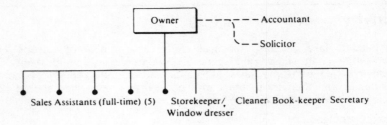

Fig 6.2   The structure of a settled small shop

6.2 The Settled Small Organisation

Once the owner of a small organisation has recovered from the excitement and worry of hiring his first employee, it is not difficult for the total number of people employed to rise quite quickly up to the point where the business could not support any more growth. By now the owner is acting in a proper managerial role, leaving a large part of the routine operations to his staff, and the organisation structure may look like that in Figure 6.2 for a large shop.

The important point as far as this, and all other simple organisations, is concerned is that all the staff report to one manager only, who is the owner or sole working director. None of the staff have any responsibilities of a managerial nature: all decisions are taken by the 'boss'.

There are two important variations on this theme, the first being the small firm which is employing technicians or technical experts. The structure of this kind of institution might look like Figure 6.3.

Again all the decisions are taken by the owner. Each 'technician' is given work to do and has an assistant to do the routine work for him. This kind of organisation may be found in, for example, a firm engaged in central-heating installation or repair, or in a technical drawing office.

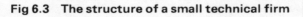

Fig 6.3   The structure of a small technical firm

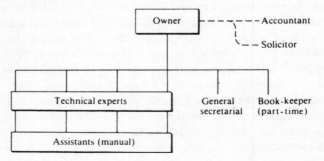

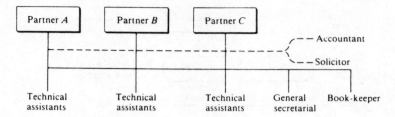

Fig 6.4   A partnership structure

The second kind of variation is the partnership where two or three individuals have come together to develop a business idea. Decisions tend to be taken collectively, but apart from that, each partner often then concentrates on his own area of specialisation – see Figure 6.4.

An organisation like this can be very strong if the partners understand and support each other's actions and aspirations but it depends for its success on effective and frequent communications. The disadvantage is that differences of opinion may slow down the decision-making process too much. The one-man operation can move much quicker because he does not have to consult or discuss – although the decisions he takes may not be as good as those reached by a partnership.

6.3 The Divided Business

Activity

Look at the first organisation chart on page 87 showing how an independently owned shop might be structured. Suppose that the business was so successful that the owner decided to open a similar shop in the next town ten miles away. How are both shops going to be managed now?

Take ten minutes to decide how the new organisation structure might appear: there are three main variations (and a lot of minor ones).

Once a business like this has decided where it is going to locate its second centre of operations, the question of managing both becomes critical, simply because the owner cannot be in both places at once. There are three basic alternatives. The first is to set up both establishments in exactly the same way and travel to and from each one, keeping an eye on things all the time, as in Figure 6.5. The owner's office would, of course, be located at *A* along with the clerical and book-keeping functions. However, because *B* is the new unit, most time would be spent away from *A* especially in the early months. So who would handle all the telephone inquiries and the sales representatives from supplier companies?

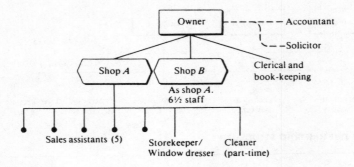

Fig 6.5   Structure of a multiple-sited retailer

To avoid this complication most small firms will take the critical step of appointing either one or two managers. It is not an easy decision to take for the first time, because the owner thinks some of their personal power is being given away; someone else is being trusted with the business they built up, and they are in effect being cut off from the 'action' and possibly from some old friends. It has to be done, because there is no way of keeping track of everything that is going on in the organisation. The owner's effective span of control was the seven or eight people on one site, not fifteen people on two sites ten miles apart.

These two further possibilities – appointing either one or two managers – are shown in Figure 6.6. The better of these two solutions would be the second, to appoint a manager in charge of each shop. However, here there is a practical difficulty: who is to be appointed manager at each location? The success of the business in the future may well hang on these appointments, so it is important to get it right. Possibly the best answer would be to promote two of the existing staff to the new managerial

Fig 6.6   Alternative structures for small, multiple-sited retailers

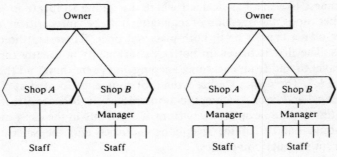

positions. This would have the big advantage that they would know the owner's values and beliefs and there would be no settling-in period. To be able to achieve this very desirable state of affairs needs considerable foresight.

All this we will discuss in relation to the rules of personnel management in Chapter 9.

Delegation: the inevitable step

The moment the owner of a small business appoints a manager, delegation is of a much more significant nature than before. All delegation is concerned with assigning tasks to subordinates; this is not difficult if the subordinates are close by, and their work is visible and easily controlled. However the act of appointing a manager involves delegating some authority and decision-making power.

This is hard for the owner and could also be dangerous. It is hard because, as we saw, he is cutting himself off. It is dangerous because the owner has to trust the manager to do the job properly.

At this stage in the development of the organisation the delegation of managerial responsibility can be the start of its success – or the beginning of the end; it all depends on who is appointed and how well he is trained.

6.4 More Divided Organisations

The example described above relates to a decision to open a second branch of an organisation in a different location. A shop was used for the example, but it could be any type of activity where the strategic plan is to grow by market expansion on a geographic basis. Dividing up an organisation is often referred to by the cumbersome expression 'departmentation', which simply means the process of splitting the business into departments. There are many different ways of doing it, and it is worth having a look at some of the main ones (this list will also apply to the problem of dividing work up between individuals).

Geographically
This is the one we have just been considering and is obviously useful where it is important to be close, physically, to the territory in which the organisation wants to operate. For instance, a company based in Britain may consider that its market is the whole of Western Europe. Rather than attempting to do everything from its head office it may divide up the sales function (and later the production function), placing a separate operation in each country, or cluster of countries.

By function

In a manufacturing organisation the main functions of the business are production and sales. It is not uncommon to find, in a very small business, that the first manager to be appointed by the owners is either the sales manager, or a manager in charge of 'operations'.

One function not easily recognised by most small businessmen is that of marketing, as opposed to sales. Very often decisions regarding the marketing mix are taken by the owner without realising that they are really marketing issues and without the appropriate knowledge. A common trap is to first have a sales manager and then call him a marketing manager without either person really appreciating what marketing actually involves. It is best to recognise both functions early. This is explored more fully in the next chapter.

By product

As organisations grow, so the range of the products or services they are offering grows. At first all the products are handled using common facilities, but there comes a time when the volume being dealt with is so big that advantages are to be gained by treating each product as a separate company. For instance the Unilever organisation's soap-powder operations (i.e. Lever Brothers) and its ice-cream business (i.e. Walls) are separate companies operating almost entirely on their own. In a department store, the products are divided up into departments because of the importance of specialised knowledge in both buying and selling.

By customer

This is particularly common in the selling function where it is felt that different kinds of customers require different treatment. For example in the food manufacturing industry there is a distinction between the small independent shop and the large multiple supermarket firm. Each needs to be approached in a different way.

By process

Many operations, both clerical and in manufacturing, are performed in sequence, and it is one of the features of organisations that the sequences have tended to be split up into more and more smaller parts. The reason for this is that each separate process requires special skills; by specialising in a limited range of work, the operator becomes highly efficient, thus raising his productivity.

To pursue this kind of departmentation to its logical conclusion would result in all kinds of absurdity. Imagine what would happen if the work of bus drivers was divided up. Driver A would start up the bus, driver B would then take the bus out on to the road, where driver C would take over. Driver D would take control on dual-carriageway roads only and driver E would be used for stopping the bus. One could even imagine a situation where yet another individual, F, would stop the engine.

Self-check

What do you think of this example? Why is it absurd?

The absurdity of the example comes about because it is such an inefficient way of driving a bus. But a more serious issue lies beneath the surface, namely how do you think the people involved feel? Would they feel a bit frustrated at not being able to do the whole job?

It is this kind of problem that has resulted in criticism of the conveyor-belt system in recent years, and which has led to such things as the Volvo experiment in Sweden. The idea at Volvo was that in the conveyor-belt method of making cars, each worker only sees a tiny fraction of the whole process and is doing a repetitive job so eventually becomes bored with it because there is no identification with the end product. To overcome this, group working was introduced, whereby a small team of workers could together be responsible for the output of a particular department or workshop, each doing a variety of jobs.

More recently, Toyota, the Japanese car-maker, has devised a system which optimises automation and human labour in its Motomachi plant. Machines are expensive and do break down. Robots are used to minimise unpleasant work and workers move along the line with the car in the assembly area, carrying out a variety of tasks. It is in this part of the process where human intervention is most useful: 'Only humans can tell if a door really fits or if the steering wheel feels right', says Mikio Kitano, director in charge of production engineering (quoted in the *Financial Times*, 9 August 1994). The conclusion is 'that workers have a stronger feeling that they have made an important contribution to the manufacturing of the car'.

By numbers

This system is used in, for instance, the army and in other circumstances where many people are required to carry out similar work to each other.

Alphabetically

A common way of dividing up work which is of a similar nature is on an alphabetic basis. This is particularly common in offices where large volumes of similar material have to be processed. One department will deal with all customers whose last names begin with the letters A, B or C. Another department handles D, E and F and so on.

Which sort of division to choose

It must be recognised that each way of dividing up an organisation has its advantages and disadvantages. Some methods are obviously completely unsuitable for the task. For instance, to divide up the management of British Rail alphabetically by name of station would be pointless. The key questions to ask include:

- Does the division tie in with overall strategies?
- Does it cost more than any other method?
- How easy will it be to co-ordinate the separate parts?
- Could it lead to interdepartmental battles? (Not avoidable in any split-up, but some are potentially more likely to result in war than others.)
- Are the members of the team likely to be motivated by the arrangement or not?

How many subordinates?

On page 88 we introduced the phrase 'span of control' with reference to the number of people working directly for the owner of a small shop. The phrase has been in use in management literature for a long time, although a more apt phrase would be 'span of management' since the idea behind it is not just concerned with control but with all aspects of managing. The question of how many subordinates a manager can handle is one which has taxed all kinds of people for a very long time; perhaps the first being the advice given to Moses by Jethro, his father-in-law, when Moses seemed to be spending all day sorting out disputes between people. Said Jethro:

> This is not the best way to do it. You will only wear yourself out and wear out all the people who are here. The task is too heavy for you; you cannot do it by yourself... You must instruct them in the statutes and laws, and teach them how they must behave and what they must do. But you yourself must search for capable God-fearing men among all the people, honest and incorruptible men, and appoint them over the people as officers over units of a thousand, of a hundred, of fifty or ten. They shall sit as a permanent court for the people; they must refer difficult cases to you but decide simple cases for themselves. In this way your burden will be lightened and they will share it with you.

> (The whole episode is in Exodus xviii, 13–17 (New English Bible translation.)

In modern times a number of attempts have been made to come up with a definite answer to the question. General Sir Ian Hamilton wrote in 1921 that between three and six is the ideal number depending on the level in the organisation. Lyndall Urwick, the management consultant, considered five or six to be ideal towards the top; and at the lowest levels in an organisation it can be as many as twelve (if these twelve do not supervise the work of others).

Surveys have revealed that the number of managers reporting to the managing director varies from one to twenty-four with the average being eight or nine. The more there are, the bigger the problem.

Self-check

Manager X has two assistants Y and Z. There is, therefore, a direct relationship between Manager X and Y, and also between Manager X and Z.

There are occasions, however, when Manager X will discuss things with Y when Z is also present, and sometimes will discuss things with Z when Y is present. These two could be called 'group relationships'.

Moreover there will be times when Y wants to consult Z, and others when Z wants to consult Y. These two could be called 'cross relationships'.

There are therefore six possible relationships:

$$\text{Two direct relationships} + \text{Two group relationships} + \text{Two cross relationships}$$

1 If there were three subordinates, how many relationships would there be in total?
● Between six and ten.
● Eleven to fifteen.
● Sixteen to twenty.
● Twenty-one or over.

2 If there were eight subordinates, how many relationships would there be?
● Less than 100.
● 101 to 500.
● 501 to 1000.
● Over 1000.

The actual number of relationships is as shown in Table 6.1.

Table 6.1   Staff numbers with the potential number of relationships

Number of subordinates	Total number of relationships
1	1
2	6
3	18
4	44
5	100
6	222
7	490
8	1,080
9	2,376
10	5,210
20	10,486,154
24	201,327,166

All this was worked out by a French consultant, A. A. Graicunas, in 1933. Fortunately it is not likely that all the possible relationships will occur in any group of people in any one day, week or even month. If it was attempted all at once, there would be a fair amount of chaos. As to the effective number of subordinates that anyone can manage – this must depend on the nature of the work and the people involved.

6.5 **The Growing Complex Organisation**

Eventually an organisation that has successfully divided itself up on a simple basis, such as we have been looking at, will find itself with another problem that comes about as it grows. The problem is known by the phrase 'chain of command'. This can best be illustrated by another example, that of a firm selling herbal bath-salts that decided to expand its sales force so that every chemist's shop in Britain would be visited once every two weeks. They calculated that they needed a salesforce of 2,160 to do the job properly. Bearing in mind the problem of the span of control, they proposed creating a structure that looked like that of Figure 6.7.

In other words, the chain of command had seven levels.

By being a little more flexible, and deciding that twelve salespeople could be comfortably managed by one manager, a revised structure was drawn up with only six levels (Figure 6.8).

Fig 6.7   A seven-level chain of command

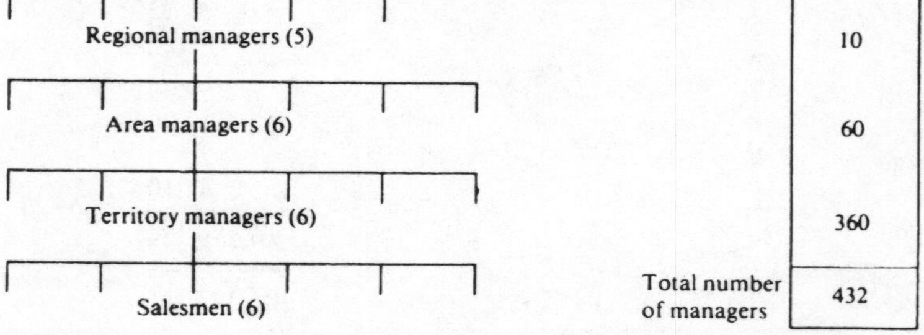

	Total number of managers at each level
Managing director	
Sales director	
Sales manager (north) Sales manager (south) (structure as north)	2
Regional managers (5)	10
Area managers (6)	60
Territory managers (6)	360
Salesmen (6)	
Total number of managers	432

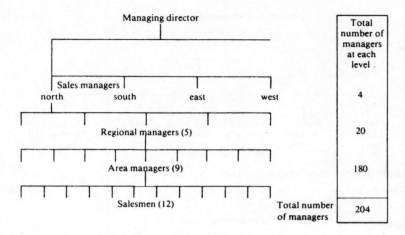

Fig 6.8   A six-level chain of command

The conclusion from this is that the wider the span of management, the shorter the chain of command. The problem with very long chains of command is that instructions, questions, suggestions and requests take a long time to pass up and down the line, especially if there is no way of short-circuiting the process. For instance, in our seven-level salesforce structure it can be seen that there are actually a total of 432 managers between the sales director and the salespeople (in the six-level organisation there are only 204 intermediate managers). If a salesperson in the south wants to discuss with a salesperson in the north a client whose factory happens to be on the borderline between the two, consider what happens. A message would in theory have to go all the way up to the top and back down the other side to the original salesperson. No less than eighteen separate communications would have occurred; highly wasteful of time, energy and money.

The shorter the chain of command, the faster the decisions get taken and the quicker problems get solved. In addition, to be a long, long way from the top, in terms of an organisation chart, results in a loss of morale – people begin to feel like numbers or 'cogs in the wheel' and rather insignificant.

The problem, then, for the growing complex organisation is how to divide itself up without losing the flexibility of the smaller firm and without creating a situation where the staff feel unimportant. Often the answer lies in the creation of self-contained divisions or separate businesses. The difference between this and simple departmental organisation can be seen by looking at their respective organisation charts (Figures 6.9 and 6.10).

The importance of the produce/factory relationship is that factory A would make produce X; factory B would make product Y and factory C would make product Z.

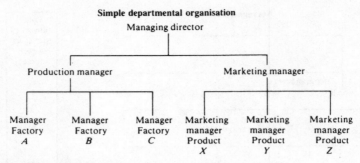

Fig 6.9   A departmental organisation's structure

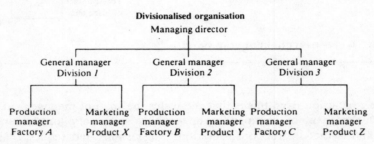

Fig 6.10   A divisionalised organisation's structure

In a divisionalised organisation the managing director is no longer concerned with co-ordinating the marketing and production functions of all the different products and factories. The responsibility has been delegated to each of the three general managers. The managing director's role can now be much more strategic in emphasis and concerned with the overall performance and prospects of each division as a separate business.

There are, however, some limitations to the divisional structure. It is not an appropriate structure for single-product companies, however large. It could lead to under-utilisation of some productive resources; the advantage of the departmental company is its ability to minimise waste and maximise capacity. Moreover the divisionalised business can spread talent too thinly across the company, whereas the departmental company puts all the expertise in a particular function together.

Activity

Consider an organisation you know well and try to work out what would happen if its workload suddenly became four times as big as it is now. It may be the company or institution you work for, or a club or society you are involved with; whatever you choose ask these questions:

● Would the present organisation structure be able to cope?
● What type of structure would be best for the organisation if it was four times as big?

The matrix organisation

An alternative type of organisation structure has come into prominence over the last thirty years which is known as the 'matrix structure'. The idea is to avoid the weakness of both the departmental structure and the divisionalised structure we have just considered. Its roots can be found in advertising agencies, construction companies and in civil and aeronautical engineering firms: indeed it can be encountered in all types of organisations which are engaged in projects – i.e. activities with a specific limited objective. It can, however, be used in more standardised forms of activity too.

The essence of a matrix structure is that the functional relationships within the business still stand. For example there would still be a production manager with three factory managers reporting to him, as in Figure 6.9. However, each factory manager would have a direct relationship with a counterpart on the marketing side, rather than an informal indirect contact. Using Figures 6.9 and 6.10, the matrix organisation structure appears as in Figure 6.11.

Each marketing manager would take on a co-ordinating responsibility for his particular product, making sure that all aspects of its production distribution, storage, promotion and sale were handled in the most efficient and profitable way. Similarly in companies engaged in project work, a project manager would be appointed to make sure that the project was a success. A number of experts would report to the project manager as long as

Fig 6.11   A matrix organisation's structure

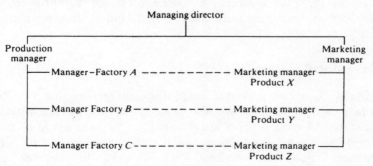

the project was in progress, and as soon as it finished all concerned would move on. In the same way advertising agencies have account executives to manage each client company's advertising needs.

The holding company

Ultimately an organisation grows so large that the only effective way it can be managed is by making separate companies out of existing divisions. This can be done in such a way that the only relationship between each operating company and the top of the organisation is the legal one of ownership, the divisions becoming 'wholly owned subsidiary' companies. The actual connections become mainly concerned with the movement of finance and the transfer of profits, and the head-office management interfere only if adequate profits are not being generated.

Many big organisations operate self-contained divisions in this way, but do not go so far as to create separate legal entities. Others only have legal subsidiary companies when they buy up existing independent organisations. Thus they have a mixture of divisions and subsidiary companies.

Centralisation *v.* decentralisation

One of the big problems in developing organisational structures is the extent to which authority should be kept at the top of the organisation or passed out down the line. In effect this implies that if all decisions are taken by the owner of a small business, or by the managing director of a larger organisation, then it may be described as a highly centralised operation. On the other hand, if the power to take decisions is passed away from the top, then it is a relatively decentralised organisation. As we have seen, the owner of the small firm has to delegate; and the more he delegates, the more his firm is decentralised.

If the organisation charts in Figures 6.9 and 6.10 fairly represent actual authority, then it is easy to see that the departmental organisation is still centralised, while the authority of the divisional company is passed down a level from the managing director to the general managers of each division. Similarly in the matrix structure, Figure 6.11, the authority must be decentralised to the project team leader if that kind of structure is to work effectively.

The line and staff problem

Early in the chapter we looked at the professional services that a small firm might hire for specific jobs. We also brought into the picture a part-time book-keeper. All these services are essential yet they are not at all directly connected with the production, distribution and marketing of the organisation's goods or services. They are like the umpires, coach, groundsmen and scorers at a cricket match: not actually in the game, but essential to its success. All organisations have to have the services of a variety of experts and, as they grow, so they bring in more and more such people. These areas of expertise are usually referred to as 'staff functions'.

The accountancy function is one of the most important of these because every transaction that the organisation makes has to be recorded and checked. In addition, the enormous sums of money flowing through companies (even the smallest) need to be carefully controlled. Finally many decisions in organisations are related (or at least should be) to improving efficiency and effectiveness and the accountancy function is best placed to help managers arrive at a good decision. Accountants do not make the product, nor do they sell it, but without their expertise the organisation would very soon collapse.

Similarly the need for experts in personnel, legal and company-secretarial, buying, market research, statistics and a hundred other areas is vital for the continuing success of the firm as it grows.

In contrast, the makers and the sellers in an organisation are known as 'line functions', because their authority is received straight 'down the line' in the chain of command.

Self-check

Which of the following jobs are 'staff' functions?

1 The maintenance engineer in a brewery bottling plant.
2 The cashier in a bank.
3 A nurse in a hospital.
4 An economist in a motorcar firm.
5 The army intelligence service.
6 An accountant in a firm of chartered accountants.
7 An accountant in British Rail.

Numbers 1, 4, 5 and 7 are staff functions. The maintenance engineer is a service function, not in the normal line of command as far as production is concerned. The economist in the motorcar firm is in an advisory position and does not, nor cannot, direct the operations of the firm. The army intelligence service is similar; it does not direct – it advises. In fact the concept of line and staff functions may well have first been developed in the army. Finally accountants in British Rail neither run trains nor look after railway stations: their work is a service.

Decentralising staff functions

The discussion on decentralisation on page 98 was in relation to the line function of an organisation. However, a separate problem exists with staff

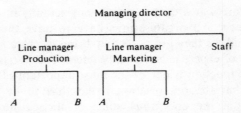

Fig 6.12   Structure of a departmental company with centralised staff function

functions, because they can easily remain centralised while the operating parts of the organisation are decentralised. The simplified organisation charts in Figures 6.12 and 6.13 illustrate the dilemma. The departmental organisation in Figure 6.12 may change to either of the two structures in Figure 6.13. The issue is: should staff continue to report directly to the top when the line responsibilities are being decentralised (Figure 6.13a) or should they be decentralised too (Figure 6.13b)? The problem can be seen at its clearest in relation to the buying function, namely: centralised buying or not?

Some large diversified organisations insist on a highly centralised buying function – a group of skilled buyers operating from the headquarters of the organisation and making purchases for the group of companies as a whole. Other organisations have merely a token buying function at head office,

Fig 6.13   Alternative divisionalised company structure with centralised or decentralised staff functions

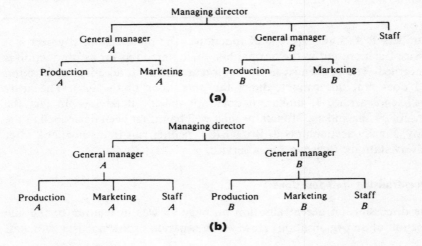

leaving all the work to buyers at the level of the subsidiary company or division. At the local level decisions can be made quickly, sudden problems can be quickly solved and the buyers have a better knowledge of the needs of the operating managers in the division. They will not, however, have the power and leverage that a headquarters buyer can exert. So what does the company do?

Each organisation has to choose whether or not to decentralise its staff functions unless they are so specialised that it is obviously uneconomic to duplicate them across all parts of the organisation. There is no right or wrong answer to this; it all depends on the needs of the organisation.

The virtual organisation

There is a large 'holiday village' (what used to be called a holiday camp in the old days) in the west of England which not only employs cooks, waiters, cleaners, entertainers and administrators, but all the trades and crafts needed to keep the place operating successfully – electricians, carpenters, gardeners, plumbers, builders, accountants, security guards and dozens of others.

However, it need not employ anyone directly; it could hire in on a contract basis almost everyone it needed as and when the service was required. If it were to organise itself in this manner, it would have the same turnover, but its costs would be less (hopefully) and the job of management would be very different. It would become a 'virtual company'.

Many organisations, both public and private, are sub-contracting out work so that they can focus all managerial activity on the main purpose. One of the best examples in the public sector is the London Borough of Wandsworth which has contracted-out most of its services. We will return to this question in Chapter 8.

How does an organisation's structure change?

Structure depends on:

- *the type of business or activity*
- *size*
- *strategies*
- *policies*
- *the values of the people in positions of power in the organisation*

Organisation structures are changing all the time as new opportunities arise, as old activities die away, and as the organisation itself develops and grows. Most of the time the structure changes gradually, but every so often it is necessary, for a variety of reasons, to have a radical reorganisation. As one expert on organisation development called it, 'Evolution and Revolution as Organisations Grow' (title of an article by Larry E. Greiner in *Harvard*

Business Review, July–August 1972). The reason why these reorganisations occur are several and will be looked at in Chapter 13 on the management of change; they grow and prosper or wither and die. There is, however, nothing to say that they have to die. Certainly, though, if they fail to adapt their structures to meet the requirements of new strategies and new circumstances then their chances of success will be diminished.

7 Policies in Marketing and Sales

The aim of this chapter is to help you to identify the key areas of choice that all business organisations face in the marketing and sales functions. You should also be able to understand and state the difference between marketing and sales, and identify the main reasons for their importance in the search for success.

Most of this chapter is relevant only to business organisations and other activities where some form of sale is involved. Purely administrative organisations, in government for instance, will not be concerned with many aspects of marketing or selling, although they should be interested in the question of promotion (see pages 109–12).

7.1 Marketing: The Key Policies to Choose

The case of the Cotoo Mineral Water Works

Ten years ago the Cotoo Mineral Water Works was a run-down old-established fizzy soft drinks firm in South Wales. The owner died, leaving the company to a distant relative who decided to put his savings into the firm and build up the business. He found that the products were tasty, the sales force were able (although they were only two in number) and the rest of the staff were loyal and keen to help in the development of the firm. The factory was entirely rebuilt on modern lines with brand-new up-to-date equipment. In total, fifteen different flavours of 'pop' were produced, all of it put in large glass bottles with a screw-top cap.

New delivery vans were purchased (and carefully painted with the ancient livery of the firm on the side). However, sales remained static and only went up whenever there was a heatwave, which was not all that often.

The overall effect was depressing because the bottling plant had finished production by lunchtime each day, and most afternoons were spent keeping the place cleaned and well maintained. In a nutshell, a lot of money had gone out and very little had come in. So the new owner called a meeting of the two staff in sales, the accountant, the bank manager and two or three older and more senior employees.

The problem of the firm was easily identified as not enough bottles of pop being sold. The underlying problem was, How do we increase sales?

Self-check

You may know nothing about selling soft drinks, but you may well have bought some (cola, tonic water or lemonade, for instance) during the last few weeks. If you were in charge of the Cotoo Company, which of the following ideas do you think would be most useful in helping to increase sales? (All these were ideas that could have come up at the meeting. Read the list twice before deciding and then choose just three. Spend about ten minutes on the problem.)

Ideas for raising sales of soft drinks
1 Sell more flavours.
2 Put the products into plastic bottles.
3 Put the products into small bottles or cans.
4 Advertise heavily.
5 Employ a bigger salesforce.
6 Redesign labels or packaging.
7 Cut prices.
8 Offer better terms to retailers if they buy in large quantities.
9 Run special promotions, e.g. 'Collect ten labels and get a beachball free'.
10 Find out more about your customers and what people want.

Note: Check back to Chapter 5 and recall the discussion on expansion strategies (pages 71–6).

All ten suggestions made above are possible ways of increasing a firm's overall sales, but some would have a much better chance of success than others. The task you were set was to choose three out of the ten, but in reality – if you really were in charge of the company – your problem would be to decide *how many* of these ideas you would employ to push sales up.

To do all these things instinctively feels wrong; and indeed, for a small company not doing very well, to attempt everything might be disastrous, simply because of the drain on limited resources (it would cost a lot of money) and the risk of failure being relatively high.

Idea **10** is the joker in the pack because its adoption would not increase sales directly. It is simply an information-gathering activity which on its own cannot sell anything. It is, however, an important part of marketing – usually termed 'market research' – and an early policy decision to be made by any organisation is how much (if any) effort should be spent on it. Market research can range from a very simple survey of, for instance, the number of shops in an area carrying a rival's product, to very sophisticated studies involving computer programs and many dozens of researchers asking questions of people in the streets. There is no rule of thumb to tell you how much market research to do; it all depends on how badly you need to know and how much you are willing to spend.

Ideas **1** and **9** are all variations on a theme – the marketing theme – and the preferred ranking of the nine (in order of best for the job) is given later in the chapter. Right now the focus has to be on the major areas of decision in the marketing function, which is the part of the business that links corporate strategy with day-to-day operations.

The key policy decisions in marketing and sales can be grouped together under a broad heading commonly called 'the marketing mix' and a convenient way of classifying the variables for which policies can be formulated is known as the 'four *p*'s'.

- *product*
- *place*
- *promotion*
- *price*

A successful marketing operation is one where the mix is working to best advantage, namely that the product is right, it is in the right place, at the right price and is being promoted in the right way. Each of the four *p*'s needs to be looked at in more detail.

Self-check

Classify each of the nine suggested ways of increasing Cotoo's sales (page 104) according to the four *p*'s.

The first three are product questions; the fifth is concerned with place; numbers 4, 6 and 9 are promotion matters (and so is 5 partly) and 7 and 8 relate to price. Each of the four *p*'s can now be studied in greater depth.

'Product' policies

Quality

Any and every product or service offered for sale can be of high quality or low quality or just average. Every type of industry or trade or service seems to produce the equivalent of a Rolls-Royce at one end of the quality scale and a cheap shoddy product at the other end. To decide where on the scale a firm's products or services will be is a fundamental marketing policy decision, the word 'quality' meaning different things in different contexts. An airline may be well known for the quality of its in-flight service; another, infamous for the lack of service.

Product range

There are very few firms that make or sell a single separate product. Even British Gas sells appliances and a maintenance service in addition to its main product, gas. Most firms find that it is easy, cheap and beneficial to offer the market a range of products or services so that there is a better chance of achieving a sale. So, for example, a bed-maker offers a range of beds of different sizes, but also of different quality too – so that different spending power will be attracted to the firm's products. Another example is the soft drinks firm that offers a range of flavours and possibly in different sized bottles.

This conveniently provides an illustration of the overlap that exists between a strategic decision and a policy decision. The strategic decision to expand by growth in the range of products or services offered (see page 72) sets the general tone of the firm's activities. It will be a decision that is arrived at with due regard to the marketing function's analysis of the markets. The policy decisions which follow are those concerned with the precise manner in which the expansion should take place. For instance, the first three ideas for increasing Cotoo's sales of soft drinks are all policy matters, and so the statement can be made, 'Our policy is to seek product expansion by developing a parallel range of products to those in large bottles, but in smaller 'mixer'-sized bottles as well.'

A variation on this theme is what is known as 'bolt-on extras' whereby customers can have a number of optional features added to the basic product if they want. The motorcar business is the best-known example of this, as it is of another similar idea called 'custom design'. Here the customer has to decide on certain features which are added to a standard basic product, making it different from the rest in some way.

Finally, there is one other basic option in this respect – namely, not to make any 'standard' products at all, but to manufacture whatever the customer wants within the broad area of technical competence of the business. A printer can come into this category, if the decision is taken to be a 'jobber' simply waiting for a printing job that may have no relationship with the last job.

The extent to which the company gets involved in these kinds of activities are very much key policy decisions.

Guarantees and after-sales service

All products from any reputable firm have some form of guarantee or warranty, and many products of a durable nature have some service arrangement built in to make sure that any faults are corrected without extra cost to the owner.

'Place' policies

In marketing terms 'place' has a very wide meaning. It not only refers to the basic question of the precise place where a customer can go to buy the product or the service, but includes issues such as the way in which the product is to be moved from the factory to the final selling point. Once the basic strategic decision has been taken defining the market in broad terms (territory to be covered), a whole range of alternatives have to be examined and decisions made about them. A set of rules in this area eliminates a considerable amount of debate and discussion.

Suppose that Cotoo Ltd has defined its overall market as South Wales; it now has to ask itself four very important questions, namely:

To whom are we actually going to sell our products?

An organisation does not have to sell to the final consumer of the product. The soft drinks firm may sell bottles of lemonade directly to schoolboys, but it is not likely that it would rely on this form of activity to achieve the sales volume it wants. However, in some contexts direct selling is probably the most appropriate method. Banks in effect sell direct and so do building societies mostly. Very few consumer products these days pass directly from manufacturer to consumer. It would, however, apply if a large order was being placed, and also in industrial markets where the product in question is sold by one firm to another firm to form part of its own product.

If it is decided that the customer (i.e. the person who buys the product) is not to be the final consumer, the choice left is:

- *an agent*; someone who finds customers for products and services, or who finds a product or service for a customer. Typically this kind of activity is found in exporting where a firm may decide that it is too expensive to set up a separate sales organisation in a particular country. By appointing an agent, in effect the firm is buying a ready-made expert.

  Other examples of businesses that work through agents are to be found in the travel and tourist world, insurance, car distributors.
- *a wholesaler*; someone who buys a range of products often in bulk, splits them up and sells to a large number of smaller customers. Newspapers and magazines typically are distributed in this way.
- *a retailer*; someone who sells a range of products to final consumers.

The policy chosen may be to sell exclusively to one type of customer, or it may be decided to adopt a 'mixture' policy. This may well be necessary if the product itself is normally sold through many different channels. For instance there are at least six or seven different types of places where you could buy a bottle of bitter lemon (e.g. shop, supermarket, pub, club, off-licence, restaurant and hotel).

How do we get our products to our customers?

Once the decision has been taken regarding who the customer will be, the next decision is related to the method used to get the products to the customer. The choice is usually between the simple method of sending the

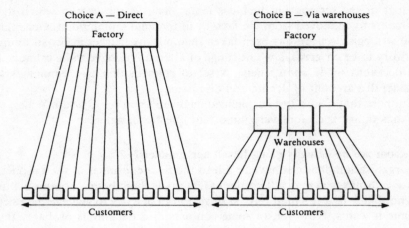

Fig 7.1   Distribution systems – direct or via warehouses

goods direct from production unit to customer or by sending the products to warehouses or stores located in suitable places. The choice can be illustrated with a simple diagram, Figure 7.1.

The factors which will affect the choice include:

- distances involved
- the size of the loads
- extent to which the products are perishable
- and, of course, the relative costs of operating the two systems.

A particularly difficult policy to formulate arises if the company decides to sell direct to the final consumer of the product. For instance:

Self-check

- Through a chain of soft drinks shops.
- Via mail order.
- Through a central warehouse.
- Around the streets, 'off a van'.

The only sensible way would be to send its van out around the streets, in effect combining the functions of selling and physical distribution. This kind of door-to-door service used to be fairly common, but it is now limited to the occasional soft drinks firm and, in the summer, the ice-cream man.

The alternatives are all possible but for the soft drinks business not the wisest alternative – partly because of the cost of setting up the system and partly because it is difficult to see how such operations could be successful. It is unlikely that customers would bother to order their soft drinks on a mail-order basis, or go to a central warehouse to collect them when similar products could be bought at the shop around the corner. Moreover demand for soft drinks is not normally high enough to make an exclusive retail soft drink shop a viable proposition.

To what extent should we try to cover the market?
This is a deceptively simple question. Suppose it is decided that the customer is the retailer and the product is therefore going to be sold in retail outlets only; the question to be resolved is, What proportion of all the retail outlets in the area are going to be asked to carry the goods? And, as a follow-up question, How often is each outlet going to be serviced (i.e. called on or phoned, or delivered to)? Cost and the pattern set by competition are key guides here, as is the desired level of service. Generally the nearer a 100 per cent coverage a firm aims at, the higher will be the average cost of a call.

What physical distribution system should we use?
This issue is a straight choice between:

- *rail*
- *air*
- *sea*
- *road* (own vehicles or hired vehicles or common carrier)

Once again there is no easy answer to this question. The policy chosen will depend on the product, the channel of distribution, distance, cost, level of service and the extent to which the firm wants to retain control over its products as they travel downstream (literally and figuratively).

'Promotion' policies

The Cotoo Mineral Water Company had an excellent range of products. The products were available widely throughout the area, yet sales failed to rise to a level sufficiently high for a decent return on the investment that had been made. If there had been no competition then the firm would have done well – there would be no choice.

There is, however, in the soft drinks business quite a lot of choice, and 'promotion' in the widest sense of the word is concerned with the whole issue of persuading the customer to choose one particular brand of product rather than another. In fact promotion goes on in all walks of life all the time, as people and institutions attempt to persuade others of the merits not merely of their products but of their services, their ideals, politics, beliefs and religions. So whenever politicians stand up to speak, their aim is to promote themselves, their party and its (or their) policies.

Similarly every manager and every organisation is concerned from time to time to get involved in promotion one way or another; the policy decisions being concerned with the extent to which promotion is carried out, and the precise way in which it is carried out.

Generally, promotion covers five elements:

- *advertising*
- *publicity*
- *selling*
- *sales promotion*
- *packaging*

and it is helpful if policies are established in each of these areas.

Advertising
The three key questions at the policy level, so far as advertising is concerned, are:

- What is the advertising going to say (the message)?
- How much is going to be spent?
- Where are we going to advertise (the medium)?

The message
The message can be almost anything and indeed marketing textbooks list dozens of different types of messages that can be contained in an advertisement. They range from the type that contains no words – merely a picture of the product in a particular location: for example, the bottle of beer in the desert sand – to, at the other end, the advertisement which is an essay persuading you of the merits of a particular product or service and includes a cut-out piece to send your name and address off either for a catalogue or to buy. The 'Become an officer in the Army' advertisement is of this type. The important thing is to be clear why advertising is taking place and when advertising will not be carried out.

Activity

Take a recent copy of a magazine, newspaper or Sunday colour supplement and study some of the advertisements contained in it. Try to work out what the advertiser is trying to tell you. For instance, he may be saying one of the following:

- 'Here is this new product; it is very good.'
- 'Do not confuse my product with anyone else's.'
- 'Buy this now, it is cheaper.'
- 'Help us.'
- 'Visit our country/hotel/shop/region.'

If you really cannot see any message, do not be alarmed; advertisers sometimes fail to 'get the message across' and the advertisement then becomes a waste of money.

How much to spend

There have to be some rules about this, otherwise no profits would be made at all because there is no obvious limit to the amount that can be spent. The relationship between the amount spent on advertising and the volume sold can best be illustrated by means of a simple chart – Figure 7.2.

This shows that, as the amount spent increases, so too does volume. However, there comes a point where the addition of an extra £1,000 of advertising has no effect whatsoever. Before that point is reached there is another point where the extra cost of advertising is greater than the extra profit arising from the additional volume; this too is unsatisfactory. Ideally therefore the amount spent on advertising is just enough to ensure maximum extra profit. This ideal can never be reached – in terms of the old joke: 'Half the amount spent on advertising is wasted; the difficulty is that we do not know which half.'

How much to spend, therefore, depends on how widely the message has to be spread; how much can be afforded and what other firms in the same line of business are doing.

The medium

There are many ways in which the advertising message can be passed on.

Fig 7.2   The profit/advertising spend relationship

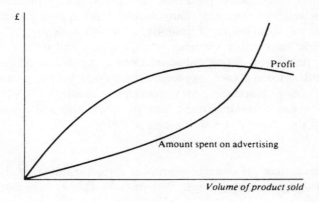

Self-check

List six different ways of advertising soft drinks. Take no more than five minutes on this.

A complete list of possible ways of advertising would include:

radio
television
cinema
newspapers
magazines
leaflets through doors
shop-window displays
sky writing
posters on buses
posters on hoardings
airships

The policy decision as to which medium to use emerges from an analysis of the market – what it is and what is the best way of reaching it.

Publicity

Publicity can be defined as free advertising, in that it means that the organisation concerned, or its products or services, gets its name mentioned in public without them having had to pay anything. This is now recognised as an important supplementary to advertising, and companies in fact take a lot of trouble to cultivate potential sources of free advertising. A brief interview on television about a new product or service can give a firm more exposure than it would get by spending £100,000 on an advertising campaign.

Some organisations shun publicity. Others welcome it and, through their public relations department, push out an endless stream of information about themselves. For instance, many annual reports of companies have been used directly as a source of quotations for this book.

In the public sector, too, publicity is often considered to be sufficiently important to justify appointing public relations and publicity officers. Most local authorities, for instance, appreciate that good publicity can help a department develop its services a lot faster than no publicity. This is because people hear about the department and its work and are amenable to suggestions if they believe it is doing a good job.

Selling

Selling, in this context, is a meeting between a representative of the selling organisation and a potential buyer. It is usually face to face but can be conducted on the telephone. The words 'salesperson' or 'sales representative' ('rep'!) cover a very wide range of activities, from someone who is little more than an order-taker, to someone who is trying to get new customers where none existed before, and to highly professional consultants whose job is to design a product for a customer as a one-off job.

The main policy decisions in this area relate to the precise use that should be made of sales people and this possibly will depend on such things as the type of product and the channels of distribution chosen. If the two extreme definitions of the word 'salesperson' are taken it can be seen how this decision is closely tied up with some other fundamental operating policy decisions:

- The order-taker tends to be – selling from a catalogue; 'standard products'.
- The technical adviser tends to be – custom-building; 'jobbing shop'.

It will be recalled that these product options were discussed earlier in the chapter under 'product policies' (page 105) and they will be met again later in the next chapter when operating policies are discussed.

Finally as regards sales people, a very important ground-rule is the one relating to the way sales people are paid for the work they do. Many people in sales are given cars – an essential tool of the trade – but some receive a salary which is very low. This type of organisation pays its salesforce chiefly on a commission basis, giving them the chance to earn sometimes more than the highest paid director in the firm. Other firms pay generous salaries and relegate the idea of a commission or bonus to a minor place in the 'remuneration package'. The choice is the company's, depending on what it considers is the best way of attracting, keeping and motivating the best staff.

Sales promotion

Sales promotion activities are everywhere – coupons through the letter-box with 5p off a tube of toothpaste; buy 10 and get a free sunshade; competitions; free samples and so on. The use is to boost sales in slack periods, encourage customers to try a new product or to clear out a product which is just about to be replaced by a new one.

Activity

Look out for a sales promotion activity, probably in a newspaper. It may be similar to those described above or it could be a bargain such as the airlines offer, e.g. 10 per cent off the normal air fare to America.

When you have found it, ask yourself if the organisation is likely to be better off (in terms of profit) by making the offer. In other words, what is the purpose of the promotion (see above) and is it likely to work?

The danger with sales promotion activities is that they may cheapen the image of the product or the organisation, and thus may run counter to all its other policies. It has, therefore, to be used carefully – the initial policy decisions being, Do we use sales promotion techniques? If so, when, and which kinds?

Packaging

Packaging is an essential part of the 'promotion mix' in that it can be an important part of the fight to get the consumer to choose one brand as against another. There are two main policy considerations:

- Minimum standard or 'expensive' packaging (in both looks and in actual quality)?
- How frequently should the packaging design be updated?

Poor packaging can turn potential customers away – that is certain. How far the reverse is true is arguable.

'Pricing' policies

Whenever a product or service is made available for sale, one of the most important decisions is the one related to the price to be charged. To have no policy regarding price – merely to 'think of a number' – is to invite trouble because some products may seem cheap and some may seem expensive. As a result the market can get confused and not buy at all.

The basic decision as far as pricing is concerned is to answer the question, At what level should we pitch our prices? A relatively high price (in relation to the competition) indicates that the product has something special about it not found in the other products. In other words the customer is expected to pay a premium for the extra-special qualities to be found in the product. This also applies to services like any form of maintenance or repair work (garages, plumbers, electricians, etc.). Unfortunately it is a well-established economic law that the higher the price, the lower the volume sold. On the other hand, if your prices are low many more will be sold.

The extremes of pricing policy are the Fortnum & Mason type and the Tesco type. Fortnum's have the reputation of high quality and service, allied with high prices, but with low volume; whereas Tesco's have average quality and service, low prices and very high volume. Both ends of the market can be equally profitable.

A related policy decision is concerned with discounts. Some organisations offer discounts out of habit, others never give any kind of discount. In the food business, especially in the non-perishable part (e.g. canned food), it is common to offer a retailer extra discounts for buying in bulk, and the more that is bought the bigger is the discount. This is known as a 'quantity discount'.

'Prompt-payment discounts' are another inducement to the customer (usually retailers), whereby if payment is made quickly (say, within ten days) the amount payable is a little less than it would normally be.

The retailer is particularly interested in the size of the difference between what is paid to the manufacturer and what the customer pays, i.e. the 'trade discount'.

Self-check

Sales rep A comes into your shop and says: 'This produce has a price of 50p on it. That is what you can charge for it. All you have to pay us is 40p.' Then sales rep B comes in and says: 'This product (very similar to product A) has a price of 50p on it. That is what you can charge for it, but all you have to pay us is 39p.' Which sales rep will you do business with?

It should be fairly obvious which you would do business with, assuming that you were indifferent about the products, and the sales rep B would win most of the time.

Another important element in the decision is how payment is to be made. Why is it, for example, that Marks & Spencer do not accept Access cards or Barclaycards or American Express, whereas British Home Stores do accept them quite readily? Why is it that some organisations demand cash with order, yet others go for cash on delivery and some others do not demand payment until the end of the month? The answer to all these questions is that each organisation has decided on its payment policy; they have decided that their particular way of doing business is best.

Follow-my-leader
For the firm with a small market share, especially where there are two or three very big firms and many small ones (like the soft drinks industry in Britain), one pricing policy decision that has to be made is whether to pitch prices and related terms at the same level as the 'big boys' or whether to go higher, or lower. There are risks whichever is chosen, but regard to the other elements in the marketing mix helps to reduce that risk.

The Cotoo Mineral Water Works revisited

At the beginning of the chapter the situation of this soft drinks company was described, and its main problem was identified as, quite simply, that its sales volume was too low. Excluding the suggestion to carry out some market research, nine specific ideas were put forward for improving the volume of sales. The ideas in the list were classified according to the marketing mix categories which we have been considering. It is now possible to look again at each idea and comment on each, deciding which

Table 7.1   The marketing mix and differing ideas for raising sales levels

Ideas for raising sales	Marketing mix type	Comments
1 Sell more flavours	Product	Probably wide enough already.
2 Use plastic bottles	Product	⎰Good idea – if equipment
3 Small bottles or cans	Product	⎱will cope.
4 Advertise heavily	Promotion	Yes – but through which medium?
5 More salesmen	Promotion/place	Possibly for better coverage of existing territory.
6 New labels	Promotion	Definitely.
7 Cut prices	Price	Not if it means no more profit and same volume.
8 Bigger discount to retailers for bulk buying	Price	Only if the present discount structure is a hindrance.
9 Special sales promotions	Promotion	May be useful temporarily.

of all the alternative actions is best. In Table 7.1, out of the nine suggestions it is possible that **2**, **3**, **4** or **6** would rank highest, with **5** and **9** as a second level; **7** and **8** are possibilities only after some research; **1** is a last resort.

There are many other ideas that could be thought out to boost the sales of soft drinks, and indeed the sales of any product or service are capable of being increased by a considered marketing approach. To have sensible policies in this area – rules that fit the needs of the organisation – improves the chances of success significantly.

Marketing in tomorrow's world

Marketing is more than increasing the sales of existing products or services: it is concerned with finding what customers want – and may want – in the future. It should also be the mechanism which takes internally-generated ideas and finds out if customers are likely to be attracted. The marketeer would love to be able to quiz all customers and potential customers about their buying intentions, likes and dislikes, and the use of computer technology is beginning to make this dream nearer to reality. Supermarkets now have instant information on purchases by customers and it is possible for the suppliers of groceries to be connected into the system so that they can receive data on buying patterns instantly, too.

It has been said (see the article 'Marketing is Everything' by Regis McKenna, *Harvard Business Review*, January–February 1991) that the marriage of technology and marketing will bring the customer inside the company, thus putting marketing at the centre of the organisation, and this will apply to public sector bodies just as much as to business enterprises.

Review

Select a manufactured product which you buy fairly regularly and try to find out how it is marketed, using these four questions as the guide to the four *p*'s.

- Is it expensive or cheap compared with the competition?
- Where is it sold?
- How is it promoted?
- Is the product 'just right', or is it not exactly what you want (e.g. in terms of size, shape, colour, durability, strength)?

8 Policies in Buying and Operations

In managing the buying side of a business and in operations management there are a number of basic choices to be made in the way the jobs are done. By the end of the chapter you should be able to identify what these basic choices are and what are the main advantages and disadvantages of each way of working.

Most people in the West eat some bread every day. Most of us never give it a second's thought, but every time we take a loaf and eat a bit we have in fact carried out a process involving a whole string of decisions. For most of us that process is automatic – we do not have to think about it – simply because some time ago we made ourselves some rules, some policy decisions, which we carry out now without any further thought.

The very first thing to decide on is whether to buy our bread requirements from the shop or make it ourselves. Maybe a compromise is reached and we decide to make a little bread at the weekend but to buy most of our needs most of the time.

Activity

Suppose you decide to make your own bread; list four or five other decisions you have to take before you can actually taste the results of your own efforts.

(Ten minutes.)

There are of course many aspects to the question of making bread at home. Among the most important are:

- How many different types of bread to make?
- What kind of flour to use?
- Which recipe(s) to follow?
- In what to mix the dough?
- Hand mixing or machine mixing?

- Where do we buy the ingredients?
- Do we buy more flour and yeast than we need for one bake?
- How much to make at a bake? (Enough for two days for example, or enough for two weeks – putting the rest in the freezer if we happen to have one?)
- What is the best form of oven heating for bread?

Similarly if we decide, on the whole, to buy our bread in the shops we have another set of decisions to think through:

- How much bread to buy at a time? (Again the question of freezer storage comes into the picture.)
- What sort of bread to buy?
- When to buy?
- From where do we buy bread?

There are not quite so many decisions to make as there are if we had decided to make our own bread. This should not be taken to imply that the decisions are easier; in many respects – as you will see – the decisions connected with buying can be extremely difficult.

It is possible to illustrate the decisions we have been looking at in simple diagram form – see Figure 8.1.

Many of the problems that have been described in relation to an individual acquiring bread are broadly similar to those encountered by managers in all kinds of organisations. There are very few organisations that can get by without having to buy something from outside; possibly the occasional commune, kibbutz or monastery may be able to do-it-itself entirely but this is very rare.

Even problems relative to specific types of equipment do not only relate to the production and distribution functions; offices too have to think these things through carefully and develop policies to handle them; and in this case, for the eighth problem, change the words in Figure 8.1 to, Which type of furniture/typewriters/data-processing equipment do we buy?

The primary problem of all – make or buy? – is there for every organisation no matter what its function. It is not an all-or-nothing decision usually, but more a question of degree: How far are we going to make things ourselves? In this context the word 'make' refers not only to products but also to services. As we noted in Chapter 6, local councils often ask private organisations to carry out certain services on their behalf, like road building, repairing council houses and so on. Always the council has a choice between buying in the service or creating the facility to do the job in-house. Some activities are almost sacred to government departments. For instance, it is unlikely that responsibility for local government finances would ever be passed out to a private firm of chartered accountants. It is, however, possible that the provision of the refuse-collection service could be handled by a private firm.

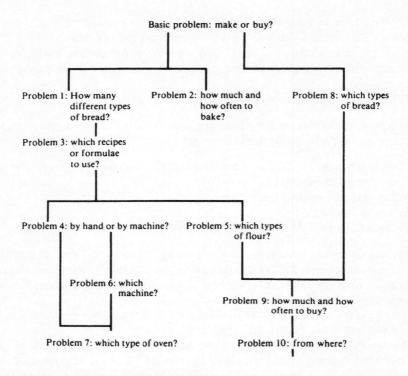

Fig 8.1   The make or buy decision tree

The decision 'Make or buy?' is a fundamental policy decision, so it will be examined first, looking at major issues in the areas of buying and operations later.

Marks & Spencer make nothing themselves; they buy all the goods they sell. Boots the Chemist manufacture some of the products they sell and buy other products from different makers. They could, in theory, make everything they sell in their own production units. Some firms in fact do make everything they sell all the way back to the production of the raw material – motorcar manufacturers making their own steel and power, for example.

As we have seen, the basic question all organisations have to ask is, Which is best: to buy the material, product, component or service from an outside supplier, or do it ourselves? To have to ask this question every month about everything bought out is very tedious and time-consuming. Instead organisations tend to have a fairly clear-cut policy on the subject. At one extreme there is the Marks & Spencer type policy of 'Make nothing, just buy and sell.' (A similar policy is, 'Buy, stick on a label and sell.') And at the other extreme there is the firm which tries to do it all itself.

Self-check

If you were the owner of a small building firm, what reasons could you have for making your own window frames? List three reasons for having a make-your-own policy, and three reasons for a buy-in policy, for window frames.

(Ten minutes.)

When to have a 'make' policy:

- If your suppliers are unreliable (e.g. if they are inefficient, strike-prone, have variable quality in their work, or if they are overseas and liable to political interference).
- If you can make it cheaper than your suppliers can supply it (not so simple a calculation as you might think).
- If your firm has competence in the technology (or can easily buy it). This is to pick up some synergy (see page 76) for a definition of this word).
- If the organisation is looking for an investment opportunity.
- If there is capacity (in space and in management).
- If control over the activity is essential (this is especially true in local government finance).

When to have a 'buy' policy:

- If your capabilities in producing the goods or services are weak (e.g. poor production facilities, no managerial experience, labour problems).
- If you can buy cheaper than you could make.
- If the cost of entry into the business is very high.
- If the suppliers are reliable and you can be sure of getting the level of service you require.
- If the future for the product is doubtful (for example, if you sell a 'craze' product like a skateboard it is risky buying the manufacturing facilities too: you may be left with a lot of useless equipment).

Activity

Mention has already been made of local councils' refuse-collection services. There is some suggestion that the service should be carried out by private firms who are contracted to do the job by the council. Using the checklist of reasons listed above try to decide which is better for the council: to provide its own dustbin men and lorries, or sub-contract the work?

Having made your own mind up, you will probably find that the subject is good for an hour's argument with your friends. Bear in mind, however, that there is likely to be a purely political element in the debate which will make the argument more exciting than if it was purely economic.

8.1 **Rules in Operations**

Once an organisation has taken the basic decision to make a proportion of the products or services it is providing, a number of other important policy decisions have to be established. These correspond roughly with the list of questions that was drawn up on pages 118–20 to illustrate the issues that have to be resolved in making bread, although managers tend to use somewhat different words. The main decisions are:

How many different products to make?

This is the problem that has already been met both in relation to the development of a strategy of expansion, and in the analysis of the marketing mix. In managerial terms it is known as the size of the product range.

To make life easy for any manager in production (or indeed in any type of operation), it is undoubtedly best to provide one product or service only. To do so would raise productivity to its highest possible level. This is because everyone concerned would become highly expert and skilled at producing that particular article. Moreover since only one product was being made it would be unnecessary to adjust or clean equipment frequently, as is a common feature in multi-product works.

To illustrate this idea consider the bread-making example. If only one type of bread is made then it is only necessary to clean the equipment at the end of production for the day. If, however, the daily production is of five different types of bread, then equipment has to be cleaned five times each day. Nothing can be produced during cleaning times and output per man (the traditional definition of productivity) falls.

The effect is similar where machinery has to be modified for each different product. Industries where this is a problem include all those where the product is made by pouring a liquid into a mould, allowing it to cool into its final hard form: for example, glass bottles, many plastic products and many metal products (i.e. those made in iron or steel foundries). In all these and similar industries, the greater the number of products to be made, the greater the number of times the equipment has to be stopped so that dies and moulds can be changed. The greater the down-time for equipment cleaning, as it is called, the lower will be productivity and the higher will be the cost. A single product would, therefore, be ideal from an operations angle, but strategically and from a marketing point of view a single product operation is often a very weak and vulnerable business.

To reconcile these two views it is necessary either:

- to have such a large demand for each line that a separate production unit can be justified for each. Unfortunately only firms with very big demand can do this;

• or management has to try to find that point where profits are likely to be greatest. The marketing manager will state that the more products that can be offered, the greater will be the sales. In contrast, the operations manager will insist that the more products that are made, the lower will be average profit per unit.

Somewhere there has to be a compromise, and a clearly established rule in this area avoids much of the trouble that can arise in arriving at the compromise.

How much to make; how often?

Having decided the size of the product range, the second key decision hangs around quantities and timing. The alternatives can be classified as follows:

1 Make the products before the orders have been placed by the customers, in long production runs (to get productivity as high as possible) placing all production into store until sales get the orders. This is known as 'making to stock' or 'selling ex-stock', and has undoubted advantages so far as production planning, productivity and distribution planning are concerned. Also sales people find it handy to be able to offer the products on an immediate delivery basis.

Many firms operate in this way, particularly in the consumer goods industries. All the products seen in the shops are made 'in anticipation of demand', and the manufacturer by doing things this way is, hopefully, keeping costs down. He is taking a risk, however, because the products he has made may never sell; in which case he would lose a lot of money. On top of this any company engaging in this kind of activity finds that it has to pay out a lot of money (in wages and for the cost of materials) often months before the sale is made. Tying up money in this way (in big stock levels) can cost a lot – especially if the business has to borrow from the bank to keep stocks high. Nevertheless, it can and often does pay off.

A related example of this kind of activity is in bread-making where the baker has to make in anticipation of customer demand. He risks not selling enough or not being able to satisfy the demand; either way, an unsatisfactory state of affairs. He does not have to carry stock, which saves him money, but it can raise his wastage rates very high if he overproduces too often.

The bread-maker has to make each product daily because bread is so perishable. If the product is not perishable, nor likely to go out of fashion, then it can be made at any convenient time and stored. Therefore making in anticipation of demand can only be justified if you can be reasonably sure that there is likely to be a continuing demand for your products.

2 At the other end of the scale, rather than manufacture in anticipation of demand, a firm can choose to wait until the customer places an order. A good example of this would be in the manufacture of oil rigs. It is unlikely that many such objects are constructed for selling ex-stock – the cost of holding it unsold and the risks of not selling at all are much too high. Instead these costly constructions are made when the customer asks for them.

Supporting issues that have to be resolved in this area involve the crucial one of whether the products will be standard lines identifiable in a catalogue, or whether the whole production operation will be a jobbing shop; in other words being willing and able to make anything within a broad area of technical expertise.

Generally the decision to make to customers' orders comes about where demand is uncertain, where the cost of stock-building is very high or where a standard product is inappropriate. Sometimes, of course, there is no option – as for instance in the case of a garage workshop – but where there is a choice it is important that a clear-cut policy is established. Firms that try to do a bit of both finish up doing nothing at all.

There is, however, an important intermediate policy which can help to overcome some of the problems of going to one extreme or another. This is where a firm makes components to stock, only carrying out the final assembly when the orders have been received.

Self-check

For each of the following five different types of product or service put a cross in whichever column you think is the most appropriate policy for a firm in that particular line of business.

	Making in anticipation of demand	or	Making to customers' orders
• Lawnmowers			
• Central heating engineers			
• Advertising agency			
• Book publisher			
• Wedding cakes			

Lawnmower-makers and book publishers produce in anticipation of demand. Central-heating engineers and advertising agencies 'make' to customers' orders and are in effect jobbers. The wedding-cake maker is building the product to the customer's order but most probably on the basis of a catalogue.

Which formula to use?

Two issues are involved in setting policy to answer this question, a formula being a recipe or specification for an article. The first ties in with marketing policy very closely and relates to the decisions on the quality of the product and its price. If it is a high-quality product or service and carries a high price tag, then the formula will be relatively high quality too. The second issue is that the firm may choose to allow the customer some freedom in this area and may either have a policy of building what the customer wants or simply offering products of one's own design or to a home-grown recipe. Clearly if the firm is making standard products or services, then it cannot also make products to the customers' own designs and specifications. If, however, the business is a jobbing shop then what the customers want can be provided.

Self-check

There are dozens of different recipes for Christmas puddings. How would you decide which to use if you had never made one before and had to?

If you had the time you would experiment until you found one that tasted good and did not cost too much. Thereafter you would guard the recipe very carefully! Firms do this too.

Make by hand or by machine?

The bread-making illustration at the start of this chapter required a simple decision as regards making dough, namely whether to knead it by hand or use a machine. The machine is quicker and makes the effort of bread-making less onerous. On the other hand, equipment is expensive to buy and there is something very satisfying about kneading dough by hand. In organisations of all kinds, the question crops up frequently, Do we use people or machines? And also (at a different stage), Do we replace people with machines?

In management language the policy decision is, What is the degree of mechanisation we should try to achieve? Another way of putting it is whether the business wants to be labour intensive or capital intensive – men or machines. The answer is difficult because there are so many elements in the equation. Here are a few of the factors to take into account.

A business that is highly mechanised avoids problems of finding and keeping large numbers of people. It avoids rising labour costs and the risks of not being able to satisfy customers because of strikes or other industrial action such as working to rule. Mechanisation speeds up the productive process, raises productivity, cuts costs and eliminates many dangerous, dirty and exhausting tasks. The robots used by motorcar manufacturers are doing all these things.

On the other side of the coin, mechanisation is very expensive to install, it requires very skilled people to operate it, it is not as flexible as a human being, it can lead to a lot of people being out of work (at least in the short run), and to make money there has to be a big enough demand for the product that the equipment is kept going for most of the time. A computer that is only used six hours a day for a five-day week is not being used for a quarter of the time it should be used.

Which machine to choose and use?

The policy decisions under this question centre on the question of the type of technology to be employed. It may be just a question of choosing a particular manufacturer's products, or it may be more fundamental; for example, where heating is important, should the fuel system be gas, electricity, coal or oil?

Within this area there is also the problem of whether to buy, rent or hire equipment; basic ground-rules must be established for this. So too there must be a clear-cut policy about maintenance of equipment. This usually revolves around the question, How much regular maintenance should be carried out with a view to preventing costly machine breakdowns? One extreme answer would be simply to wait until the equipment actually seized up, then fix it. Another extreme would be to have a huge team of maintenance men continually fine-tuning the equipment so that it never, ever, broke down (a solution both very costly and probably impossible).

Finally as regards equipment and machinery there is the important decision as to how fast it should be replaced. Do you run it until it collapses in bits on the floor or do you deliberately buy new every two or three years, or whenever the latest model appears?

Review

Many of the points raised in this section could relate to running a motorcar. Make your own policy decisions about a car, in relation to the following items (assuming that you can pay).

- Which manufacturer?
- Which model?
- Buy or rent?
- Which maintenance policy?
- What replacement policy?

The final set of policies that have to be established in operations are those that revolve around the purchase of the components and materials needed to make the products and help provide the services. These policy decisions are broadly similar to those which are required if the organisation was in the 'buy' not 'make' category and can therefore be considered at the same time.

8.2 **Rules in Buying**

On page 47 the story of an unfortunate trip to the coast was described; the sequel to that story is just as unfortunate.

There was just about enough petrol for the journey home, but to be on the safe side I decided to fill up the tank at the first garage we came to. When we got there we found the price to be 2p higher than I would normally pay at my local garage. So we decided to drive on to the next one and when we got there we found that the price was 3p higher still. So we drove on to the next garage; and at each garage the price was higher than at the one before. In addition we were held up in a traffic jam and it began to get late. Garages we came to were closed and the atmosphere inside the car became very strained indeed as the needle on the petrol gauge hovered near zero. In the end we had to stop at the first open garage irrespective of the price. We found one in the end ten miles from home, so only one gallon went in the tank, but it cost me 8p more than if I had bought it at the seaside.

You may have had a similar experience yourself, either as the driver or the passenger. It is much worse being the driver because there is no way of avoiding the blame; all the passengers have to do is sit and glower.

Self-check

What should I have done to prevent such a situation happening? (There are several possibilities, but two ideas will be enough.) (Five minutes.)

Possible ways of avoiding running out of petrol:

- Carry a gallon can of petrol in the boot.
- Fill up the tank every 100 miles (or some other regular interval).
- Study the price of petrol in the garages on the way out, so that you know which is cheapest on the way back.
- Calculate before you start how far you intend to travel, work out how many gallons you need, add 10 per cent for emergencies and fill up accordingly.
- Having arrived at the second garage and found it more expensive, you should not take a chance, but fill up, pay up and smile.
- Fill up before starting off on the homeward journey.

There are a few more, but they all have one characteristic in common, namely they all indicate the need to think ahead.

My experience was not too critical – we did get home safely, but imagine if I had been the captain of a jumbo jet or a supertanker, and my plane or ship ran out of fuel ten miles from home. That kind of situation cannot be allowed to happen. Similarly organisations that try to take chances as far as buying is concerned may be lucky and scrape home but often they find themselves paying a heavy price to get there. Naturally the aim is to buy as cheaply as possible. The skill of the buyer includes achieving this aim without having to live in fear that the wheels will stop turning because insufficient has been bought.

The six ideas listed above for avoiding trouble are different ways of buying petrol. If we decide that we will always fill the tank up after 100 miles of travelling – irrespective of the price – we have, in effect, chosen a particular policy for buying petrol; we have a rule.

Since all organisations have to make purchases of one kind or another, even if it is only on paper, someone has to be responsible for the activity simply because of the huge sums of money that can be involved. A small shop can find itself buying goods and services worth over £100,000 a year these days. In 1993 Rolls-Royce's outside purchases of materials, consumables, components and services amounted to over £2 billion. A 1 per cent cut, through better buying, would have raised operating profits by over 30 per cent, from £76 million to some £99 million. Marks & Spencer buy over £5 billion's worth of goods and these are goods for resale in their stores. It is here the importance of the buyer can be most clearly seen. To get the right products in the right place at the right time and with the right quality, all this is the aim of buyers because if they fail to get the elements right they can ruin the organisation.

Self-check

Can you see any connections between the last sentence and the 'marketing mix' discussed in the last chapter? (See page 105.)

What, then, are the key issues that buyers have to deal with and for which rules can be established? There are four main ones.

Choosing suppliers

In selecting a suitable policy regarding suppliers, two basic issues have to be resolved. The first is, How many suppliers should we have? And the second is, How do we choose which organisations will supply us?

One supplier or more?
The advantages of the single supplier are:

• Often gives a better service (delivery, goods on credit, etc.).
• Gives a better price.
• Helps to establish a relationship and is therefore more likely to respond in a crisis.

- There may be economies in repair and servicing if the product is of a durable nature.

For instance, to have a fleet of aircraft consisting of just one type (say twenty Boeing 737s) is considerably less costly, in terms of holding spares and parts and in having a skilled maintenance department, than if the twenty planes consisted of six different types from four different manufacturers.

The advantages of having several suppliers are:

- Safety – if one firm goes broke or on strike, delivery is still assured. Flexibility is added.
- One supplier may not be able to supply all the different types needed.
- A single supplier may become wholly dependent on your organisation if the quantities involved are particularly large. It may be advisable to 'spread the favours'.
- Can often obtain very good buys by only taking up 'special offers'. This is similar to the shopper who looks in all the shops each week and decides where to buy the groceries on the basis of the best discounts going at the time.

How to choose your supplier(s)
The main factors affecting choice of supplier are:

- price;
- ability to deliver the goods on time;
- 'after-sales service';
- the extent of technical support services;
- the amount of credit given (how long is it before they want to be paid?);
- the quality of the goods;
- any exchange arrangements (will they buy from you?);
- the supplier's financial 'health';
- ability to meet urgent orders;
- friendship (this can override quite a few of the others).

Buying to stock or not

Activity

Everything used regularly can be bought just before it is needed. This is known as 'hand-to-mouth' buying. Or it can be bought in bulk and stored, i.e. buying 'to stock', and it is possible to buy three months', six months' or a year's consumption in one big purchase.

What are the advantages and disadvantages of buying a year's supply of cheese (or butter or bananas) at one time?

BULK BUYING OF FRESH FOODS

Main advantages	*Main disadvantages*

- Cheaper to obtain (bulk discount).
- Protected against a shortage of supply due to labour problems, weather, war, etc. In a factory this would ensure that production would not be held up.
- The cost will be much higher by the end of the period (this assumes inflation will happen).
- Ensures that a sudden big increase in demand can be met.

- It costs money to store the goods.
- It means spending a lot of money a long time before any comes in (it may mean borrowing too).
- The goods may go bad.
- The goods may 'shrink', which is a polite way of saying that they get pinched.
- The goods may become unpopular and only saleable as waste.

It appears therefore that the disadvantages outweigh the advantages of bulk buying, at least as far as fresh food is concerned. With other products the opposite may be the case. The buyer of wine for a big hotel or off-licence group has to buy some wine in bulk many years before it is fully mature. He has to bear all the disadvantages just mentioned, because in the end the wine can sell at considerably higher prices and moreover is then unobtainable on the open market.

Even if the only goods supplied to an organisation are paper and other stationery items, a policy decision has to be made – do we buy when we need it, or carry stocks in anticipation of demand for it?

If the answer is to buy to stock, a further important rule has to be established, namely:

How much stock to carry?

The easy answer to this question is 'just enough to make sure that we can always satisfy the customers' requirements instantly'. The only problem is that to be absolutely 100 per cent sure of doing this the quantity and range of stock that would be needed to be carried would be too expensive in relation to the likely overall demand. A simple example of this is in Uncle James's shoe shop. Each men's shoe can be in, say, ten different sizes with five widths for each size. That makes fifty different sized shoes for one style. If only twenty styles are carried there are one thousand different boxes of men's shoes. Even then at least two pairs of each have to be carried – probably five or six for the most popular fittings, giving a grand total of four or five thousand pairs of shoes. Even then there is a possibility a customer could come in just after the last pair had been sold. It would not make economic sense to carry so much stock.

The policy decision to be made is the level of customer satisfaction to be aimed at (whether the customer is a person who comes in and buys or is a department being supplied within the same organisation). A 10 per cent satisfaction indicates that most of the time stocks are very low, which may not be a bad thing if everything is built to suit the customers' own requirements. But to try to satisfy most of the people most of the time (say 80 per cent) tells the buyer to go out and spend a lot of money.

An associated policy decision is called the 'economic order quantity' or 'EOQ'. Properly decided and applied, the EOQ avoids embarrassing shortages on the one hand and a squirrel-like hoarding on the other.

The concept of 'Just-in-Time' (JIT) has grown in popularity in recent years, originating in Japan, where it is called 'Kanban'. The aim is to have an arrangement with suppliers so that an item of material, or component, is delivered just before it is needed on the production line, and so no stock need be held – a great saving of money and space. The disadvantages are that the suppliers have to carry stock (who pays?) and you have to be sure you will not be let down at the last minute. In the same way, as we saw in relation to marketing and the use of technology, supermarkets can cut the amount of stock they are carrying because they can tell as soon as an item is bought – and re-order immediately.

Centralised storage or not?

The final major policy to be settled regarding buying is, Where do we store the material (or goods) when they have been delivered?

With a single-unit operation like an independent shop or a small workshop, there is no problem; the goods flow in at the back door and into a storage area. If there is more than one operation, however, there is a choice between a central store for all units or smaller stores attached to each of the operating areas. The choice for a two-unit operation, in diagrammatic form (assuming similar products or services in both areas), is shown in Figure 8.2.

The choice will depend on such things as the distance between the two operating areas, the amount of storage space alongside each operating area and the cost of carrying a full range of stores at each location.

Self-check

Looking at the diagram of system X and system Y in Figure 8.2, state which you think would be best in the following situations

- Operations 1,000 miles apart.
- No storage space near either operating unit.
- Very cheap materials.

If two operating units are 1,000 miles apart, it is often better to have separate storage facilities in each place, unless some other factor makes this impossible. So system Y is normally preferred here.

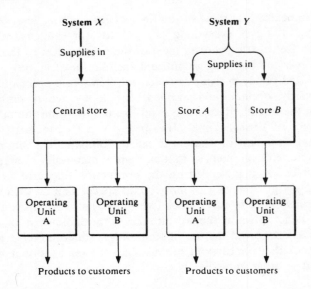

Fig 8.2   A centralised storage system compared with a local storage system

---

In contrast, if there is no convenient storage place nearby, system X has to be employed: there is no choice.

Finally if the materials being stored are cheap it may be no problem to store them at both locations (Y). This is more easily understood if we had been talking about jumbo-jet engines – no airline can afford to keep spare engines at every airport they visit; the cost is prohibitive, and so a central store is used.

Review

Turn back to Figure 8.1 on page 120, which describes the various choices that face everyone in deciding how their bread supplies should be obtained. Now that you have read more about policy decisions in operations and buying, answer the ten questions posed in the diagram according to your own circumstances.

---

9 Policies in Personnel and Industrial Relations

All organisations depend for their success on people or, in management jargon, the human resource. The aim of this chapter is to examine the key issues for which policies need to be developed in the area. The chapter will help you appreciate what these key issues are and why they are important.

One of the most effective ways of finding out about human resource management is to build a house or an extension on an existing house. There are three ways of going about the task. One is to employ a reputable firm of builders who will see to everything on your behalf. Another is to do everything yourself from plumbing to bricklaying to the wiring. The first of these is expensive; the second is considerably cheaper but you need to be very practical and have far more spare time than most people care to give to such activities. The third alternative is to hire all the skills you need, when you need them, for as long as you need them only. It is a halfway position: you save money and save time, at least in theory.

The first of the three approaches requires some human resource management skill and the second only a little. But the third alternative contains many of the personnel and industrial relations issues that will also be found in the biggest firms. In the first place there are the purely organisational matters that come up when these questions are asked: What are the different tasks that need to be carried out to make sure that the job gets done properly? and, In which order do we want the tasks carried out? Once these have been answered, it is necessary to get answers to a range of other questions all of which fall into the category of 'policy issues'.

Self-check

Can you think of three or four in five minutes?

Possible policy questions would include:

- What sort of people are we going to hire?
- Where do we get them?
- How much are we going to pay them?
- Are we going to offer them any other compensation?
- Are we going to bother if they are trade-union members or not?
- For how long do we employ them?

It is of course perfectly possible to operate on a purely arbitrary basis, deciding the answer to each of the questions as and when needed. But this can lead to some odd discrepancies in the treatment of employees, so that some may get free overalls for instance and others do not. If significant, these discrepancies can lead to trouble – a situation which is hardly uncommon in the post-war British industrial relations scene. Indeed there is a good deal of evidence to suggest that those organisations that have had well-developed personnel and industrial relations policies for many years are the firms that have least trouble and the greatest success. 'No policy' is bad policy.

The areas of personnel and industrial relations which need clear policies can be classified into four, namely:

- *recruitment and selection*
- *pay and conditions*
- *training and development*
- *industrial relations*

and within each area several aspects need a policy decision.

9.1 Recruitment and Selection

Activity

Assume that you have decided to build a house and you are going to hire in people to do the actual work. You have the drawings, the money and the planning permission. In addition, all the materials you need have been delivered to the site.

Which of the following ways of hiring people would be most appropriate in the circumstances?

- Place a large sign in front of the site saying, 'Men wanted for building work. Apply within'.
- Ask your friends for names of reliable individuals with special skills (carpentry, bricklaying, etc.).
- Look for these skills being advertised in the local paper.
- Advertise in the local paper.

(Ten minutes.)

Simply to advertise for 'men' would be to invite trouble on two counts. First, the Sex Discrimination Act of 1975 forbids that kind of advertising. Most jobs must be open to both men and women. Second, to advertise for people without specifying what type of skills and experience are needed attracts large numbers of people who are quite unsuitable for the jobs needed. The first possibility is therefore out. The second and third possibilities are common for small jobbing work: to have someone working for you who has been recommended is reassuring and often a good arrangement. The fourth and fifth choices are also possibles, but these require a careful screening process to ensure that the people that are taken on are competent to do the job.

This example illustrates the point that the recruitment of staff is chiefly concerned with these three questions:

- What sort of people do we need?
- How are we going to get them?
- Where do we get them from?

What kind of people do we need?

This question is not as simple as it appears at first glance. Obviously an organisation that does no planning at all is asking the question daily, as work fails to get done on time, if at all. Most organisations, however, try to establish well in advance what their staffing requirements will be. This activity is known as 'personnel planning' – a highly complex, and necessary, function.

The personnel planning operation has to work within the broad strategic framework of the organisation and in accordance with the policy decisions made in the various functional areas such as sales and production. These factors determine both the types and quantities of staff needed at specified dates in the future, the need arising partly because staff will have to be replaced from time to time (as they retire or get promoted or leave), and partly because of changes in the strategies of the organisation.

The policy decisions which will help to make the personnel planner's life easier are four in number. First, the kind of age profile the organisation wants. This has already been looked at as part of the analysis of internal strengths and weaknesses (pages 33–4). It should be kept in mind, however, that organisations may want a corporate age profile that is unusual for many reasons. For instance, one company may not want to hire people over the age of thirty, whereas another may never recruit anyone under that age.

The second policy decision in this area is concerned with qualifications. Again there is a choice. Some organisations may be prepared to take on anyone who has the ability and experience to do the job; others will insist on certain minimum qualifications as well. For example many large companies insist that promotion to a managerial grade is only possible if that person has a university degree. Another example is the organisation that insists that all its accounts department staff should be members of the Institute of Chartered Accountants, not hiring staff who are members of other similar institutions.

The third area where a policy decision needs taking is that related to experience, some preferring no experience of the work so that training can be related to the precise requirements of the organisation, others looking for experienced people who can adapt.

Finally, there is the question of hiring people who have potential for higher posts within the organisation. Some firms recruit people in relation to the specific job that is vacant without regard to any future requirements. Other firms try to employ people who seem capable of taking on greater responsibilities after a few years' experience.

Activity

Some organisations only recruit their typing and secretarial staff straight from college, 'before they have picked up any bad habits'. Others prefer to employ experienced staff 'because they know what it is all about'. Which do you think is best?

How are we going to get them?

The policy choice which is built into this question is, Do we recruit the people we need, when we need them or do we try to develop our own staff in anticipation of need?

The first course of action (a hand-to-mouth policy) has the advantage that there is more chance of getting a better-qualified person than if the only people available were home-grown. Moreover there is some argument for bringing in new people from outside in that new blood is good for the body. The disadvantages are that often it is more expensive to obtain new staff than to promote existing personnel, and there is a risk that the new staff member may not in the end be suitable for the job. A sensible policy regarding recruitment of new staff is clearly needed and this should minimise the chances of getting a dud, but even so the risk is there.

In contrast, the advantages of the planned development policy are, first, that it is cheaper; second, it increases the chances of getting the right type of person for the job; and, third, the person appointed can be effective more quickly in the new post because there is little or no settling-in time. Finally, the prospects of promotion from within, if strong, may well provide a motive for better work.

The disadvantages of growing one's own talent are, first, that the talent may leave the organisation after being trained; second, an organisation that tries never to recruit from outside (especially at the managerial level) runs the risk of producing an inward-looking top management team, short of ideas.

Where do we get them from?

The main policy decisions that need taking in this respect are whether recruitment is to be open to all, or limited in some special way by, for example, only advertising in local newspapers or only in *The Sunday Times*. A further decision is whether to recruit directly oneself or use the services of an agency.

There can be innumerable rules regarding staff selection. The preceding discussion has concentrated on most of the main ones, but very often particular organisations will have to develop rules about all kinds of selection matters, such as racial or sex discrimination; health; working for a competitor; and even religion.

Finally there is the question of getting rid of staff. All organisations must have clearly set out rules for dismissal and redundancy. It must be made known to every employee under what conditions they could be dismissed, and a policy must be established for dealing with staff who are surplus to requirements – either because of a trade recession or because the nature of the business has changed. It is also worth deciding in advance if the policy on redundancy is 'first in, first out' or 'last in, first out'.

9.2 Pay and Conditions

'Pay and conditions' is a shorthand phrase for all the benefits an employer brings (or could bring) to an employee, ranging in importance from basic wages and salaries through bonus systems and hours of work to such intangibles as the physical conditions of the place of work. There are several important policy matters relating to this aspect of personnel management, as follows:

General levels of pay

While many organisations (but not in the public sector) try to have general pay levels roughly similar to 'the going rate' to be found around and about, many firms have a policy of deliberately paying higher (or lower) rates of pay than ordinarily found. The high-rate-of-pay policy is to be found in the organisation that believes it is only by paying high wages and salaries that it is getting the best people. The economic justification is that the 'best people' will actually make the firm much more profitable, thus more than paying for their high cost. While this may be true in some cases, there is also some evidence to suggest that a very high level of salaries and wages is no guarantee of much improved performance in a firm. It does seem, however, that a higher than average level of pay can lead to a reduced level of industrial action, such as less strike action.

In contrast a low-rate-of-pay policy is one where the firm has decided to take a fairly tough attitude towards pay increases and works hard to keep general awards in line with the minimum to be found (such as the trade union's minimum wage). The economic justification for this policy is that by keeping total wage costs low, general price increases can be kept low too. Thus demand for the company's products or services will remain high, ensuring work for all the employees in the firm.

In the public sector much is heard these days of 'comparability studies'. This is especially relevant for those employed in the Civil Service, local government and for teachers and hospital staff. The need for this type of activity is to ensure that general levels of pay do not fall too low in relation to private business, so that there is no drift from the public to the private sector. The comparability study aims to identify the pay someone would receive in private business for doing a job with similar responsibilities in the public sector.

Many informal comparability studies also take place, especially within an industry or trade, and also in specific areas such as trading estates or any place where several firms can be found.

Internal pay consistency

Activity

Imagine what would happen if whenever someone was hired in a large company like ICI or Shell the persons making the appointment were able to fix the pay of the newcomer. Within a very short time there would be a great deal of trouble. Similarly, imagine what would happen if you were working in a firm and the boss called you into his office and told you he was giving you an immediate rise of £20,000 a year, and then a few days later you discovered that all your colleagues had been given increases of £22,000 a year. How would you feel? What would you do?

A debate which often comes up in this connection is concerned with geographic differences. For example two secretaries work in the same firm, doing identical jobs. One works in London, the other in Leeds. Should there be any pay differential? Many organisations, both public and private, recognise the need to adjust pay if the cost of living is higher in one part of the country than in another. In Britain the 'London allowance' is quite common, and organisations like the United Nations have very complicated allowances adjusting pay from country to country depending on relative living costs.

Merit awards

It has been recognised for a long time that some individuals work harder and with a higher quality of results than others. It is a matter of policy if, and how far, this should be recognised and rewarded. It is not difficult to establish relative efficiency where individuals' work can be measured precisely, such as for salesmen. There it is normal to give the salesman a small percentage of the value of every order over a certain minimum quantity. In the same way in factories if output exceeds a certain basic level those achieving the excess share a bonus.

The problem is more difficult in offices and in other situations where it is difficult to identify diligence and superior work. Many public service organisations have no merit award system for this reason, arguing that it is the diligent and 'better' employee who gets promoted.

Activity

Imagine a bonus system for firemen, surgeons and soldiers. What would the 'efficiency' ratings be based on?

Profit-sharing schemes

A popular form of bonus is to give all employees a share in the profits of the firm. This may be a fixed percentage of the profits of the firm, so that if the firm had a bad year no bonus would be given, but in a boom time, the bonus could be high.

While everyone likes a 'free gift' of money, objections to such a policy are that it cannot be fair. If the sum is distributed on the basis of basic pay (e.g. 5 per cent of pay) or if it is a flat sum (e.g. £500 per head) someone is bound to complain. Someone else would complain if it was given 'on merit'. Profit sharing is not uncommon, but needs careful handling.

Shares for staff

Many companies these days have schemes whereby employees can obtain shares in the firm. Shares can be given to staff instead of a cash bonus and usually held in trust for five years after which there is no tax liability. Also, some firms have 'Save-as-you-earn' schemes, whereby staff can obtain shares in the future at an earlier price. Share options, too, give staff (usually senior management) the option to buy shares in the future at the existing price on the date the option was granted.

All these methods result in employees being shareholders too and in some cases staff hold a significant proportion of all shares in the firm. For example, in Texaco, the giant oil company, 9 per cent of shares were owned by staff at the end of 1993 and, it would appear, not a dissimilar percentage in J Sainsbury, the supermarket group.

Fringe benefits

It is a matter of policy whether an organisation gives its employees any other benefits besides basic pay. Such benefits include cars, pension funds, free or cut-price meals, interest-free loans, long holidays and shorter working hours.

Some of these are taken for granted, like holidays and pension funds. Some organisations add on many items in an attempt to get hold of the right kind of staff. How many fringe benefits, and how far to go, are important decisions and will be based partly on the following considerations:

- Is it normal for the type of business?
- Can I get the staff only by offering such attractions?
- Is the profit of the business likely to be higher if I give out many benefits?
- Who in the company will enjoy the benefits and who will be left out? And what do I tell the ones who are left out?

Other conditions

While minimum health and safety standards are set out by law for people at work, through such legislation as the Health and Safety at Work Act 1974, there can be a world of difference in the standards of the working environment in one organisation as compared with another – not only in connection with health and safety matters but in such things as the location of the organisation, the standard of décor, furniture and fittings.

As always there are merits and demerits of a policy to ignore or foster considerations such as these. Often the decision hangs on whether the top management in the organisation believes these elements to be of importance in recruiting, keeping and motivating staff. This itself is discussed in Chapter 11.

9.3 Training and Development

From the discussion earlier in this chapter it will be obvious that training depends largely on various other policies in the personnel area. If an organisation intends to hire people simply for the immediate job that needs to be done, then any training is optional. In contrast, firms that recruit in anticipation of need, or that have a policy of growing their own talent, will by definition have to get involved in training to a much greater extent.

Several different types of training can be identified in all organisations. These are:

- Training for the immediate job to be done; for instance, helping a new sales assistant in a shop learn how to deal with customers.
- Training in understanding the immediate environment of the employee; for instance, giving that sales assistant the opportunity to learn more about the company and how it operates.
- Training to prepare for promotion. The sales assistant attending training programmes for sales supervisors would be a common example of this. A more sophisticated way of handling this would be to expose the assistant to some of the supervisor's normal work load and get them to do it. This is sometimes known as 'action learning'.
- Training for general all-round improved efficiency and understanding. This could be where the same sales assistant is given the chance to learn more about business generally, or to keep up to date, or to acquire new skills – for instance in computer programming.

In all these situations, the organisation has to determine the extent to which it is going to encourage staff at all levels to develop. This to some degree depends on the future needs of the organisation and also on how rapidly the environment is changing. A company at the forefront of technology, in information processing for example, may find its staff being called upon to possess new skills and knowledge quite suddenly. This could be fatal if that firm had not been developing its key staff in anticipation.

Not only is the problem one of extent, but there are other key issues. Are we going to train our people inside the organisation? Are we going to rely on external agencies to train for us? How much time and money should we give staff who want to go away and train themselves?

Activity

If you work in an organisation, do you know:

- who is being trained, or has been trained, to take over from your immediate boss if that individual gets promoted or retires?
- who will take over from you, if you leave?

If you do not work in an organisation, do you know if:

- the Prime Minister has anyone trained to take over in case of an emergency?
- anyone is being developed to take over running any of our national sporting teams when the present team-managers retire (or get fired)?

In all four cases there should be someone ready to take over. Is there?

Training and development of managers

Particular emphasis needs to be placed on the training and development of managers. It is, of course, entirely up to the organisation how much time and money it puts into managerial development, but there are very few sound arguments against doing no training. On the other hand there are a number of very good reasons for putting considerable effort into the activity.

The arguments against include:

- It costs too much.
- Once trained they will leave.
- Once trained they will be discontented.
- Once trained too many questions will be asked.

The arguments for are:

- The increasing complexity of organisations requires that managers have to be knowledgeable about more and more things to be effective.
- Managers have to understand, or have a thorough working knowledge of, all aspects of the part of the organisation for which they are responsible. Top managers by definition need to know about all aspects of their organisation.
- Without adequate preparation for higher levels of responsibility, managers can be promoted beyond their level of competence (this is known as the 'Peter Principle': Laurence J. Peter, in his book *The Peter Principle*, Souvenir Press, 1969).
- Only if managers have some understanding of other parts of the organisation will they be able to communicate with each other and gain their trust and goodwill.
- The environment is changing so fast that it is not reasonable to expect the managers to keep up to date in all the things they should be up to date on: an out-of-date manager being a dangerous animal.

9.4 Industrial Relations

When anyone starts working for an organisation it is normal to establish precisely what pay and conditions will be given to that person in exchange for his time, skills and effort. It is, in effect, a contract between an employer and an employee and is reviewed and renewed at least once a year. In very small organisations the process can be carried out on an informal basis between individuals and senior management; each person effectively doing his own bargaining and negotiating.

As organisations grow, however, individual bargaining becomes impracticable and so systems are developed for classifying groups of employees into categories for pay and conditions purposes. Changes in the levels of pay within categories or grades are handled by representatives drawn from employees or by representatives of a trade union. In essence, therefore, industrial relations policy matters are concerned with the relationships between the organisation and trade unions or other staff representatives.

The choices that exist for management can best be seen by looking at a number of specific questions which have to be answered if sound rules for negotiations are wanted:

To what extent do we want our staff to have their pay and conditions negotiated by trade unions?
Often this question is irrelevant because it is traditional in many sectors of the economy for unions to carry out negotiations. Where this is not the case, a choice exists and the answer will depend on the efficiency of existing negotiating systems, on the track record of the unions involved, on the wishes of the staff themselves and on the attitude of the decision-makers towards trade unions in general.

What should our attitude be towards the unions?
A whole range of possible answers can be given to this question. At one extreme there is the 'necessary evil' attitude, which results in considerable effort being spent in trying to frustrate the work of the union in such matters as the disclosure of information to staff on company performance or plans ('Don't tell them anything') or deliberately putting off decisions about fringe benefits.

At the other extreme there is the co-operative approach which views the role of the unions as essential for the future wellbeing of the business. In this situation full consultation takes place on all matters, small requests are handled quickly and information is offered freely before it is requested.

There are many shades of attitude between these two extremes and it has to be remembered in choosing a particular policy that it is often very difficult to move from a 'hard' position to a more co-operative relationship. This is because attitudes may be so well dug in on either side of the relationship that change is almost impossible.

How far should we involve the unions?
This question clearly stems from the last one. Again, the extremes can fairly easily be identified: there is the 'pay and hours only' school of thought which is the traditional view of collective bargaining, representing one extreme. At the other end there is the view that there ought to be some employee representation on the highest decision-making bodies in the organisation. In other words, employees should have a say in the future shape of the business. This idea is found in practice in Germany, but has been seriously considered in Britain only since 1977 when the Bullock Report was published (*Report of Committee of Inquiry on Industrial Democracy*, HMSO, 1977). Although the committee's conclusions have been attacked from many

quarters and largely ignored, the contents make interesting reading on the merits and demerits of employee representatives taking a seat in the boardroom.

In the event of a dispute how far should the organisation try to avoid damaging industrial action?

Even in the best-run organisations (from an industrial relations point of view) serious differences arise from time to time between the claims of the employees and what the management side of the negotiating table considers appropriate. For instance if the union asks for a 35 per cent increase in basic pay and the company considers that only 5 per cent is justified, a situation is in the making that could lead to trouble. Some organisations adopt a policy of giving the union as much as possible, irrespective of the cost: an 'anything for a quiet life' policy. Other organisations, at the other extreme, try never to compromise but are actually prepared to tolerate strike action, rather than appear to be giving in. Again the extent to which an organisation veers to one or the other extreme depends not only on the nature of the business, but, more important, on the attitudes of the participants in the bargaining process.

Review

How important do you think the four aspects of personnel management are in the organisation you know best?

- Recruitment and selection
- Pay and conditions
- Training and development
- Industrial relations

There are no right or wrong answers to this, but your estimate of the importance of each aspect should be the same as the organisation's – especially if you have an important position in it.

10 Policies in Money

Money, like the human resource, is a resource on which the success of the organisation depends. The main difference between money matters in the public service sector and in the business sector is that, in business, money is used to make more money. In government, the town hall and in institutions like hospitals, in contrast, money is used to make the service work better and more efficiently.

By the end of the chapter you will be able to see what particular aspects of money need policies, why we need to have them and what should be the basic considerations in making the choice between the alternatives.

Most people, as individuals, have dealings with money. Even school-children receiving pocket money each week have to learn to handle it and soon realise that because there is a limited amount of it, care has to be taken with what they do with it. As adults, the quantity of money passing through our hands is usually a lot more than a schoolboy's pocket money; unfortunately adult needs for money are greater than the schoolboy's. The problem is that the quantity of money coming in rarely seems enough for all the needs we have, needs that only money can satisfy. Occasionally more money comes in than we need and when that situation occurs we have the different problem of deciding what to do with it.

All organisations are faced with exactly the same problem, the main difference being the sheer size of the numbers involved. Whereas the average British wage-earner will bring home several thousands of pounds in a year, the biggest British companies pull in from sales hundreds of millions of pounds in a year (say, £5,000,000,000).

There is, however, another difference that exists between individuals and public service organisations on the one hand and commercial organisations on the other. This is that commercial organisations usually have to spend money before it comes in from trading. For instance the baker has to buy his ovens and premises, his flour, yeast and salt. He has to buy all of these things before he can sell his bread. Until he sells the product no money can come in. Unfortunately he has to spend before he can receive money, but there is no guarantee that he will sell anything at all; he could make 1,000 loaves of bread only to find that the weather takes a turn for the worse, storms and gales keep people indoors and no bread gets sold. The bread goes stale, it is thrown away and the baker has lost money.

It must be remembered too that the amount of money actually in an organisation is not the same thing as profit. Profit can be defined as the difference between what is sold and the cost of making the sale. If the baker sells a loaf for 60p and the ingredients cost 50p then his profit is 10p on a loaf. By selling 1,000 loaves he would make a profit of £100 out of which he has to pay all the wages and the other overheads of the business. Then he can calculate his profit. But as to how much money he has – it could be anything. All the bread might have been sold on credit, and the baker would have bought next week's flour and put it into the storeroom – that particular transaction does not get included in the profit calculation until it is turned into bread and sold.

The wage- or salary-earner in contrast does at least know that the pay will arrive at the end of each week or month and approximately how much will be in the pay packet. Similarly the hospital, school or fire-brigade does know at the start of each year how much it is able to spend during the following year – their income is guaranteed by the appropriate government department. The butcher, the baker and all have no such guarantee. They have to set themselves up to trade at their own expense. They are risking their own money and that of their fellow shareholders.

Policies regarding money, usually known as financial polices, therefore, revolve around two basic questions:

- From where do we get money?
- How should it be used?

In financial language these two questions are referred to as dealing with the sources of finance (or funds) and the uses of finance (or funds).

10.1 Sources of Finance

For any commercial organisation there are four main sources of finance. It may come from the owners of the business (the shareholders); from lenders such as banks; from a sale of part of the business; or from the firm's own trading activities. Each of these has merits and demerits, and if an organisation wants to raise money it may be guided by pre-established policies. The main factors influencing the choice for each are considered in the following pages.

10.2 Finance from the Owners

All business operations begin with finance supplied by the owners. As we saw in Chapter 2, this is usually called the share capital of the business and this simply means that anyone who buys a share in a company becomes a part owner.

For example, at 31 March 1994 Marks & Spencer had 2,779 million shares of 25p each, in the hands of over 300 thousand shareholders (according to the 1994 Annual Report and Accounts).

If Marks & Spencer or any other company wanted to get more share capital into the firm it would have to:

- Make sure it could legally sell more shares.
- Offer the extra shares at a specified price on the market. This is usually done by inviting existing shareholders to buy extra shares at a favourable price. This is known as a 'rights issue', and is offered to shareholders in direct proportion to the number of shares they already hold.
- Be fairly sure that the existing shareholders will be willing to take up their rights (in other words the dividend and growth record has to be attractive).

As long as these three conditions are fulfilled, then a policy of raising money via rights issues is relatively simple and inexpensive.

Activity

Rights issues of shares are not uncommon, so look out for reports about companies that have announced plans for such an issue. You will find the arrangements discussed in the financial pages of the papers. Follow the story to see if the company succeeds in raising the sum it wants. Also try to find out what it needs the money for.

An alternative way of raising new finance in the form of share capital is to offer additional shares on the open market. This policy, usually these days referred to as an 'offer for sale', is used when large sums of money are involved or where, for some reason, it is felt that a rights issue might not succeed. It can also be used in the process of turning a privately owned company into a public company.

The policy decision to raise more share capital depends partly on the overall financial structure of the business (which will be examined later), partly on the sum of money required, partly on the acceptability of the company as a good risk (i.e. the chances of losing your money are not too high), partly on its prospects and partly on whether the present owners are prepared to lose some of their control of the business (in terms of ownership).

Finance from lenders

The policy issue in raising money by way of borrowing can be summarised in the following question: How much should we borrow?

From time to time every organisation finds that it needs to borrow some money. The need may be temporary, such as when a farmer has to buy the fertiliser and seed early in the year, or it may be on a much longer-term basis, such as when an airline borrows to buy new planes, paying back the borrowing over several years. These two different types of borrowing are usually referred to as short-term borrowing or 'current liabilities', and long-term or 'loan' capital. The total amount borrowed is sometimes referred to by the American term 'debt'.

Short-term borrowing
There are two kinds of short-term borrowing. One is where the organisation does not pay its bills (having actually received the goods or service; and may include a tax bill too!), the other is where money is actually borrowed to pay the bills or wages or the tax man.

Some organisations have a rule that no money should be owed for more than a few days and that borrowing on a short-term basis should be avoided if at all possible. The main reason given is that short-term borrowing is very expensive in terms of the high interest charges that have to be paid on the amount of money borrowed. In addition, paying your bills very quickly can sometimes save money. Some suppliers allow 'prompt payment' discounts, so that if the bill is paid up within seven days a small percentage can be taken off the total owed.

To be able to pay all the bills on time and avoid having to borrow from the bank requires the organisation to be fairly sure of receiving money in (either through sales in the case of a commercial organisation, or through the rates in the case of a local authority). In addition it has to have well-developed cash forecasting systems to make sure the money paid out never exceeds the amount flowing in.

At the other end of the scale there are many organisations that put off paying their bills as long as they possibly can and do not seem to mind how their overdraft is at the bank. There are, however, limits to all this borrowing. Banks do have rules to prevent overdrafts getting too high and suppliers can stop supplying if their bills are not paid. The limit depends on the amount of money flowing in and how trustworthy and stable the organisation is (known usually as credit-worthiness). Within these limits, however, it is a key organisational policy decision how much short-term borrowing to undertake.

Self-check

Would you try to borrow any money, if you were any of the following?

1 The owner of a popular hotel in a busy seaside resort who wants to repaint the outside of his hotel just before the season starts and who has no other debts outstanding.

2 A small shopkeeper who is making £500 a week on average (after tax) but who owes suppliers £50,000 (the sum to be borrowed).
3 J. Sainsbury.

(Fifteen minutes.)

Answers

1 *Yes: borrow.* On the assumption that there were no odd factors to influence the decision it is normal for a business with a highly seasonal trade to borrow from the bank before the season starts. If the trading history of the business is good then it makes sense for the bank to lend for a few months to pay for repairs, renewals or building up stocks – activities which will help ensure a successful season for the firm.

2 *No: do not borrow.* If the bank lent this business £50,000 at 15 per cent interest, its profit would fall to approximately £356 a week because of the interest payments. At that rate it would take nearly three years to pay off the debt. Meanwhile if your livelihood depends on the profits of the business how are you going to survive if it is all going to the bank? It would be better to try to reduce the debt gradually, only borrowing if a supplier becomes troublesome.

3 *Yes: borrow.* Sainsbury's happens to be a very interesting example of what an organisation can do if it has a high level of credit-worthiness. At 12 March 1994 the accounts of Sainsbury's show that it owed:

- its suppliers etc. £1,018 million;
- the tax man £256 million;
- its shareholders (dividends to be paid) £136 million.

These, together with some other amounts due to be paid off quickly, amounted to £1,483 million. In contrast, its liquid assets (cash, debtors and other items that could easily be turned into cash) amounted to only £371 million. So its current debts far exceeded its liquid assets, yet it had also borrowed £300 million from the banks. Conventional accountancy reckons that the relationship between liquid assets and all current liabilities should be about 1 to 1 (this is known as the 'acid test'). Yet here is Sainsbury's with an acid test ratio of only 0.21 (i.e. liquid assets ÷ current liabilities).

At that level, not only would most firms not get any more overdraft from the bank, but their suppliers might wonder whether they would get the money owed them, and so stop supplying any more goods. Lending short term to Sainsbury's is safe because the business is profitable and sales revenues in relation to these sums of money are very high (e.g. the overdraft is equal to under ten days' sales).

Long-term borrowing

Organisations borrow money on a long-term basis when they want to grow but either do not have sufficient of their own or cannot raise more from shareholders. Some companies have a policy of never raising finance in this way, preferring to plough back the profits of the business. The big advantage of borrowing is that it enables the firm to grow faster than if it relied on its own, and the shareholders', funds. This is not to assert that fast growth is automatically desirable, but it is sometimes necessary if, for instance, a competitor is planning to attack one of the firm's best markets; there has to be a quick response to the threat, and borrowing enables the firm to meet that threat faster.

Another advantage of long-term borrowing is that it should increase the amount of money available to each shareholder. This can be better appreciated if we look at the case of Len's Launderette.

Len owned a very busy, old-established launderette which produced for him a profit last year of £8,000 after tax had been paid. Normally Len took most of this profit out of the business, so that the equity capital of the firm hardly rose year after year.

One day Len was offered another launderette on a prime site for £40,000. On its own this business could bring in £8,000 as well, but by combining the two shops together the total profit could be as much as £20,000 after tax, because of the effect of synergy (see page 76). Len could not afford to buy this second launderette himself, although he really would have liked to. He spoke to his brother-in-law, who immediately replied that he would gladly find £40,000 and put it into the business, in exchange for half of all the profits.

Len thought about this for a long time. Half the profits of the total business was £10,000: quite a bit more than his present earnings; it sounded an attractive proposition. However, he decided to have a chat with the bank manager whom he had known for a long time. The bank manager heard Len's story, then gave his opinion that a loan would probably be available to Len if he wanted it.

'What about the interest?' asked Len, to which the bank manager replied that even if it was at 15 per cent a year Len would still be better off because he would not have to share the profits. He then proceeded to prove his point with some simple figures:

First situation: using brother-in-law's money

Trading profit before tax:	£30,800
Less: Tax at 35% (approx.):	−£10,800
Profit after tax:	£20,000
B-in-law's share (i.e. half):	−£10,000
Left for Len:	£10,000

Second situation: using borrowed money

Trading profit:	£30,800
Less: Interest on £40,000 at 15%:	−£6,000
Profit before tax:	£24,800
Less: Tax at 35% (approx):	−£8,700
Profit after tax:	£16,100
	All for Len!

The bank manager went on to explain about the type of loan that could be made, the security for the loan, some other tax angles and how the loan could be made. In the end, Len agreed that it sounded the best possible alternative – but he said, 'the trouble is, it sounds risky to me'.

Self-check

Why does the deal sound risky to Len? (Clue: it is not directly connected with either tax or the rate of interest.)

The risk, and this applies to *all* borrowing, is that there is no guarantee that trading profits will turn out as high as planned. What *is* certain is that the interest payments will have to be made, and if trading profits fell enough, Len could end up worse off. Even more difficult would be the situation that trading profits turned out to be less than the interest due.

Self-check

Calculate what the effect would be for Len in both situations if trading profit fell to £10,000. (The answers are given later, on page 155, but try to work them out yourself before reading on.)

All organisations that choose to borrow face a similar risk. The decision that has to be taken at the policy level is: at what level of borrowing does the risk become acceptable? To put it another way, if we borrow more, what are the chances of our trading performance deteriorating (because of intense competition, recessions, strikes, changes in fashion, etc.) to such an extent that we cannot pay out any dividend to shareholders or, even worse, be unable to pay the interest?

Finally, in respect of long-term loans, it should be noted that once the major policy decision is taken regarding the extent of such borrowing, further policy decisions have to be taken regarding the precise type of borrowing. There are many different types of loan: preference shares, debentures, mortgages, secured and unsecured loans, medium-term to long-term, fixed or variable interest rates, loans raised at home or abroad, and so on. All have to be discussed, analysed and ranked in terms of which are most suitable for the company. Needless to say each type has its merits and drawbacks, but that is beyond the scope of this book.

Finance from selling off part of the business

There are two aspects to this method of raising money, and neither actually produces new additional capital, but merely converts existing assets into cash. First there is the 'sale and leaseback' arrangement where an organisation that owns some land or a building sells that asset to (usually) an insurance company or pension fund. At the same time a contract is drawn up enabling the firm to lease the asset from the new owners for a fixed term of years. The seller gets the capital value of the asset and its use, in exchange for what amounts, in effect, to a long-term rental agreement.

A policy to engage in this kind of activity to any extent must naturally correlate with the basic 'rent not buy' policy of the business. This type of policy, where the company chooses to lease or rent as much of its fixed assets as possible, has the advantage of not requiring so much capital, but it does naturally result in lower profits because of the rental or leasing costs. A company that chooses a 'buy not rent' policy will not normally want to get involved in sale or leaseback activities unless it is in a 'cash flow crisis' and other sources of finance are not possible.

The second aspect to selling off part of the business is where the firm needs finance and chooses to get rid of some activity it no longer considers to be suitable. A variety of policies are found in practice; for instance:

- Hang on to it as long as it brings in a little money.
- Get rid of it if it fails to make 15 per cent return on the capital invested in it (or some other percentage).
- Sell it while it is still a very profitable activity (i.e. before it gets old, in the case of an asset, or before the product's life-cycle stage is reached when it is on the wane), to get the best possible price.
- Get rid of it if we can find something else that will make more money.
- Sell it if it no longer fits our overall product and market strategies.

These are deceptively simple choices; in fact the mathematics involved in what has become known as the 'abandonment decision' are fairly complex. Suffice it to say that an organisation that sells off assets or activities because of financial pressure cannot succeed like the firm that has a clear policy regarding the timing of the sales.

Finance from trading activities

Most firms obtain most finance as a direct result of their trading activities. The amount that becomes available to companies is closely tied up with a specific policy decision about dividends, and this is discussed first.

Dividend policy (How much should we pay the shareholders?)

In Chapter 2 (page 27) we noted that profit after tax is available to the company to pay out to shareholders in the form of dividends or to put back into the business to help provide funds for tomorrow's expansion plans. The way in which the total after-tax profit is divided is up to the top management of the business – in the shape of the directors. In law they recommend to the shareholders at the annual general meeting of the company how much dividend should be paid out. The shareholders can agree or decide to reduce the dividend; they cannot vote to raise it, and usually they take the directors' advice.

It is therefore up to top management to decide how much will be given out and how much kept. The decision can be simplified by following a particular predetermined policy and there are several to choose from.

Always pay a fixed percentage of the profits
This implies that the shareholders' dividends will rise and fall as the profits of the firm rise and fall. In good times dividends are high, in bad times dividends are low. This kind of policy, sometimes referred to as the 'constant payout percentage', may be good when business is expected to do well in the foreseeable future. The disadvantage is that the shareholder never knows what dividends to expect, making his planning more difficult. The result of this kind of policy is that the shares, if quoted on a stock market, are not likely to be popular.

Always try to pay a bit more each year. Figure 10.1 illustrates how this might work in practice. Dividends grow as profits grow, but not as fast, so that if profits slump there is still some margin for the shareholder.

It will be noticed that the dividend line in Figure 10.1 is only gradually rising when profits are forging ahead, but as profits slip so the company tries to keep the dividends at least at the level of the earlier years. It would not actually matter if profits in year six fell below the dividend line, because a company can pay dividends out of earlier years' profits if it wishes – a policy not to be pursued too often, as this is in effect reducing the size of the firm.

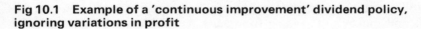

Fig 10.1   Example of a 'continuous improvement' dividend policy, ignoring variations in profit

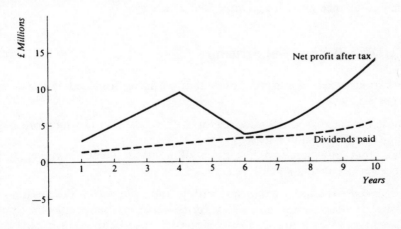

This type of 'stable dividend' policy is fairly popular these days in Britain, although there are a number of variations on the basic theme. Some firms will pay out a fixed proportion of the profits in dividends as long as profits are rising (usually a low proportion). If profits fall, the actual amount of dividend paid out is maintained at the previous year's level.

The advantages of the stable dividend policy are that shareholders know where they stand and are more likely to support a request for further finance. The disadvantages are that in a very good year the firm may retain more profit than it needs, and in a poor year may have to dip into earlier years' profits to pay the dividend. (It should be noted, in trying to work out what dividend policy various British firms have, that during the 1970s there were government limits on what companies could pay out as dividends. This distorts the record historically.)

Give the shareholders what's left
The third broad type of dividend policy is really a non-policy, since it has regard first to the needs of the company and only then considers the shareholder. It is sometimes referred to as the 'residual dividends policy', hence the belief that the shareholder is not the prime beneficiary in the business but the last beneficiary or the 'residual legatee'.

Money comes from being efficient

Finally as regards raising finance from operations, there is the simple but very important expedient of trying to be more efficient all round. If a company cuts its costs while maintaining standards and overall sales, then there will be more profit available for retention and future growth. Similarly selling off surplus capacity, as we have seen, generates money which can be put to better use. In the same way careful housekeeping in relation to stock levels and money outstanding from sales (i.e. debtors) can also generate money to finance growth and improved efficiency.

10.3 **Overall Financial Structure**

The various ways of raising money that we have discussed fall into two categories:

- those that increased the total size of the business (i.e. raising more share capital; additional borrowing);
- those that only increased the amount of money in the business (i.e. selling off assets; reducing stock levels).

Financial structure is concerned with the first category – the question of the size of the business in money terms – and refers specifically to the different ways that a firm can raise money. It may be thought of as a wall

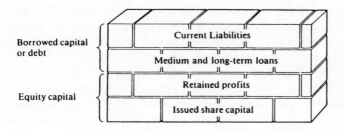

Fig 10.2   The capital structure of companies

---

consisting of several different types of brick – see Figure 10.2. The merits and demerits of each row of bricks have already been discussed. There is, however, one main issue where a policy decision is needed and that is the question of the relative size of the 'debt' part of the structure and the relative size of the 'equity' part; in financial terms the relationship between debt and equity is called 'gearing' (in America it is known as 'leverage'). (There are many definitions of gearing, and many ways to measure it; take care.)

The advantages of each type of finance have already been described, but to follow either the debt or the equity path depends first and foremost on the overall financial structure the business is prepared to accept. Briefly the alternatives are:

- We will borrow as much as we can lay our hands on.
- We will always try to get by with as little borrowing as possible.
- Our aim is to have a gearing ratio of 1 to 1 (i.e. equal amounts of debt and equity).
- We will raise finance when we need it whichever way is cheapest.

Remember Len's Launderette on pages 150–1? If Len had borrowed the money he would have been more 'highly geared' than before and he would have made much more money. But if his trading profit fell to £10,000 his results would have been

	Using borrowed money	*Using b-in-law's money*
Trading profit:	£10,000	£10,000
loan at 15%	−£6,000	–
Profit before tax:	£4,000	£10,000
Less: Tax at 35%	−£1,400	−£3,500
Profit after tax:	£2,600	£6,500
	(All for Len)	(Of which £3,250 for Len)

The conclusion is that, by borrowing, Len would be better off in good times and worse off in bad times compared to his position if he had raised the money by means of extra equity capital. His decision is based on how much risk he was prepared to take and whether he wanted to keep total control of the business.

The problem for organisations is this: in any new venture there is an ordinary commercial risk that the idea may be a failure. If the project has been financed out of borrowings then there is, in addition, a financial risk. The more a firm borrows, the higher the financial risk (but equally the greater the possible profit).

Self-check

Len's Launderette, Part 2: Len decided to borrow the money to buy the second launderette, and after it had been operating for several months it was obvious that the profits would be even better than expected – thanks partly to the fact that inflation had put the charges up. So Len went to the bank manager again and asked if it would be possible to borrow another £40,000 to £50,000 for a third launderette. What do you think the bank manager said after he had seen the figures?

He would probably have advised Len to wait a couple of years, pay off some of the existing debt and plough some of the profits back to form the basis for the finance of the third launderette. Borrowing an extra £40,000-plus would put Len's gearing too high, bearing in mind the uncertainty of profits.

The example neatly leads into the other type of policy question regarding finance that was put early in the chapter (page 146), namely How should money be used?, or 'to what uses can finance be put'.

The basic rule is that short-term finance is used for short-term needs. For instance, the bank overdraft facility is used to tide people and companies over a temporary cash shortage; it is not recommended for use in buying factories or houses.

As far as long-term finance is concerned (whether it is debt or equity) the rule is that it should be put to profitable use within the organisation.

This clearly depends on the overall strategies that the organisation has already chosen. However, the specific uses will be determined by the different operating functions within the organisation, like operations or sales. Even so, each part of the business will come up with many proposals for spending capital on new ideas – the problem is choosing which to adopt. To help in the decision, some basic policy decisions have to be made, setting up rules which have to be complied with in making the selection.

Activity

Suppose you had £1,000 which you wanted to try to increase by investing in some activity and you are given four alternatives shown below. List the four in order of the amount of money you might get back if things worked out right (you do not actually need to work out how much you would get – just which could bring in most, and least).

- Put the money on a horse in the Grand National at 100 to 1.
- Put the money in a deposit account at the Midland Bank for a year earning 5 per cent interest.
- Buy shares in Tesco Stores at £2.50 per share, for a year.
- Invest in a company that has been set up to look for gold in Australia.

The racehorse could give you the best return. If you won you would get £100,000. The gold mine could also do you very well too; if they did hit gold the £1,000 of shares would be worth a lot of money and you would eventually get some handsome dividends – but only once production had begun.

Buying shares in Tesco for £1,000 at £2.50 each would give you 400 shares. The value of these could rise to anything (or fall to anything!) in a year, but in addition you might receive dividends of, say, 8p a share. You could therefore receive dividends of £32 in total together with the value of the rise in the shares from £2.50. If the share price rose to £3.00 you would receive 50p × 400 shares = £200, giving a grand total of £232.

Finally, putting the money in the bank at 5 per cent for a year would give £50.

Activity

Now rank the four possibles in terms of risk: which is the least likely to give you anything and which is the most likely?

Clearly the racehorse is the riskiest – the biggest gamble of all – and some may feel that the Australian gold-mine venture is not far behind, but it has probably less risk if you know who is actually involved in the operation (and also where they are exploring). Tesco is a fairly safe bet, but the bank is even safer, the least risky of all (if an unknown bank had been chosen instead of the Midland Bank, the risk would have been greater. Would you put your money in the 'Bank of Antarctica'?).

The problem can probably be seen by now; it is that the higher the return (potentially) the greater is the risk, and the lower the risk, the lower the return.

The decisions that all organisations have to make regarding investing are:

- To what extent are we prepared to risk money in uncertain commercial ventures?
- What basic returns are we expecting on our investments? (Some firms state for example that 'we will invest in anything as long as it gives us a return of more than 20 per cent'.)

- To what extent do we go for a 'mixture' of investments bearing in mind that there is this relationship between risk and return?

These decisions may refer to separate activities within a total organisation or they may refer to certain characteristics of products within an operation. What is often sought is a balanced portfolio of sub-activities, or products.

One method of classifying a product portfolio has been developed by the Boston Consulting Group. (This concept has recently been reviewed thoroughly in the *Financial Times*: See Further Reading.) They have identified four basic product characteristics (see Figure 10.3), like this:

'Stars' are products that are growing very fast and, because of the company's high share in the market, are likely to do very well in the future. However, at this stage the product is sucking money in (for development costs, extra advertising and so on). 'Cash cows' are products that have passed through the high growth stage, are now mature and no investment in them is needed. They simply 'make money'.

'Problem children' products could do well if the growth continues but the investment required is greater than for stars. There is a chance of success if it turns the low market share into a high share. There is also a chance of them turning into 'dogs'. Dogs are products to get rid of; their volume is too low to fully utilise the resources assigned to them and they are probably not contributing much by way of profit to the business. All firms need to have policies with regard to the extent that their products fall within these categories and to make sure that the product range portfolio does not get out of balance.

Policy decisions in the area of finance are clearly important. Some organisations operate on a hit-or-miss basis, simply taking financial decisions in an *ad hoc* way as and when they occur. This is neither particularly clever nor wise since the risks involved are very often too high to

Fig 10.3   The Boston Box

	Company market share	
	High	Low
High	1 Stars	2 Problem children
Low	2 Cash cows	4 Dogs

Growth rate of the product

be left to unplanned decisions. The wise organisation – whatever its size – has financial plans carefully worked out to coincide with its strategies and aims, and has a series of rules already taken, to meet most eventualities. Many of the rules cannot be discussed here – such things as holding foreign currency, how much to carry in the bank and what to do about customers who do not pay. Nevertheless they, and the ones we have discussed, are important because the ultimate success or failure of a business (or even an organisation's ability to survive) will depend in the end on its financial strength and prospects.

Review

In this chapter several concepts have been introduced that may be unfamiliar. The main ones are listed below, together with the number of the page on which they appear, if you wish to check on any of them.

If, however, you feel you would like to become more familiar with the broader picture of this area of management, read Chapter 2 again and then this chapter; the two are closely related.

Part IV

Everyday Managing: Getting the Job Done

This part of the book deals with some of the most important elements in the daily workload of practically every manager. Most managers have staff responsibilities and this implies the need to have the skill of leadership and the ability to motivate. Managers have many problems to solve and many decisions to make about all kinds of things. The more senior the job the bigger the problems faced.

Finally the manager's job is concerned with change and it is one of the keys to success for a manager to be able to handle it.

11 Motivating Staff

In this chapter you will be able to read about the different views that exist on the subject of motivating people. By the end of it, you should be able to identify some of the main theories on the subject, and appreciate their main features.

There once was a farmer who bought a donkey from a neighbouring farm. The following morning the farmer went to its stable, saddled it up the best he could since it was sitting down on the straw, and then he tried to get it to stand up and walk into the farmyard. Sad to relate, no matter what he did he could not get it to move. He talked to it; he whispered in its ear; he cursed it; he offered it carrots and candy (which it ate). He beat its backside with a stick, but all in vain, it would not budge.

In desperation he called his neighbour on the phone, who said he would go over and fix it straight away. A little while later the neighbour drove into the farmer's yard, looked at the donkey sitting peacefully in the stable and gave a big sigh. He went to the car and from it produced a huge sledgehammer. He went over to the donkey and walloped it over the head with the hammer. Immediately the beast rose and walked into the yard and backed into the cart waiting to be harnessed to it.

'That's amazing,' said the farmer. 'Why did he respond when you hit him on the head?'

'That's easy,' replied the neighbour. 'All he needed was motivation.'

There is not much doubt that most people would not be motivated in the same way as the donkey, yet it is odd that sometimes even the most tempting offers fail to have the desired effect on human beings. Motivating people is not seriously under question itself; it is generally acknowledged to be important. However, it is not easy to achieve, although it is very easy to destroy.

Activity

Try to imagine what situation at work could cause you to lose completely any motivation you might have for your work. What would cause you to give up trying, to do the minimum required of you, and eventually leave the job?

There are many possible answers to this problem. To have your wage cut to a tenth of what it is now would do the trick very nicely. So might making you work outdoors (if you now work inside) in all kinds of weather. You might well be demotivated if you were asked to do something illegal or against your principles; or if your boss started insulting you and your character; or if you were continually being held responsible for things going wrong that had nothing to do with you. It may have been that the job was boring, or that you were not given clear instructions about what to do. All these and many more are possible ways of becoming demotivated, of losing the will and inclination to do more than the absolute minimum.

What, though, is the situation if we turn the question on its head and ask about motivation, not demotivation?

Activity

Think back to a time when you were performing extremely well. What were the factors that caused your high level of performance?

Once again there are many different answers to this question. It might have been something to do with the job itself – interesting, exciting or challenging, for example. It might have been because of the pay and conditions – a very good wage or a super place of work. It could have been that your colleagues were a 'great crowd' and you enjoyed their company and they enjoyed yours.

Another possibility is that the organisation itself seemed to be the kind of outfit it was a pleasure to work in; the atmosphere inside and the image outside all contributed to a morale-boosting environment.

Finally it could have been the people for whom you were working, or to give it a fancier title, the leadership style. Words that spring to mind here might include trust, encouragement, recognition, consultation and freedom.

It would seem, therefore, that there are many things that could turn people off and there are many things that could turn people on. It is odd that factors that turn people off are not always the opposite of the factors that turn people on. For instance a cut in pay may easily demotivate someone, but a big rise in pay may not cause them to work any harder or better.

Activity

Were the factors that turned you off opposites of the things that cause you to work well?

Many people are known to reply 'no' to this question: the things that caused them to work well are not the opposite of the demotivating things. Equally, others will have had very different experiences and can say 'yes' to the question: there is a single factor. If it is there they feel highly motivated; if is absent they lose that motivation.

Motivation is therefore a highly complicated problem and there is no magic formula that can be applied to everyone. Over the years many people have pondered the problem of motivation and suggested solutions – some of which seem to work better than others. In the following pages some of the key personalities in the debate will be looked at and their ideas discussed. To begin with we have to go back almost 200 years, to the early days of the Industrial Revolution.

11.1 Robert Owen

Although there is a view nowadays that Robert Owen was paternalistic, there is no doubt that this amazing Welshman was way ahead of his time. During the early years of the nineteenth century, Owen's textile mill at New Lanark in Scotland was the scene of some novel ways of treating people. His view was that people at work are not all that different from machines; if a machine is looked after, cared for and maintained then it is likely to be more efficient, reliable and longer lasting than equipment that is neglected. Similarly people at work are likely to be more efficient and reliable if they are well looked after than if they are treated badly. Robert Owen practised what he preached and introduced such things as employee housing and a company shop. His ideas on this and other matters were too revolutionary for the times and many of his innovations were opposed.

11.2 Jeremy Bentham

Possibly the essence of the traditional view of people at work can be best appreciated by a brief look at the work of this English philosopher, whose ideas were also developed in the early years of the Industrial Revolution, around 1800. Bentham's view was that all people are self-interested and are motivated by the desire to avoid pain and find pleasure. Any worker will work only if the reward is big enough, or the punishment sufficiently unpleasant. This view – the 'carrot and stick' approach – was built into the philosophies of the age and is still to be found, especially in the older, more traditional sectors of industry.

11.3 Elton Mayo

The work of Elton Mayo represents a significant landmark in the development of ideas about the behaviour and attitudes of people at work. Mayo was born in 1880 – forty-eight years after Bentham died – and although trained as a psychologist in Australia, he eventually moved to the United States where he became professor of industrial research at the Harvard Graduate School of Business in 1926. Two years before this, he had started the series of experiments which have become so famous and are now referred to as the Hawthorne Experiments.

The Hawthorne Works of the American Western Electric Company was in Chicago, where over 30,000 employees were working, making telephone equipment. Mayo and his team were called in because, in spite of many 'progressive' employee schemes in the firm (like a pension scheme and other facilities), there was poor productivity and a good deal of dissatisfaction. The idea behind the first experiment was that if conditions of work improve, so productivity will improve. It was decided, therefore, to begin by improving the lighting for a group of female employees.

To be sure that the results were scientific a 'control' group was set up – another team of employees whose lighting would not be changed. Nobody was surprised when the output of the experimental team went up, but everyone was very surprised when they discovered that the output of the control group had also risen. The lighting continued to be improved and output continued to rise and then came the second big surprise. The lighting was gradually reduced but output still rose. Eventually it got so dark that hardly anything could be seen at all – at that point, at last, output dropped.

Further experiments over several years all pointed in the same direction. Five-minute rest pauses were introduced and output rose. Then these were extended to ten minutes and output rose significantly. When six five-minute pauses each day were introduced, output fell and the girls complained that their work rhythm was being interrupted too often. The two-rest-pauses system was reintroduced with a free hot meal in one of them, and output went up again. Later the girls were sent home at four-thirty instead of five p.m. and output went up, but when they were sent home at four p.m. output stayed the same. Finally all the improvements were taken away and the group went back to the situation as it had been at the start.

Self-check

Guess what happened.

Incredibly, output rose yet again, finishing up over 30 per cent higher than it had been at the start.

Self-check

The experiments that have just been described produced an unexpected phenomenon, which has now become known as the Hawthorne Effect. The effect is that there is something else besides working conditions and an individual's physical wellbeing that determines his productivity. Why do you think this effect occurred?

The conclusions that have been reached is that motivation is a very complex subject and is not just about pay, conditions and how tired people are, but involves psychological and social factors as well.

The girls at the Hawthorne Works knew that they were being involved in some experiments that were of interest to the management. Throughout the experiments an observer sat with the girls and kept them informed of what was going on, how the experiments were doing and also listening to their views and complaints. The view now is that the girls responded to the interest being shown in them and their work. Although Mayo's researches have been criticised from many angles, there is not so much argument about his central conclusions, namely:

- People are motivated by more than pay and conditions.
- The need for recognition and a sense of belonging are very important.
- Attitudes towards work are strongly influenced by the group (since work is frequently a group activity).

11.4 A. H. Maslow

Maslow developed his Theory of Human Motivation in the early 1940s. Until then, apart from the ideas that we have looked at, most of the work on motivating people had been confined to economists, and psychologists like Freud, Adler and Jung. Maslow's idea was that there are many human needs, and motivation comes from an individual's desire to satisfy these needs. He classified the needs into a 'hierarchy' (i.e. grades) as follows:

1 *Physiological needs.* These needs are the basic ones and include, primarily, the need to satisfy hunger and thirst. In some societies these needs are not totally satisfied, but in most industrial economies by far the majority of people do not have to concern themselves too much with this kind of need. Once these needs have been satisfied, they no longer operate as primary motivators and people concentrate on other needs.
2 *Safety needs.* In Maslow's terms, safety not only consists of the kind of safety that comes from a fear of being attacked, but includes shelter, clothing, and protection from all the potentially dangerous or uncomfortable things like the weather, machinery, vehicles, fire and flood.

Activity

Do you think that people spend a lot of time, effort and money in protecting themselves, their families and possessions? (Do not forget the money paid out in tax and rates, for defence, police and fire services.)

In addition to the physical safety factors, there are also psychological safety factors, which have been considered to be very important motivators. Psychological safety includes pensions, health insurance and unemployment benefits. In addition, the problem of the 1980s – namely high unemployment – gives rise to another safety need: the need to avoid redundancy.

3 *Affection (or social) needs*. The need for affection and love can be described as the social needs of wanting to belong to a group, not only the family but also the group in which the individual works (or plays). It has been noticed that loyalty to a small work group and the need to belong to the group can weigh heavily in discussions about changing an organisational set-up.

4 *Esteem needs*. The need for esteem includes self-respect and the feeling that something useful has been accomplished. In addition, esteem includes the need to get recognition for what has been done and to have someone express their appreciation.

Activity

- How would you feel if you had just discovered the cure for the common cold?
- How would you feel if nobody took any notice of your discovery?

5 *Self-actualisation needs*. Maslow used the expression 'what a man can be, he must be', which really means that this need is concerned with self-fulfilment – being able to do what you really want to do. Examples of this can be found in music, in art and in sport, where people spend all their time and energy involved in the things they most love to do.

In considering the hierarchy of needs it is important to bear in mind that individuals do not necessarily satisfy the first need, then move on to the second and so on until they reach the top of the hierarchy. People are much too complicated for that to apply; what happens is that there is, in most people, a mixture of needs at any time. Some will be stronger than others and there are plenty of examples of people who are so motivated by, for instance, the need for self-actualisation that more basic needs are ignored.

11.5 Frederick Herzberg

The work of Dr Herzberg is more recent than that of Maslow, his findings only being made widely known towards the end of the 1950s. Herzberg was interested in the question of 'job satisfaction'. Specifically, several hundred accountants and engineers were interviewed and asked about the way incidents at work affected the way they felt about the job. From the answers, Herzberg developed his theory that there are two factors at work in determining job satisfaction. He called these two:

● *hygiene factors*
● *motivators*

Hygiene factors, according to Herzberg, include pay, working conditions (accommodation, lighting, etc.), pension funds and fringe benefits; in fact all the items we considered in the chapter on personnel policies (pages 133–4). Herzberg made the point that these factors have to be present and adequate otherwise there can be job dissatisfaction. On the other hand, an abundance of hygiene factors does not necessarily lead to a highly motivated staff.

Activity

Look back at the question on page 138.

● Would that huge rise in pay motivate you for more than a few days? (According to Herzberg's research, it probably would not.)
● Would your colleague's even bigger increase *de*motivate you, or cause you to be dissatisfied? (It might well do so!)

The 'motivators', on the other hand, are factors that have to be present if there is to be job satisfaction. These factors are associated with such things as responsibility, a sense of achievement, challenge and self-improvement. In other words, all these things motivate people to work effectively, and without them, no matter how good the hygiene factors, there will be no improvements in productivity or efficiency.

Another interesting conclusion from the studies was that as long as the motivators are there in abundance, people will put up with all kinds of deficiencies in the hygiene factors.

Activity

Try to think of real-life situations you know about when the following conditions applied, and try to decide whether people were, or were not, highly motivated at the time:

- High-level hygiene factors; high level motivators.
- Low-level hygiene factors; high level motivators.
- High-level hygiene factors; low level motivators.
- Low-level hygiene factors; low level motivators.

11.6 Douglas McGregor

McGregor's book *The Human Side of Enterprise* first appeared in 1960 (published by McGraw-Hill). In it he describes two extreme views about the way people inside organisations are managed. There is the traditional view, which McGregor calls Theory X, and there is a more modern view, Theory Y.

Theory X (the traditional view)

Every management decision is taken with certain specific views about human nature and behaviour. These are:

- The average human being has an inherent dislike of work and will avoid it if he can.
- Most people have to be coerced, controlled, directed and threatened with punishment to get them to make an effort in the direction of the organisation's goals.
- The average human dislikes responsibility and has little ambition, prefers being directed and wants security first and foremost.

  McGregor points out that most organisations provide for the physiological and safety needs of their employees. This being the case, he asserts that staff will be seeking to satisfy higher-level needs; if they do not succeed in this aim then it is not surprising that they behave in the ways suggested above (with indolence, passivity, resistance to change, unwillingness to take responsibility).

Theory Y

There are a number of basic assumptions about human behaviour which McGregor uses to support this theory:

- Physical and mental effort at work is as natural as rest or play.
- That the threat of punishment and controls are not the only ways of achieving the goals of the organisation. People do exercise self-control and self-direction if they are committed to those goals.

- That the average human being is willing to seek out and take responsibility under certain circumstances (note here McGregor's qualifying words 'average' and 'certain circumstances').
- That many (not a few) people are capable of exercising a lot of imagination, ingenuity and creativity in solving the problems of the organisation.
- That the way things are organised, the average human being's brainpower is only partly used.

Self-check

How many of the five statements made above do you think are correct.

- in respect of other people generally?
- in respect of yourself?

An organisation that is run on Theory X lines tends to be authoritarian in nature, the word 'authoritarian' suggesting such ideas as the 'power to enforce obedience' and the 'right to command'. In contrast a Theory Y organisation can be described as 'participative', where the aims of the organisation and of the individuals in it are integrated; individuals can achieve their own goals best by directing their efforts towards the success of the organisation.

Theory X and Theory Y have come in for considerable criticism, mainly on two counts. First of all both theories are wide generalisations about work and human behaviour. Theory X has been described as 'organisations without people' and Theory Y as 'people without organisations'. The two theories represent extremes and such generalisations do not fairly represent what is actually going on. Psychologists and sociologists have established that few people correspond with the descriptions set out in each theory. Secondly it is clear that to have a Theory X organisation does not automatically lead to failure; on the other hand, a Theory Y set-up is no guarantee of success.

11.7 Rensis Likert

While Theories X and Y represent extreme views, Likert has developed a refined classification, breaking down organisations into four management systems:

- System 1: primitive authoritarian
- System 2: benevolent authoritarian
- System 3: consultative
- System 4: participative

Likert writes:

> A steadily mounting body of research findings is demonstrating that System 4 achieves substantially better results than do other ways of managing, not only in business, but in school systems, universities, hospitals, military establishments and elsewhere. The chief executive officers in firms that are using System 4 or moving closer to it are obtaining results that confirm this pattern. I know of at least 50 papers published in recent years that report similar results. (Letter to *Management Today*, February 1977)

He goes on to say: 'Firms find that as they move from System $2\frac{1}{2}$ (the position of most firms) to System 3 to System 4, their productivity increases by 20% to 40%; quality improves and labour relations are much better.'

11.8 Victor Vroom

The work of Victor Vroom and others in the 1960s has led to the development of an even more sophisticated theory of motivation – known now as Expectancy Theory. This suggests that two separate things need to be working to motivate an individual. First there is the usual view that people want things. They want not only the basic things in life, but lots of other things like promotion, status, power and so on. Some of these 'wants' are strong desires, but others will be merely a 'liking' for something. The relative strength of someone's preference for one thing as against another is called the 'valence'. So if we say, 'Promotion has a high valence for Joe', what we mean is that Joe wants promotion very much indeed.

The second element in the motivation equation is called the 'expectancy'. Expectancy is an individual's own estimation of his or her chances of achieving what they want. 'I'll never get promotion' is a statement reflecting a very low expectancy.

The important thing about expectancy theory is that it sees motivation as similar to an electric current. If the strength of the current is too low, there is not enough power in it to make a motor turn. In the same way motivation has to reach a certain strength to lead to action – see Figure 11.1.

The importance of the X sign between valence and expectancy in Figure 11.1 is this: if either of these two elements is absent (or negative) then no motivation can possibly result. For example, salespeople may be offered a wonderful holiday in Hawaii as the prize for achieving a sales target. If they want that holiday badly enough and are convinced they can get it, then they will be motivated. Alternatively, if they see it as an impossible dream (or a trick) they will not bother.

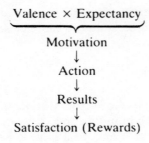

Fig 11.1 Expectancy theory of motivation

11.9 Clayton Alderfer

Alderfer's work is very recent, but is considered significant. It is called the ERG Theory, the letters standing for three different sorts of needs: Existence; Relatedness; Growth. This is similar to Maslow's list of needs, but in three groups, instead of five. Moreover instead of seeing the needs as a hierarchy, Alderfer considers them to be on a continuum, and people move along it all the time (see Table 11.1).

Activity

Having read about the ideas of some of the people who have made a significant contribution to our understanding of motivation, take a breather and review their ideas. Below is a list of some of the ways in which an individual might be motivated. This list was suggested on page 164 in answer to the question, What was it that motivated you most?

- The nature of the job itself.
- Pay and conditions.
- Colleagues – the work group.
- The organisation.
- Leadership style.

Which do you think is the most important to develop if a highly motivated work force is wanted? You may want to rank them in order of importance, but however you decide remember that there is no right or wrong *general* answer to the question. (Fifteen minutes.)

Table 11.1

Existence	*Relatedness*	*Growth*
Material desires (physiological needs; security; money)	People relationships (social and esteem needs)	Self-actualisation (creative desires)

Of all the aspects of motivation noted above, the work group, the job itself and leadership style need to be examined more closely.

11.10 **The Work Group**

One of the conclusions that emerged from the Hawthorne Experiments was the importance of the group in motivation. A work group may be a small two- or three-person team or it may be a large department in a factory or office. In the world of music it ranges from a group of four musicians (like the Amadeus Quartet and The Who) to the 1,000 singers and players normally required for a performance of Mahler's Eighth Symphony. At either extreme the numbers of the group are all pursuing a common goal.

In music-making, if one or two individuals fail to perform as well as the rest, the performance as a whole suffers; this is no less true of any work group though usually less obvious. The effect is known as failing to live up to the group norms and, as found in the Hawthorne Experiments, there can be a very strong pressure on individuals to adjust to and accept those norms.

Group atmosphere

Research carried out in recent years has demonstrated that the atmosphere of a group often has a considerable influence on the extent to which the individuals in the group perform, and therefore on the performance of the group as a whole. There are many aspects to the idea of group atmosphere but they include the extent to which the group is:

- friendly
- enthusiastic
- supportive
- warm
- satisfying
- interesting
- productive
- co-operative
- successful

Activity

Try to recall when you were a member of an effective group. To what extent were the factors mentioned above present?

If you have ever been part of an unsuccessful team you may have found that the atmosphere tended towards the opposite of these factors, e.g. unfriendly, cold, unproductive, unenthusiastic, hostile and boring.

Group working

An example of group working was given in Chapter 6, when the Volvo experiment was discussed. Instead of each individual doing a highly specialised task within a department, all members of the department are encouraged to learn each other's job. This is known as 'multi-skilling' and can lead to an increase in motivation because jobs are wider and therefore less boring. In addition productivity can rise partly because the absence of a single member of the team does not now hold up the whole process. (For a review of this, see the *Financial Times*, 19 April 1985: 'The Volvo Experiment ten years on'.)

11.11 Team Roles

Another way of looking at work groups or teams is to consider the different attributes and personal skills different people bring to the task. The main research in this area has been carried out by Dr Meredith Belbin who identified eight team roles:

1 Co-ordinator (leader) – someone who is good at organising and works at making sure resources are used effectively.
2 Plant (ideas person) – the innovator and one who is creative.
3 Team worker (team builder) – these folk foster team spirit and keep things going; they build on others' ideas.
4 Monitor–evaluator (critic) – analysts who calculate the feasibility of ideas, useful for balanced decision-making.
5 Implementer (doer) – sorts out the details, fixes things, translates plans into actionable tasks.
6 Shaper (driver) – keeps things on track, co-ordinates activities.
7 Resource investigator (contact person) – finds out what's going on outside, brings in ideas.
8 Completer–finisher (inspector) – pays attention to details, ensures team's effort is 'perfect'.

Nobody can have all these attributes; indeed only a few possess more than two or three roles to a high degree, though most have some capabilities in most roles. Belbin has discovered that a really effective team consists of a balance of all these attributes. Too often, though, there is no choice in the team with whom we work and in these situations it is important to be aware of what's missing. At least we can then make an effort to compensate.(For a recent update on Belbin's work, see *The Independent*, 18 June 1991, where the team roles of some famous people are used to illustrate the concept. For example, Prince Charles is a 'Plant'.)

Activity

What do you think are your team roles?

11.12 **The Job Itself**

If responsibility, self-fulfilment and achievement are motivators then it is not likely that a boring, repetitive job is going to be a highly motivating experience. 'Job design', as it is called, works on the assumption that these motivating factors should be built into the job, whether or not it is done as part of a group working scheme or not. A concern for the quality of working life (QWL) is increasingly being seen as an important contribution to greater efficiency and the two expressions that have come into prominence in this area are:

- *job enrichment* and
- *job satisfaction*

Job enrichment

This is also sometimes called job enlargement and is the process of making jobs more interesting by increasing the amount of responsibility each individual has and by giving them greater opportunities for self-development. Many of the ideas about job enrichment came out of the motorcar assembly industry. Studies revealed a high level of boredom, a low level of job satisfaction and considerable dislike of the job. This was because the speed of the assembly line determined the pace of work, the skills needed were very low and because the individuals felt isolated.

Job enrichment, especially when built into group-working schemes, has been seen to have beneficial effects, but it has to be remembered that the success of such a programme will depend on the background and attitudes of the individuals involved.

Job satisfaction

This has already been looked at in connection with the work of Herzberg (page 169). There are many more studies in this area and especially interesting are those which have tried to establish a relationship between job satisfaction and productivity. It seems that job satisfaction comes about from doing the job well. However it also seems to be the case that unless individuals' work is designed to be satisfying, then high productivity is unlikely to result. Good job performance leads to job satisfaction, leads to better job performance and more job satisfaction, etc. Conversely, poor job performance leads to less job satisfaction, leads to worse job performance and even lower job satisfaction, etc.

All this does not imply that managers can avoid the issue: their responsibility is to create an environment that is conducive to a high level of job satisfaction.

11.13 Leadership Style: Follow-My-Leader

To lead an organisation or part of an organisation successfully is one of the hallmarks of the effective manager. Real leadership by definition implies a willingness of others to follow or, as we saw in Chapter 1 (pages 3, 10), to be directed. If leadership is poor, or absent, the individuals in the group or the organisation display all the characteristics associated with low motivation. They are not willing followers and they will only perform to the minimum standards. In contrast, if leadership standards are high, the motivation and performance of members of the organisation or group are also high.

These effects can be seen in relation to the management of football teams, where the performance of the team is tied up very closely with the team manager's own leadership skills. The team without a manager or with a weak manager performs less well than teams that have stronger managers. It is worth noting, though, that sometimes a successful manager transfers to another club and finds that his successful leadership formula no longer works.

This kind of experience is found in every kind of organisation; sometimes a manager is a success and sometimes he is not, and it would seem that it has a lot to do with leadership style in relation to the organisation's own values, beliefs and requirements.

Leadership style means the personal way in which the leader of a group relates to his subordinates. There are many classifications of leadership style. Some divide it into two broad categories: the leader who is orientated towards people, and the leader who is orientated to the job in hand and getting it done.

People-centred leadership

An extreme view of a people-centred leader would be the manager who strives above all to make the individuals for whom he is responsible feel that their needs are all being looked after. The aim of such managers would be to run a 'happy ship', on the principle that if all the members of the crew are happy then the ship will be easy to sail in the right direction.

Work-centred leadership

A totally work-centred leadership style would probably correspond to Theory X (page 170) and would be described as 'scientific management'. This idea was introduced in Chapter 1 in connection with the work of F. W. Taylor, the first person to study people at work using scientific principles (page 12).

These two styles represent extreme views: clearly there are many other styles. An alternative classification was suggested by two writers, Tammenbaum and Schmidt, in 1958 ('How to Choose a Leadership

Pattern', *Harvard Business Review*, March–April 1958), a classification that has gained considerable support. It has been described as a 'leadership continuum' and contains a range of styles, including:

- Autocratic – where the leader dictates what he wants.
- Persuasive – where the leader sells his ideas, using the morale and enthusiasm of the team members.
- Consultative – where the leader discusses with the team members but then takes the decision himself.
- Democratic – where the leader involves team members in discussion and in decision.

The full continuum can be illustrated as in Figure 11.2.

The appropriate style of leadership to use for maximum motivation will depend on a number of factors:

- the size of the organisation;
- whether the workforce is highly skilled or not;
- whether there is a high degree of interaction between members of the group;
- the personality of the members of the group;
- the knowledge and ability of the leader;
- how quickly decisions need to be made;
- what team members feel most comfortable with;
- the current state of the organisation (is it up or down?);
- the normal style of the organisation.

The need for leadership

Since Tammenbaum and Schmidt wrote their 1958 article, many writers and researchers have tried to establish what makes a good leader. There is no

---

Fig 11.2   The leadership continuum

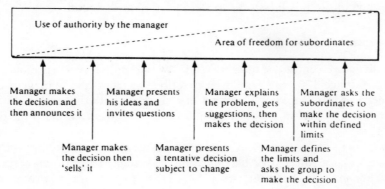

doubt that it is vital to have a leader, but what type of person, how strong, how visible, what style is right?

In the 1980s a popular book on leadership was *Leadership and the One-Minute Manager*, by K. Blanchard *et al.* (Willow Books, Collins, 1986). Here the view is that the leader's style needs to be appropriate for the situation – a directive style will be needed where subordinates' skills and experience are low, and a supportive style is needed where individuals' interests and motivation may not be strong. The validity of these styles is particularly useful in dealing with small groups.

About the same time, the sequel to the now famous book *In Search of Excellence* by Peters and Waterman (see Further Reading) was published, called *Passion for Excellence – the Leadership Difference* by Tom Peters and Nancy Austin. Many of the excellent companies identified earlier had strong leaders who transmitted drive, enthusiasm and got commitment from staff. Also it has been noticed that more successful organisations tend to have leaders who have been in the firm a long time and who know 'what makes it tick'.

Peters and Waterman assert that leaders are not born but that they emerge when organisations form new problems and that effective leadership can move organisations from current to future states. In other words, effective leadership is needed to drive strategy forward. (See also the article 'The Lust for Leadership' by Simon Caulkin in *Management Today*, November 1993.)

Action-centred leadership

Another very useful way of looking at leadership, developed by John Adair (see *Effective Leadership* by John Adair, Pan Books, 1984) and called 'Action-centred leadership', is illustrated in Figure 11.3. The leader's role is threefold:

Fig 11.3   The three circles model: what a leader has to do

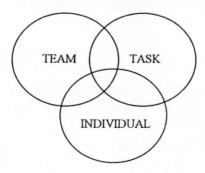

- to define and achieve the task
- to build and maintain the team
- to develop the individuals

'Task' is concerned with such things as setting objectives and determining strategy and tactics. 'Team' refers to the group and ensuring that it operates as a cohesive unit, pulling together and with the members supporting each other. The 'Individuals' aspect relates to motivation, education and training in the members of the group, so that each is confident, competent and capable. If any one of the three aspects is underdeveloped or neglected, then it is very difficult – if not impossible – to achieve desired results.

Self-check

Try to picture a situation where one of these three elements is underdeveloped; maybe from your own experience. Do you think it could lead to success? Who is responsible if any of the three elements are underdeveloped?

A good example of differing leadership styles is given by Sir Winston Churchill in his book *The Second World War*. He describes how General Montgomery would not eat with his subordinates, but would have a sandwich by his car. Napoleon too would have kept apart (but eating better!) whereas Marlborough and Cromwell both would have fed with their officers. There may have been different techniques, but the results, says Churchill, were the same.

Activity

- Find out more about the leadership style of such people as Lord Montgomery, and try to discuss how he went about remotivating his troops.
- Do you think that such styles as are normally found in the army could work in civilian institutions (this is a 'forever' discussion)?
- Should a leader change his style to suit the situation?
- Read the quotation about Chris Bonington again (page 62).

Face-to-face leading

One aspect of every manager's job as leader that needs to be kept in mind is the way in which individuals are addressed, both in speech and in writing. Consider these two examples:

- 'Your trouble, Smith, is that you don't seem to want promotion and you don't push hard enough. Don't let people push you around so much.'

- '*To all salespeople*: You are reminded that all salespeople must inform my office of their movements before setting out on their journeys. Failure to do so could result in loss of commission.'

Self-check

Do you think these two communications will motivate or demotivate?

Neither statement seems very encouraging and helpful, does it? Yet this kind of communication can be seen and heard every day. Good managers who motivate staff pick their words carefully and avoid being negative like the above examples are – even though the speaker in the first one actually seems to be trying to help. There are obviously times when individuals or groups have to be told unpleasant things. At such times most people would appreciate straight talking, but most of the time people are looking to be treated like adults and given positive help when they need it. Techniques such as Transactional Analysis are concerned with looking at alternative ways of saying the same things, so that instead of feeling bad, you feel good – all part of motivation.

A quote to remember
   You can't have a happy ship unless it is an efficient ship; you can't have an efficient ship unless it is a happy ship.

   (Admiral Nelson)

12 Making Decisions and Solving Problems

Managers have to make decisions; it is their responsibility. Moreover the problems that seem to beset all managers often cannot be ignored or passed on; it is their responsibility to solve them. By the end of this chapter you should have a better understanding of the process of solving problems and appreciate how good decision-making works, so that you should be able, yourself, to take decisions more easily.

One evening, not so long ago, an argument broke out between my three children. This, itself, is not such a rare occurrence and at first I was inclined to ignore it, hoping that they would resolve their differences themselves as they usually do. Unfortunately the argument developed into a full-scale shouting match and I had to intervene. It turned out that the cause of the row was that each wanted to watch a different television programme from the other two.

My first act was to find out what the programmes were about and who wished to watch what! It was by then obvious that it was me who was going to have to resolve the dispute and make the decision, so the merits and demerits of each of the three programmes were argued out in front of me.

I next checked that my wife was not particularly interested in watching any of the programmes and, as I did not want to watch either, the issue was wide open. There was just five minutes to arrive at a conclusion and make a decision and these were the alternatives that presented themselves (bearing in mind we had only one TV set):

- Leave them to fight it out.
- Draw lots for which channel to choose.
- Switch the television off.
- Choose the least unpleasant/most sensible programme and watch that (classifying the programmes was a separate decision taken easily on the basis of personal bias).
- Watch the most unpleasant programme.

- Send two children to neighbours who would be watching two of the programmes (a quick phone call would establish who was going to watch what).

Theoretically there were other alternatives like going out and buying more TV sets or a videotape recorder. These options were ruled out because of earlier 'family policy' decisions. So the choice narrowed itself down to six alternatives. The three programmes were *Coronation Street*, an old *Carry On* comedy film and a documentary about timber wolves.

Activity

By now there were only three minutes left. What would you have done? Make a decision within three minutes.

How did you arrive at your decision? You could have picked one of the six possibilities at random, or your decision could have been based on the answers you got to some test questions, such as:

- Would the decision seem fair to them all?
- Is the decision capable of being carried out?
- Which would I watch if I had to watch?
- Can I give a good reason for my decision?
- Would a decision help solve the problem (which in this case was the threat of a minor civil war)?

By applying the test questions I reduced the alternatives to two:

- switch off the television (thus satisfying nobody); or
- watch the documentary (thus satisfying one only).

In the end I chose the documentary because I could justify it in terms of my own system of values. This does not mean that it was the only correct decision. Some of the other choices could be justified in exactly the same way, and it is quite likely that if I had been given more time I might have come up with a different conclusion.

The actual decision itself is not as important, for present discussion, as the way in which the decision was taken. A number of distinct steps in the process of making the decision can be identified:

Step 1 Identify a problem which is my responsibility to solve.
Step 2 Find out the facts and establish the cause.
Step 3 Look for some solutions to the problem.
Step 4 Narrow the choice of alternative courses of action.
Step 5 Take the decision.
Step 6 Implement the decision.

The process of arriving at a decision is usually referred to as 'problem solving' and there are many different ways in which the steps can be classified. All, however, will include the following basic elements which correspond to the six steps listed above:

- Recognise that there is a problem.
- Diagnose the cause or causes.
- Develop some possible solutions.
- Evaluate the possibles.
- Choose (i.e. take the decision).
- Implement.

Each of these elements has to be looked at in more detail.

12.1 **Recognition of a Problem**

The dictionary defines 'problem' as a 'doubtful or difficult question' and it would be very nice if all problems were presented to us on paper in the form of a question. For instance, consider this question:

The word *icedions* is an anagram of what?

This is a problem; it is written down in the form of a question which has to be considered and given some thought. Unfortunately it is very rare for a manager to receive his problems like that; usually he receives his problems like this:

In this carpeth you need to use your arbin.

At first glance the sentence is meaningless because there are two words in it you do not recognise. Immediately a question forms in your mind, What do the words mean? At that moment you recognise that you have a problem.

In exactly the same way a manager receives information which does not make sense or does not ring true in some way. It may be obvious that there is a problem. 'John, John. The warehouse is on fire!' is instantly recognisable as a problem. Other problems, however, tend to creep up on the manager without realising that there is a problem. For example, the following information may arrive from a salesperson: 'The XYZ Company has decided to start advertising on TV.' A quickwitted manager may well decide to check out that story because if it is correct it could spell out a big competitive challenge. It is not a problem now, but it might be one very soon.

The very first thing to do, therefore, on receiving some information is to find out if it is actually a problem. Everyone does this all the time with the information they receive, but usually it occurs subconsciously and it is not necessary to actually ask the question out loud. This is because most information we receive is not in conflict with what we expect. It is only where some information conflicts with our knowledge or experience that mental alarm-bells ring, and this is what happened when you read the words 'carpeth' and 'arbin' above. There is, however, a grey area where the alarm-bell is very muted and it is then that it is important to have asked this question: Is there a problem?

The second part of this step is to ask the question, Is it really my problem? Too often, managers find that they are handling problems that really are someone else's responsibility. This can happen in many ways, one of the commonest being where subordinates refer problems upwards to their boss, in spite of having full authority to take a decision (and probably knowing the answer too). 'Passing the buck' is a favourite pastime in large organisations but a good manager will encourage subordinates to solve their own problems and settle their own differences. A weak manager, however, is regularly being invited to look at, comment on, get involved with and generally waste time on problems which others are perfectly capable of handling.

12.2 Diagnose the Cause

It is one thing to be able to recognise that there is a problem; it is an entirely different thing to be able to identify the basic cause of the problem. For instance the strange word that was used on page 184, 'carpeth', is an easily identified problem. We can tell from experience that the cause of the problem is that the letters of a real word have been mixed up, and this particular kind of problem is called an anagram.

Since most problems faced by managers are not so easily labelled this diagnosis stage is very important, for to get it wrong can easily lead to the wrong decision. As we saw in Chapter 3 with the example of your neighbour who tries to remove your tooth (page 38), snap diagnosis is to be avoided. That chapter was specifically concerned with the analysis of an organisation's strengths and weaknesses, but the approach can be the same for any organisational problem: be sure to find the basic cause of the problem. Find out the facts.

Spring Clamps (1): a case for diagnosis

John Brown arrived at the office a few minutes after 9 a.m. on Monday. On his desk was this note from the supervisor of the morning shift:

> *John,*   *8.35*
>
> *Nearly all this week's supply of spring clamps are no use – if we don't get some more we'll have to shut the line at 2 p.m.*
>
>   *Ted*

John immediately went down to the stores and examined the clamps which had been delivered during the previous week in accordance with the terms of the contract his firm had with the suppliers. Sure enough they were nearly all faulty.

John returned to his office in a bad temper. 'Get me Fred Smith at Spring Clamps right away. It's very urgent,' he said to his young secretary, who was a bit irritated by this tone of voice and went off to phone feeling none too happy herself.

Fred Smith was an old friend of John's and as the firm was only twenty miles away there was a good chance of getting some more clamps over by 2 p.m. At about ten o'clock John's secretary came into his office and announced that she had been having difficulties in getting through to Spring Clamps Ltd. However, she had just managed to speak to Fred Smith's secretary, who said that Mr Smith was not in and she did not know where he was. 'Keep trying,' said John. 'I must speak to him soon. I've got the Safety Committee in my office at 10.15 so pull me out of it as soon as you get him.'

The meeting ended without interruption at 11.30 and John's secretary continued to try to contact Fred Smith whenever there was a free line – John's incoming calls being particularly heavy that morning.

At 12.30 John sent his secretary to lunch, tried Spring Clamps Ltd himself and discovered that both Fred and his secretary were at lunch. So he left a message with Fred's assistant telling him the problem and asking that Fred phone him instantly on his return.

Then John ordered up some sandwiches from the canteen and sat glowering at the telephone, wondering how to keep the production line going after 2 p.m.

Activity

- What is the main problem at 12.30?
- What is its basic cause?
- How many other problems can be identified?

(Fifteen minutes.)

Stated simply, the problem (at 12.30) is that it looks as though the production line will stop at 2 p.m. because the supply of spring clamps will be exhausted.

Turning this into a question, How can we get hold of more spring clamps to keep us going after 2 p.m.?

As to the basic cause of the shortage, there could only be two reasons at first glance: either not enough had been delivered or those that had been delivered were wrong.

Since the correct quantity was delivered but the quality was wrong there must have been a lack of inspection when they arrived. In other words the crisis should never have occurred: the fault should have been noticed last week and dealt with there and then. The basic cause is, therefore, inefficient inspection on delivery.

You may have identified a whole string of secondary problems. Arriving after 9 a.m. when the shop-floor people start earlier may be one that came to mind. So might the question of being bad-tempered with a secretary, or not giving her full instructions, or continuing with a meeting when there was an urgent problem. In addition there is the problem of trying to get hold of one particular individual in an organisation. Does John have to speak to Fred and Fred alone?

In thinking through the diagnosis, what emerges is that there are two main problems, not one. There is the immediate problem of sorting out the shortage so that production can carry on after 2 p.m., and there is the second problem of finding a way of making sure the situation never arises again.

The whole process of diagnosis is best appreciated if the example of a doctor is considered. Often by listening to the patient's explanation of the problem the doctor can diagnose the complaint. Indeed a good explanation of a problem is often a sufficient diagnosis in any situation.

How to get a good explanation of a problem

- Write it down.
- Turn it into language you can understand.
- Turn it into numbers if possible – graphs and diagrams too.
- Be careful to avoid opinions as opposed to facts.
- Get a good information system, i.e. a way of making sure that facts are fed to you regularly and systematically.
- Avoid classifying the problem too soon (e.g. as an industrial relations problem or as a marketing problem; these are risky assessments to make early on because they limit your thinking).
- Ask questions like, What caused such-and-such to happen? Why did it happen? What possible causes could there be?

The objective of this stage of the exercise is therefore to be able to state clearly:

- *the problem*
- *the cause of the problem*
- *the restatement of intention or aim*

At the end of the case of the spring clamps, John Brown was left staring at the telephone. He knew what the problem was and he soon knew the cause. Then came his restatement of intent: 'I must find a way of keeping the production line going and then I must find a way of preventing it happening again.' At this point he moves on to the next stage of the exercise.

12.3 Develop Some Possible Solutions

This stage in the exercise involves the use of the brain, i.e. we have to do a bit of thinking, which we may or may not enjoy depending on the nature of the problem. Some people love crossword puzzles and enjoy thinking about how to solve them; others cannot bear such things and do not even attempt to think about them. Unfortunately managers have no choice – they have to solve the problems they are set whether they like them or not. So the first thing to be sure about is that to be an effective manager some difficult thinking has to occur from time to time.

Developing solutions to problems means having some ideas, and there are all kinds of examples of how people have had their ideas. It is generally agreed that once the information has been gathered and a clear aim has been established there comes a stage which has been called 'incubation' where the individual plays around with the information, trying to work out how it might solve the problem. For instance with an anagram, we may write down the letters in a different order two or three times to see if the answer comes up. Another process that can be useful here is to let the subconscious mind take over. This can follow a period of active thinking about a problem when no obvious solution turns up. People have been known to go for a long walk, go to bed or do something totally different, and then to find on returning to the problem that 'the answer is there staring me straight in the face'. Such moments have been called 'the flash of insight' or 'moment of inspiration' and when they come up can save a lot of time and effort.

Consider two ways of solving the anagram 'ucer'. Either we can just look at it and hope to see the answer in a flash. Or we can write down all twenty-four possible combinations of the letters on a piece of paper, then search the list till we find a word we recognise. The first way may sound a bit risky, whereas the second seems to be logical and very systematic. Unfortunately if we had a ten-letter word in an anagram form there would be 3,628,800 possible combinations of the letters to work through and that would take a fairly long time to work out.

One of the advantages of living in the last part of the twentieth century is that there are computers which can solve complicated problems like this very fast indeed. A computer will not necessarily be able to give him the final answer, but will produce a range of possible answers from which the manager must make his choice.

Often, though, the computer is either not available or not yet capable of processing the information. John Brown's immediate problem was not the sort that could be handled by a machine: it needed his brain; and he could either try to develop a systematic, logical approach (sometimes called a scientific or deductive method) or he could let his mind explore the problem in a random fashion. This kind of approach has been called 'lateral thinking' and can be very useful in this kind of situation (see *Lateral Thinking for Management* by Edward de Bono, McGraw-Hill, 1971).

Ask and it shall be given you

Remember two other things in looking for possible solutions to problems. First, someone else may well have faced the problem and can remember how he solved it. Second, people are often willing to give advice (especially when they have no responsibility for taking the decision). The role of adviser is old-established and still common in government circles. The manager can rely on his own skill, knowledge and experience (including what he has read about others in the same situation) or he can ask. Either way he is still responsible for the decision in the end.

12.4 Evaluate the Possibles

This stage of decision-making is a bit like a filtering process: gradually eliminating options until only two or three are left. The first is to get rid of obviously unsuitable possibilities.

Spring Clamps (2): the likely alternatives

John Brown wrote down some ideas on a piece of paper in an attempt to solve the problem of the lack of spring clamps. By 12.50 he had seven possibilities. These were:

1 Do nothing.
2 Phone his own boss.
3 Phone Fred Smith's boss.
4 Phone Fred Smith's assistant again.
5 Phone someone else at Spring Clamps.
6 Drive over to Spring Clamps.
7 Send out a search party for Fred.

Self-check

Which of the seven alternatives should not be given a lot of attention?

(Five minutes.)

To do nothing (1) would probably prove to be a bad mistake in the circumstances. Presumably by doing nothing the hope would be that the assistant would use his initiative and send some more clamps, or that Fred would return soon. Both possibilities cannot be relied on, so ignore this option.

To drive over to Spring Clamps (**6**) would achieve little; it was twenty miles away and even with a motorway running from door to door there would hardly be enough time to go there, find someone, get enough clamps for the rest of the day and get back in time for 2 p.m.

To send out a search party (**7**) would be fun but pointless too.

This preliminary screening reduced the alternatives to four. (You may have one or two more left, or a couple of alternatives fewer. This is a matter of judgement.) Each involved making a telephone call. One way of reducing the alternatives even more would be to ask the question, Which call is most likely to lead to the fastest delivery of clamps? The answer to this is that it could possibly be any of the people at Spring Clamps (**3**, **4** or **5**). Phoning his own boss would do little good, partly because he too may be at lunch, partly because if he were available he would then have to phone Spring Clamps, and partly because it would reflect adversely on John Brown's own administrative set-up.

This filtering process reduces the options to three: which of the three individuals to choose to phone at Spring Clamps? We are not told enough about the relationship John Brown has with other people at that firm, but it seems obvious that John is most likely to ask himself this question: Who else do I know, who would do me a favour and who has the power to take action? He may also build in a condition, especially if he is particularly friendly with Fred and does not want to lose that friendship, namely, Which phone call is least likely to harm Fred?

At this point in the filtering process, the questions that have to be asked of each alternative must be relevant and must help too in arriving at the decision. In effect a scorecard is kept of each option and the answer to each question will add to, or subtract from, each alternative's overall score. As we shall see in Chapter 19, if the alternatives can be stated in number form it is much easier to arrive at a decision. This was highlighted in Chapter 10, when the case of Len's Launderette was discussed (page 150). There the two options (borrow or use brother-in-law's money) could be turned into numbers and it was not difficult to see which of the alternatives would be the best in the circumstances.

Fig 12.1   The probability continuum

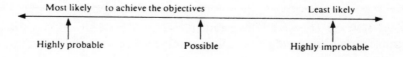

The difficulty in making the decision, so far as Len was concerned, was the fact that he could not be certain that the forecasts would actually turn out according to the calculations. In other words there was an element of risk, and this applies to all decisions. We can never be sure about the future, and this is what makes many decisions difficult.

Probables, possibles and unlikelies

On page 48 we looked at the way future events are unpredictable (remember what the weather was going to be like in Liverpool on 2 January 2010?). Sometimes we can use numbers to help obtain better forecasts and reduce the uncertainty a little; this will also be studied in Chapter 19. There are, however, many situations where every manager has to rely on his own judgement. In other words the alternatives have to be put on to a kind of scale, as in Figure 12.1.

12.5 Take the Decision

All of us are taking decisions all the time. Generally we are not even conscious of doing so because we do not need to evaluate the alternatives each time. We have established for ourselves rules or policies which steer us in one direction or another. For instance in pages 118–19 we listed the main decisions that have to be taken in baking bread at home and buying bread in the shops. The decisions need to be taken once only consciously. Thereafter they become rules and our actions in future are geared to these rules. This kind of decision has been described as a 'programmed' decision – it is routine, repetitive and subject to established policies.

A non-programmed decision, on the other hand, is the kind of decision that causes most difficulty. However, if the preceding steps have been taken seriously, then often the decision itself is not difficult to make: it becomes obvious which course of action to take because of the process of elimination that has already been undertaken. Peter Drucker has described how the decision-making process operates in Japan: 'The Japanese do not focus on giving an answer; they focus on defining the question' (*Management*, Pan Books, 1979, pages 374–9). Even so the decision has to be taken. It may be perfectly obvious which course of action is the best, but there is often some hesitation before 'pressing the button'.

It has been said that the successful decision-maker has to have courage, and indeed in conditions of great uncertainty where the decision will affect many people, the need to act courageously is essential. The decision of General Eisenhower during the Second World War to go ahead with the D-Day invasion of continental Europe required a great deal of courage.

Most managerial decisions are nowhere near so far-reaching in their effects, yet a degree of courage is required for all but the most simple decisions. Indecision comes not only from not being able to decide on most likely results, but also from fear of the consequences – even if the only result of the decision is to be extremely unpopular. Generally, however, it is surprising how little reaction there is to most decisions, and if people have been involved in the earlier stages of the problem-solving activity there will be even less reaction (see Drucker on Japanese decision-making here too). Indecision and uncertainty often upset people more than an adverse decision.

Finally it is as well to remember that when dealing with people it is sometimes impossible to please everyone all of the time. In fact there are occasions when a few have to suffer so that the majority may benefit. If this kind of situation appears then the decision must not be avoided. Similarly there are times when a decision which may lead to long-term benefits causes short-term aggravation.

Activity

Politicians in the government take many decisions which are usually announced in Parliament. Often these are greeted with howls of disapproval by the opposition or by the newspapers and the politician concerned will be told that the decision was wrong or bad or stupid.

Pick a handful of controversial governmental decisions. Make a note of them, what they were, who announced them and when. Then see for how long there is a fuss. You will be surprised how quickly most storms blow over. It has been said that a week is a long time in politics and the same is true at work.

12.6 Implement the Decision

Implementation turns the decision into action; it is the step that actually makes something happen. At a simple level we may look at a crossword-puzzle clue and when we think we have solved the problem we take a decision. But only when the answer is written down is the task completed.

In the same way, a managerial decision has either to be acted on by the manager himself or he has to communicate this to others for action. The importance of communications will be looked at in Chapter 18, but there is another implication: a decision often means a change, and that, as we shall see in the next chapter, may need handling with care.

John Brown at Spring Clamps took the decision to phone Fred Smith's assistant. Obviously that, on its own, was insufficient; John had to get on the phone and talk to the assistant. He did so and it was only a matter of minutes before a supply of clamps was *en route* for John's works.

Get the timing right

Whenever a decision is taken, the manager can either implement it immediately – if, for example, it is urgent – or he may decide to keep the decision private for a while. There are good reasons for taking this course of action and they include situations where some preparatory work has to be carried out first. For instance, a company may decide to buy a plot of land but it will need first to carry out some inquiries as to the ownership of the land, likely cost and also make sure adequate finance is available. A premature announcement would possibly drive up the price or result in a competitive bid.

Equally inappropriate is the decision that is implemented too late – or at the eleventh hour. There is possibly nothing more annoying than having to rush through arrangements for some event because the decision was not made known until very late in the day. An essential ingredient in the planning process is the allowance of adequate time between the decision and the event itself. Generally the rule should be that the more complex the event, the longer the time given to its preparation.

12.7 Two Views of Decision-Making

One writer on the subject of decision-making who needs a special mention is H. A. Simon. He considers that there are two distinct views of man as a decision-maker. The first, a 'classical' view, is that people have the following decision-making characteristics:

- completely rational
- perfect knowledge about the problem
- unconflicting objectives
- a clear view of the alternatives
- seeking an acceptable solution.

In contrast, Simon has suggested a 'behavioural model' which sees the manager overcoming problems in a much less idealised way, often by compromise, by muddling through, by not developing long-term plans. Certainly he will not be completely rational and will not have perfect knowledge. What we are faced with is the difference between what should happen and what often does take place.

Many decisions appear to be taken irrationally because they are taken under pressure; because the manager has not had sufficient time to think the problem through and evaluate all the alternatives properly. This kind of situation cannot be entirely avoided but the frequency of such events can be diminished:

- by proper, careful planning;
- by establishing good, comprehensive (yet flexible) decision rules; and
- by thinking ahead.

The last activity is mainly anticipation. In other words, to avoid having to take hasty decisions try to anticipate what might happen, as we noted in relation to strategic planning.

Chester Barnard, one of the most important early thinkers on management, wrote in 1938 (Barnard, *The Functions of the Executive*, Harvard University Press, 1968) that in 'the fine art' of decision-making there are four situations to avoid:

1 Do not decide questions that are not pertinent.
2 Do not make a decision too early.
3 Do not make a decision you cannot do anything about.
4 Do not make a decision somebody else should make.

To bring all this closer to home, here are examples of each of the four 'do nots':

1 Do not decide what you are going to do with your football pool winnings (until you win!).
2 Do not decide now how much money you are going to spend on your holiday in five years' time. Your information is not yet complete about the cost of holidays, and about your own financial status.
3 Do not decide how to get water to the Sahara unless you can actually do something about it.
4 Do not get caught in the trap that people lay for you when they ask: 'What shall I get my mother-in-law for Christmas?'

Three quotes to remember
Not to decide questions that are not pertinent at the time is uncommon good sense, though to raise them may be uncommon perspicacity.
(*Chester Barnard*)

It is quite a three-pipe problem.
(*Sherlock Holmes*) (See 'The Red-Headed League', *The Adventures of Sherlock Holmes*, by Sir Arthur Conan Doyle, one of the best problem-solvers of all time.)

I can't find anyone to make a decision.
(*An absent executive's secretary in a well-known company*)

13 Managing Change

In Chapters 4 and 5 there was discussion about the way in which the environment is changing and what happens if organisations do not change. This chapter's aim is to help you appreciate how changes affect individuals, and by the end of it you should be able to identify the main ways in which managers can achieve changes in their organisations without creating conflict and trouble at the same time.

You will recall the case of Bert's Buses, which was discussed in Chapter 5. The key point of the case was that Bert failed to change anything inside his organisation (except prices) and fairly quickly the firm went broke; if he had failed to raise his prices as well he would have gone broke even faster.

The reasons for the decline were many and varied and they were listed as 'internal' or 'external' causes. In other words, although Bert tried to change nothing, nevertheless the organisation did change and the environment in which the firm was operating also changed; it moved on and the firm went backwards.

We have already noted that organisations have to change because their environment is changing, and it should now be clear that failing to change will sooner or later be fatal. We have also looked at the way systematic planning can help an organisation adjust to the new set of circumstances continually being created by the world outside. However, a number of questions still need to be solved about this notion of change, such as:

- Where does change come from?
- What is its effect on individuals as well as organisations?
- Why is there often resistance to it?
- How should this resistance be handled?
- How can organisations make changes work?

Each of these questions needs to be examined in some detail if the nature of change and how to manage it are to be properly appreciated.

13.1 **Where Does Change Come From?**

Activity

Go back to the case of Bert's Buses (page 66). Some of the reasons why the firm failed were listed on page 67. The list was split into two, 'internal' and 'external', and five examples of each were given. Each situation mentioned was a change from the early days of the firm when everything in the garden had seemed lovely.

- Which of the ten causes were directly Bert's fault (i.e. he should have prevented them)?
- Which could he do nothing to prevent?
- Which could he have avoided by taking earlier action?

(Ten to fifteen minutes.)

Bert should have prevented wasteful spending, the old coaches continually breaking down, the lack of efficient booking arrangements and the poor financial control over money borrowed from the bank. On the other hand there was nothing he could have done to prevent the new competition with its de-luxe coaches and its new tours; nor the changing tastes of his former customers; nor a lack of money in the economy.

By taking earlier action he could have avoided having his coaches taken off the road because of the smoke pouring out from them and he should have made sure that he had some relief drivers who would take over when the regular drivers were sick.

Changes may therefore be classified in two ways:

- those that occur within the organisation *v.* those that originate outside in the environment;
- those that can be controlled *v.* those that cannot be managed or controlled directly.

Changes starting inside the organisation

Some changes inside organisations occur naturally, and cannot be controlled. People, machinery and buildings get older day by day and this process cannot be prevented. Some changes may be preventable to a greater or lesser extent, such as the rate at which people leave the organisation, the number of accidents that occur or the frequency with which equipment is replaced.

Other changes that emanate from inside organisations are those that are deliberately started (apart from those that are the result of necessity). People inside organisations change things for all kinds of reasons, sometimes unnecessary. Most of us have come across motorcar 'tinkerers': people who love adjusting, fine-tuning and playing with their cars generally. In exactly the same way some people inside organisations are forever tinkering with the system, simply because they are always conscious of the inefficiency of things.

Generally, however, changes are introduced because someone inside the business is dissatisfied with the *status quo* – the way things are. Interestingly, this may be the result of an individual on his own or, quite possibly, some committee decision. A manager on his own may decide to change nothing: working in concert with a group he may well have the courage to take a 'change' decision. As an individual, or as a group, the term used is 'change agent'.

Changes starting in the environment

We have seen how the environment is changing in many different ways and we have also seen how the different environments can affect organisations. It is possible to consider four kinds of environmental change.

1 Irrelevant changes – those that are unlikely to affect the organisation. For example a revolution in South America will not affect your local pub's trade.
2 Changes available for invitation – those that will affect the organisation only if the organisation chooses to get involved. Every organisation has the choice of using a new technology or ignoring it. Similarly a revolution in South America may lead to a decision by an exporting organisation to open up a market in that particular country.
3 Stoppable changes – those that will affect the organisation unless it takes evasive action or counter-measures. This occurs where a rival company brings out a competitive product; unless something is done to offset the impact of the new product, there could be a drop in the company's market share.
4 Unstoppable changes – those that the organisation cannot avoid. This class includes legislation and social trends.

In addition it should be noted that very large or powerful organisations may actually be able to influence their environments to some extent and thus protect themselves against adverse changes. Just how far this is possible is open to speculation.

13.2 What is the Effect of Change on Individuals? How do They Respond to it?

A case for consideration

Axelrod Grime ran a small fleet of taxis and was fairly successful at it. There came the point, however, when he had to change the cars he was using for new ones. He decided on the model of car he wanted and on all the other optional features that the manufacturer was offering. The only thing he had a problem over was deciding whether or not to have automatic gearboxes fitted.

He calculated that the extra cost of fuel that results from using an automatic gearbox is less than the cost of repairing the car's clutch and the loss of profit because the taxi is off the road. However, the problem that was holding him up was that he did not know how well, or badly, his drivers would accept the idea of automatic gears. He himself wanted the change: would the drivers? He decided to ask them for their views one day after lunch.

Self-check

What would your reaction be? (If you aren't a driver, ask one for their reaction.)

Your reaction might have been one of complete indifference, but it is more likely that the announcement would have provoked a fairly strong response. There are those who consider that a car without a manual gearbox is not a car at all and would never drive one without. And at the other extreme some people feel that an automatic gearbox makes driving so much easier and less tiring that they would never do without it.

Once again we have a continuum of attitudes ranging from the extremely favourable to the downright hostile. (See Figure 13.1.) Some will be pleased, some annoyed, some upset, and this kind of mixed reaction is likely to occur whenever a change is suggested in all kinds of situations. In addition there is the individual who thought of the idea in the first place – the generator of the change.

In connection with attitudes towards change, therefore, people can be classified into a number of categories. It should be borne in mind, however, that people do not fall exclusively into one category or another; a person may be demonstrating considerable hostility towards one new development inside an organisation and at the same time welcoming or even initiating some other change. It would seem, though, that individuals tend to lean more towards one category than another.

Fig 13.1 How people's attitude and response to change varies

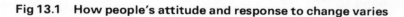
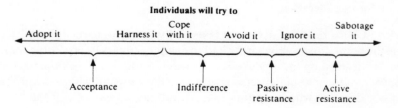

People who cause change to take place

These are the individuals who have bright ideas, who suggest different ways of doing things, who seem never to be content with the *status quo*, and who are not satisfied with the way the future prospects of the organisation appear to be shaping up. They range from the original thinkers of history, the inventors and the revolutionaries, to businessmen, entrepreneurs, politicians (of all parties) and research scientists.

Business organisations typically start up with an individual who has a bright idea, and it is not uncommon to find that companies with innovators at their head are continually changing – their products, markets, structure and ways of operating. Richard Branson is an excellent example of this kind of individual and there are many more.

As organisations grow and the original entrepreneurs retire, so this type of individual is less and less popular because of his tendency to rock the boat. Yet there is always a need for the innovator because his ideas today may well create the things that will save the company tomorrow. Successful organisations have strong teams in the marketing and design functions and, where there is manufacturing, in research and product development. The pharmaceuticals company SmithKlein Beecham is a very good example of a company which places a lot of emphasis on the kinds of people who can cause change.

In the public service it is often said that there is no room at all for the innovator and that bureaucracies develop only in size and as a means of protecting the existing state of affairs. Given that the work of public institutions is clearly established, then fundamental changes in, for example, levels of service cannot be made. However, many internal changes can be made in such organisations in such things as the efficiency of the systems that are being used. Without some innovators in the public service there would be no computers in use, no electric light in offices and wearing bowler hats would be compulsory.

Activity

Do you know an organisation with very few (or no) change generators? If you do, try to assess how long it will survive.

People who accept change

People who accept change are to be met in all walks of life. At one extreme these are the people who were the first to have pocket calculators and video-cassette recorders at home. At work they are the people who are continually pushing for new equipment or new facilities. These people take a creative idea, encourage it and develop it. In this sense they are the true 'agents of change', responsible for making sure that ideas get implemented. They are, undoubtedly, a great asset in any organisation that needs to make changes because their enthusiasm for the new ideas can carry along the more reluctant members of the group.

On the other hand to have too many enthusiastic adopters about could fairly quickly result in a haphazard organisation with new ideas being developed before the old ones had time to settle down and make a contribution.

At the other extreme within the general category of acceptance there are the people who simply accept change and harness it for their own use. These are the people who quietly take the new development into their own area of influence and make sure that it works.

People who tend to be indifferent to change

This classic attitude towards change is best described in the expression 'So what?' Many changes within organisations are met with indifference, even apathy, especially if the people concerned perceive that their own overall state will be unchanged. Such people learn to cope with the change when it arrives ('We can live with it'); or will try to avoid it as long as they possibly can.

The danger in this kind of attitude is the assumption – the perception – that their own state will be unchanged. This is a particularly dangerous assumption for a group of people to make, especially at senior management level, regarding changes that are taking place outside the organisation. The attitude will bring to mind once again the discussion earlier and in Chapter 5 on the 'do nothing new' strategy of Bert's Buses.

People who resist change

People who resist change may do so passively or actively. Passive resistance will include those who will not learn about new ideas or who will do everything to avoid having to be faced with something different. Elderly people do not take readily to computers, and old-fashioned organisations try to avoid or ignore the implications of microprocessors.

At the extreme end of the spectrum there are the actively hostile resisters. These individuals will be expressing their resistance in such activities as a 'go-slow', strikes, 'spoiling' products, or even acts of deliberate sabotage, thus perpetuating a tradition started by the Luddites in 1812, who smashed up textile machinery.

The range of responses to change that have been described can be called 'behavioural effects' because they are alterations in the way people perform their work. It should also be remembered that there may also be psychological effects – where a change is so dramatic that it causes a mental disturbance – and also physiological effects, where the person concerned becomes physically ill. Alvin Toffler, in his book *Future Shock*, gives many examples of the effect of change. He quotes some research which shows that individuals who have experienced a dramatic change in their lives are more likely to be ill than people whose lives are more stable. Similarly, techniques recently developed by the British Safety Council show that accidents at work are often connected with high levels of stress; stress itself being caused by significant changes in personal circumstances such as divorce, death of a spouse and even stopping smoking.

Why are there different attitudes to change?

In the case of the taxi firm, the idea was suggested that the individual drivers would differ: some would welcome change, some would resist and some would be indifferent. It is easy to label such reactions as 'dangerous radical', 'dogmatic conservative,' and 'the lazy apathetic', but this is neither helpful nor particularly accurate. Many factors have been proposed which might account for a particular individual's attitude towards a change, and any manager wishing to make a change should be aware of these underlying influences.

- *An attitude towards change in general.* This is something to do with personality that makes for either a general resistance to, or acceptance of, changes.
- *Cultural values and beliefs.* Individuals, organisations and groups build up their own value systems, codes of conduct or behaviour, and a change which in any way runs counter to these is likely to be met with stiff resistance. At a simple level it may be accepted practice to stop work a little early on Friday afternoon, and good luck to the new manager who attempts to change that! At a much more significant level are efforts to get people to do things which are contrary to their moral or religious beliefs.
- *Feelings of insecurity.* These are also personality traits, and often result in strong opposition to change, even though this may be quite irrational.
- *Relationship with organisation/leader.* Where an individual has a high regard for the organisation in which he is working, and especially for his boss, his attitude is going to be different from that of the person who does not trust his boss or the organisation.
- *The pattern of past events.* Individuals evaluate changes that affect them by looking for similar occurrences in the past. 'Last time they did that it was a disaster' is the kind of statement made about a prospective change and is to be heard in politics quite frequently about the other political parties' views. The alternative belief from a supporter is 'Last time our people did this it was a great success.'

Why is there resistance to change?

It has been said that people do not resist change itself. What they are resisting are the implications behind the change (whether real or imagined) that somehow they are going to be harmed. This harm may be one, or a combination, of various factors including:

- *Economic*. If a change is perceived as going to affect the money in the pocket, or in the amount of work required to produce the same money, then it is likely to be resisted. One of the problem areas in recent years has been the question of new technology and its impact on individuals. While people may clearly understand how increasing productivity (through more technology) can raise wages, there is still resistance because of the fear of losing jobs.
- *Inconvenience*. Resistance may be greater if it seems as though it is going to make life more difficult. This often occurs when offices or factories are moved from one place to another. The Location of Offices Bureau, which used to have the responsibility of encouraging firms to move out of London, could demonstrate the economic and social advantages without too much difficulty. Even so, many firms would not move because of the perceived inconvenience of being away from the capital.
- *Freedom*. If an individual feels that his freedom is going to be diminished, he will resist the idea. For instance, to try to introduce clocking-in and clocking-out into an organisation which has never known such things would have very little chance of success; it would be like trying to move from McGregor's Theory Y back to Theory X (see page 170). Greater control may be desirable in certain circumstances, but that may not be how the individuals see it who are going to be controlled.
- *Security*. If a proposed change suggests that there may be a threat to the security of jobs, then it is likely that there will be some resistance to it. Once again it may only be how the people concerned *imagine* what is going to happen, even though the planned change may have no intentions in this respect.

Activity

It is said that the trade-union movement is opposed to change. It is also said that trade unions are in favour of change, but are put in the position of having to oppose changes because management has tried to introduce the change without considering the feelings of the individuals concerned. Take a specific example of resistance to a change (general arguments do not help very much here) and try to decide which is the most likely cause. This is good for a two-hour argument.

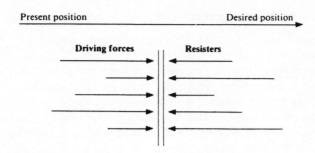

Fig 13.2   The force-field and managing change

Estimating resistance

Any manager planning to make a change should first of all try to assess the extent to which the change might be resisted. One man whose involvement in this kind of work is significant is Kurt Lewin. He developed the technique called 'force-field analysis', which is a useful way of identifying the resisting elements in an organisation, on the one hand, and the forces in favour of the change, on the other. The technique is specific to any one change, the 'forces' being different for each change that is proposed.

The technique also shows the relative strength or weakness of each element in the equation and is often expressed in the form of a diagram – Figure 13.2. This diagram illustrates clearly how the driving forces that are seeking to achieve a change come up against a number of restraining or resisting factors. The relative strengths of the driving forces and of the resisters are indicated by the length of the arrows. In order to achieve the desired objective either the driving forces have to be strengthened (which can lead to more conflict) or attempts have to be made to reduce the strength of the resistance (or remove it altogether).

13.3 Reducing Resistance to Change

There are many ways in which any individual's or group's resistance to a planned change can be made. You will have seen films at the cinema or on television where *A* is trying to persuade *B* to change or do something they do not want to do! The manager does not normally have to go so far as to get on bended knees and plead with his subordinates to change. On the other hand it is unlikely that they will revert to the method used by the owner of a small company who reputedly called his staff together and said, 'Now look, it's time you changed your attitudes.'

Among the more sensible approaches are these:

- The change should have the full support and commitment of senior management.
- The change is more acceptable if the ideas come from the team that has to change and is a group decision based on a group diagnosis.
- It helps if the change appears to reduce workloads.
- The change should not threaten livelihoods or income.
- Changes that sound interesting and exciting will meet less resistance, i.e. of benefit to the participants.
- Changes ought to be in harmony (as near as possible) with the values and ideals of the participants.
- Economic incentives are helpful but mainly where the resistance is on economic grounds. An economic incentive may not succeed in overcoming resistance caused by other fears.

Activity

Add to the above list whenever you can by observing people trying to persuade others to accept things. Notice particularly what the 'seller' of the idea is appealing to in the prospective 'buyer's mind. It may well be power, glory, fame, money or a more subtle approach; watch out for them all.

13.4 Making Change Work

We have seen that change in an organisation is either the result of some outside event, imposing its effect on the organisation, or it comes from within the organisation. Some internal changes cannot be planned (such as the sudden death of a key manager) although their impact can be lessened by perceptive planning. However, most internal changes are the result of a decision taken by an individual or by a group and it is these that need most attention. As Chester Barnard pointed out, there is absolutely no point in deciding to change something if the change cannot be made effective.

Force-field analysis gives information as to the likely extent to which resistance will be felt, but even if the resisting factors are reduced there is no guarantee that the decision will be successfully implemented unless a number of other steps are taken.

Keep people informed

It is easy to inform people of a decision to make a change and it is just as easy to inform them of the reasons for the decisions. Keeping people in the dark encourages rumour and speculation.

Get the group involved

In Chapter 11 the 'leadership continuum' was introduced which ranged from the autocratic to the democratic. Group decision-making is a useful way of introducing change because it increases the commitment of the members of the team, increases their interest and is likely to be effective faster. The qualifying points made in Chapter 11 should be borne in mind though: that a sudden switch in leadership style will be viewed with suspicion; that unless the group are qualified and willing they may not be able to take proper action.

Group involvement is not a recipe for the successful introduction of a change in all circumstances, although it is always useful to obtain the group's reaction to an idea.

Reversible changes

On occasions it may be possible to introduce a change on a provisional basis, making it clear to all concerned that the idea is experimental and to run for a limited period of time. There is a lot to be said in favour of a pilot scheme if such a scheme will provide answers to questions which are needed for a proper decision. Experimental systems and pilot schemes also enable everyone concerned to get a feel for the new proposal. On the other hand a pilot scheme can be very expensive and the delay in taking the decision to go the whole way may spoil the chances of ultimate success.

Self-check

Which of the following would be suitable for introducing on an experimental basis, for a limited length of time?

1 A new kind of footwear into a shoeshop.
2 A 'jumbo' supersonic jet-plane.
3 A coffee machine in the corner of the office, club or shop.
4 A completely different system of paying wages, including a new commission system.
5 Introducing a computer to take over all clerical work.

(Ten minutes.)

Did you decide that **1** and **3** were suitable for introducing on an experimental basis? Neither would cost too much, cause too much upheaval or cause a lot of bother if abandoned as a result of the feedback from customers or users. On the other hand the opposite effects would be apparent if the other three ideas were introduced on an experimental basis.

All changes are capable of being reversed in the long run but the cost of returning to the old position may be very high in terms of both money and personal inconvenience, as it would be if computers were introduced for a limited period of time. In making the change, therefore, it is worth spelling out the extent to which the change is reversible.

Fast or slow change?

Slow change is often recommended because it is less disruptive than rapid change. Taking things a step at a time is commendable where a great deal of retraining is needed or where resources cannot match the requirements of a full, comprehensive launch. This might occur, for instance, where a company wants to introduce a new revolutionary product throughout Europe. The cost of training all the sales people and providing adequate promotional support is very high and so may have to be introduced in stages more slowly. In addition, slow change is worth considering if it is necessary to get the individuals involved used to the idea, especially where the new idea is not likely to have been experienced before. For instance, someone who has always used a gas cooker needs some time to get familiar with an electric cooker.

The disadvantage of slow change is that by moving slowly the opportunity may pass without your being able to take full advantage of it; moreover it is possible that by the time the change is fully implemented the new system is already out of date and inappropriate. Nowhere is this problem more acute than in the case of technological change; an airline that gradually replaces its planes slowly finds that by the time it has replaced all its aircraft a completely new generation of planes is on the market: the firm is now flying brand-new, obsolete planes.

Finally, changing something quickly has the advantage of reducing uncertainty: the state of not knowing what is going to happen – one of the causes of stress.

How much change?

Some organisations exist in relatively stable environments. A hospital, for instance, need not change and adapt too much because the environment in which it is operating does not change too much from year to year. Changes that it makes are mainly by way of improvement rather than of major strategic importance. Other organisations exist in turbulent environments, where the future is unpredictable and where the way the firm operates (its system) may need to be changed frequently, such as in computer and communications technologies.

Change for the sake of change is not often a good rule. On the other hand failing to change at all is equally dangerous. An inflexible manager, group or organisation stands at risk from the changing environment just as surely as the dinosaurs failed to adapt to theirs.

There are therefore two elements in the answer to the question, How much change?, namely:

- the speed and size of change in the environment; and
- the flexibility and readiness to change of the individuals within the organisation – are they ready and able to change?

These elements can be seen in Figure 13.3. The ticks indicate favourable combinations; the crosses signify problem states.

Training

Where an organisation needs to change, but where the individuals in it do not have the flexibility or willingness to change (the top right-hand side of Figure 13.3), then there is a problem, since attempts at change will be resisted. Short-run solutions may be effective for smaller changes, but to achieve a fully flexible, forward-looking organisation individuals will have to be trained to be more adaptive and forward-looking too. It has been suggested that 'organisations need to provide the appropriate climate to allow managerial growth and the development of change-responsive managers' (Basil and Cook, *The Management of Change*; see Further Reading).

Change that hurts

Inevitably there are times when changes have to be made that cause problems for individuals. At worst there is the difficult decision to fire someone because of his unsuitability or because his services are no longer needed. These changes cannot be avoided, but their impact can sometimes

---

Fig 13.3   How to match environmental turbulence and group flexibility

Individual/ group		Environmental turbulence (speed and size)	
		◄——— Lower ———	——— Higher ———►
F L E X I B I L I T Y	Lower	✓ Little change needed: little change sought	✗ Much change needed: much resistance
	Higher	✗ Little change needed: disruptive effects	✓ Much change needed: much change achievable

be softened by the way in which the decision is communicated. A swift announcement given openly and with appropriate compensation is better than an ill-timed decision communicated by hearsay or signs.

Managing the transition

Sometimes a change is so big that it takes a lot of time and effort to implement. In these situations it is useful to have a transition team appointed whose responsibility is to make sure that the change takes place with the minimum of fuss and bother. Sometimes the team consists of outsiders (or even a single consultant), but often it is drawn from key personnel within the organisation who fall into the category of enthusiastic adaptors that were discussed on page 199. The team should consist of individuals representing all the different levels and functions that will be affected by the change, so that no group of individuals is left unrepresented.

Planned change (as opposed to natural change) is therefore an important managerial function. All managers must spend some time deliberately thinking about making changes and then actively causing the changes to take place. The key steps can be summarised as follows:

1 *Develop a concern*. Ask questions such as, Could we do it better? Do we need to change anything? Will we need to change things tomorrow?
2 *Share the concern*. Involve others in answering the questions.
3 *Define and solve the problems*. What should we do that is new?
4 *Recognise the effects of change on individuals*.
5 *Assess capability*. Make sure the organisation and the individuals can cope with the changes proposed.
6 *Train*. Individuals may have to learn to cope with an increasing amount of change.
7 *Implement*.

Activity

Consider a change that ought to take place in the organisation you know best. Spend twenty minutes working out how it could be introduced effectively.

A quote to remember

Even more important than any specific lists of advanced information, however, is the habit of anticipation. This conditioned ability to look ahead plays a key role in adaptation. Indeed, one of the hidden clues to successful coping may well lie in the individual's sense of the future. The people among us who keep up with change, who manage to adapt well, seem to have a richer, better-developed sense of what lies ahead than those who cope poorly. Anticipating the future has become a habit with them. The chess player who anticipates the moves of his opponent, the executive who thinks in long-range terms, the student who takes a quick glance at the table of contents before starting to read page one, all seem to fare better. (Alvin Toffler, *Future Shock*)

Part V

Keepings Things
Under Control

So far the emphasis has been on making plans and on effective ways of making sure that things get done. Objectives, strategies, rules and getting on with the job in terms of solving problems, motivating, managing changes are all vital, but there is one other ingredient in the recipe for success, namely control. If it is absent, the final outcome may well be to negate much of the hard work put in at the other stages. On the other side of the coin, too much control can act like a boa constrictor and stifle the life out of an organisation.

14 Key Elements Needed for Good Control

In this chapter our concern is with the questions:

- What is control and why is it necessary?
- How can we make sure controls are effective and really work?
- What are the features of any control that make it effective?

One of the most famous sketches to appear on television or film concerns the man at the end of a conveyor-belt in a large factory. His job is fairly simple, consisting of making some small adjustment to the product passing in front of him. For instance, he may be pasting a label on to a carton which has already been filled with the items made further back down the line. It is not an uncommon scene; the job is repetitive but the operator has enough time to moisten the labels, make sure each one is securely fixed to the carton and is the right way up. The sketch we see involves the gradual increase in the speed of the conveyor-belt. We are never told the reason for the change in the conveyor's speed, and the operator is powerless to do anything about it. At first he does not complain, because the increase is so small that he can cope with only a little extra effort. Gradually he finds he cannot label each carton properly – some get missed completely, some have labels on upside-down or sideways; he tries to push the cartons back only to cause them to pile up on top of each other. Eventually the situation gets totally out of hand, the conveyor-belt grinds to a halt with cartons all over the place and the factory looks as though a tornado has been through it.

The key phrase used to describe what happened is 'out of hand'. An equally common expression would be that the situation got out of control. Every day we come across situations that are out of control – either in our day-to-day work, or we read about them or see them happening. Typical examples are the racing car that spins off the track, the ship that runs aground, a rioting crowd or a fire that cannot be put out.

All these are highly undesirable situations, and it is probably true to state that any situation that is out of control is also undesirable, although it may not be as dramatic as those quoted above.

We describe these situations as having got out of control, or out of hand, because things were not turning out as expected or as planned: things are turning out quite different from what we expected – usually with a worse result – and we are powerless to do anything about it.

Conversely, control is making sure that any small change in the way things are working is sorted out quickly before it can do any damage. It is to stop the ship going on to the rocks, to prevent the factory from having its machinery jammed up, and to make sure that we do arrive at our destination without incurring excessive cost.

As far as the manager is concerned, it is part of his job to make sure that things do not get out of hand in the areas for which he is responsible. If he is wise he will invent (or have created for him) a method or system which will reduce the risk of things getting out of control.

Activity

Suppose you are the manager of the factory described at the beginning of the chapter. What would you do to ensure that things never get out of hand?

(Ten minutes.)

The essential ingredients for the manager of our imaginary factory to give him a system of control over the flow of goods along the conveyor are:

- A standard or 'normal' speed for the conveyor.
- A device for measuring the actual speed of the conveyor.
- Something or somebody checking that the actual speed is not faster than the standard speed.
- The checking has to be done at regular intervals, e.g. every five minutes.
- A method of informing the manager if the actual speed of the conveyor exceeds the standard speed by a specified amount.
- The information has to get to the manager as fast as possible.
- An ability on the manager's part to be able to do something about the difference in speed.
- The manager must do something!

From this list is possible to draw up a list of the elements which are needed if there is to be an effective control system of any kind.

1 There must be a plan of some kind. This may be expressed as a target, as a standard or as some other statement of what is wanted. However identified, it must be capable of being compared with what is actually happening. Usually this implies the use of some numbers, but there are many other ways of exercising effective control. This will be examined in more detail later.

2 There must be a comparison between planned performance and what is actually happening. A good example of this is the control that the captain of a ship exercises during a voyage. He sets out with a plan which consists of a port (the destination), a route, times and speeds. Continually during the voyage, he is checking to establish exactly where he is and comparing it with the plans he made at the outset. At this stage all that is going on is 'monitoring' performance.

3 The comparison has to be made often enough to ensure that any variation is identified before serious adverse effects take place. In some situations it may be only necessary to make the comparison monthly. In others continuous monitoring may be advisable.

4 Having made a comparison, the next step is to report any significant variation to the manager responsible for the activity. This implies that the responsible manager is the person in the organisation who can actually do something about the situation. It will not help the ship to arrive at the harbour by telling the cabin boy you are off course. Nor does it really help to solve the difficulty telling the sales manager's secretary that sales have dropped by 40 per cent – not unless she goes and tells her boss the bad news straight away.

A key phrase to be noted here is 'significant variation'. There is little point in wasting a manager's time with information that the sales force expenses amounted to £5,001 last week compared to an estimate of £5,000. The difference is insignificant. If, however, expenses had actually turned out at £5,200 then the manager concerned must know what has happened.

5 Speed of reporting is also essential for an effective control system. If a significant variation is found then the quicker the fact is reported to the manager concerned, the more likely something can be done to solve the difficulty. The longer the period of time between the event and the reporting, the greater the likelihood of a disaster.

6 Faced with a significant variation in performance, the wise manager will choose a suitable course of action. How quickly this is done depends on the nature of the difficulty; some things have to be dealt with instantly, other problems can best be solved if a little time is taken to think them through and discuss them with some colleagues. There are only three possible courses of action:

(a) Do nothing at all. This is only recommended if the reason for the problem is a unique occurrence and is unlikely to happen again; when, for example, a thunderbolt causes a fire in a storeroom.

(b) Change the plan. Events occur outside the control of anyone in the organisation. If, for instance, the buyers are working to a target price for a particular raw material of £100 a kilo and a revolution in the country where the material comes from puts the price up to £150 a kilo, in that situation alternative plans must be made.

(c) Adjust operations. The problem may have arisen because part of the organisation is not working up to normal efficiency. The manager must identify quickly the underlying cause of the problem, then take steps to cure it. For example, if your car suddenly begins to use oil, it can be expensive to do nothing; adjustments have to be made.

7 Finally the cost of operating the control system must be justifiable. The expensive control systems in a jumbo jet are justified on not merely cost, but because human life is involved. Most systems are concerned with costs, or quality, or safety, and always the potential loss involved should greatly exceed the cost of running the system.

Activity

Imagine you are running a small road-haulage business. You have three vans and three drivers and you operate out of a small yard which has a petrol pump. Each day the vans are topped up with petrol and sent off to carry out the jobs which have been sold to customers on previous days.

In road haulage, the basis for pricing a job is partly on the distance to be travelled and partly on the length of time the men and the van will be away from base. This is because some costs like petrol, oil and tyres vary according to the number of miles travelled, and the size of other costs (like drivers' wages) depends on the amount of time to be spent on the job.

● What do you think are the two most important aspects of the day-to-day operations of a road-haulage business that need to be kept under control?
● How would you control the two items you named, keeping in mind the seven key elements already described?

(Twenty minutes.)

The answer to the first question above is that the two biggest aspects of a road-haulage operation that need to be controlled are time and the consumption of petrol.

The basis of setting a price for a haulage job is:

● The estimated time for the job multiplied by a cost per hour. These are known as standing charges.
● The number of miles to be travelled multiplied by a cost per mile. These are usually called running costs and the most important cost element is fuel.

Two things can go wrong on the standing charges side of things, assuming that costs are fairly predictable. The job could have been incorrectly timed, or there could be some time-wasting, which results in more wages being paid out for that job than estimated. Clearly, time has to be controlled.

On the running costs side, fuel consumed has to be carefully monitored because excessive fuel consumption can occur in four ways:

Table 14.1   The seven elements of a control system

Key requirements	*Control of time*	*Control of fuel*
1 Plan in measurable terms	Estimated number of hours for job	Estimated miles for job; average miles per gallon = estimated gallons
2 Comparison of plan *v.* actual	Estimate *v.* time sheets	Estimate *v.* pump records
3 Frequency of comparison	At the end of the job (if completed within a day) or daily if job takes more than one day	Weekly (or more frequently if there is a hint of a problem)
4 Report significant variations	To the manager in charge of the vehicles and/or the drivers	
5 Speed of reporting	He ought to know before the grapevine hears about it, i.e. within a couple of hours in a small firm	
6 What action to take	Action will depend largely on what the cause of the problem was. It is too easy to place the blame on the driver – but the estimates could be wrong and the lorry could need servicing. It is possible to find ways of rewarding prompt timing. Also if people know controls exist they are less likely to 'try it on'	
7 Cost effective?	A system such as this would be fairly simple to operate – most of the paperwork is there anyway. So there is little extra cost as against large potential losses	

- The lorry is operating inefficiently.
- The estimated mileage was too low.
- The driver took some unnecessary 'detours'.
- The fuel tank 'leaks'.

To effectively control these twin aspects of time and petrol, the seven elements shown in Table 14.1 can be used.

14.1 Problems and Benefits of Control

So far we have been looking at the ingredients that are needed if anything is going to be controlled successfully. People often talk about a 'control system', meaning a way of keeping something under control. It is possible to draw a diagram illustrating the system (see Figure 14.1) – and this will apply to anything, from a large business organisation to your central-heating system:

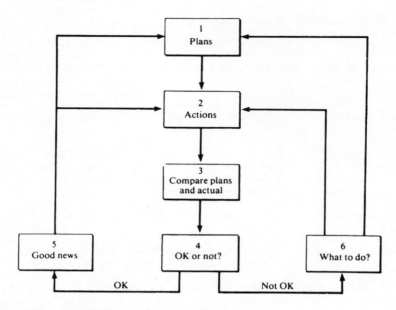

Fig 14.1   How a good control system works

The start is the plan (box 1). This is the stage when someone in charge says, 'This is what we want to do, and this is how we are going to do it.'

This will lead to action (box 2) – the 'get on with the job' stage. Box 3 (comparing the plan with the actual events) can be summed up by the expression 'This is what we want – this is what we got.' Box 4 (OK or not?) follows box 3 closely and asks the question, 'Are we getting what we want?' If the answer is 'yes' ('OK'), then box 5 – the 'good news' box – is used. The process does not end there but runs back up to the plan box and the action box, in effect passing the message on 'What you planned and what you did have worked out well.' If the answer in box 4 is 'not OK' then box 6 is used: 'What to do?' As we saw, there are only three possibilities: either it was a freak, in which case do nothing, or something is being done wrong, in which case inform the 'action' men in box 2. The third possibility is that the plan is impossible – so inform the 'planners' in box 1.

It all sounds too easy, but there are problems as well as benefits, and control systems can do more damage than they prevent, if not properly managed. Each of the six boxes has points to bear in mind.

Plans

The existence of a plan is necessary for successful control. However, the existence of a good control system is no guarantee that the plans are any good. Think about the mad yachtsman whose control over the speed and direction of his boat were superb. Unfortunately, he was so mesmerised by the compass that he forgot to look up – and hit the harbour wall; he had miscalculated the direction to travel.

As noted earlier, it aids the control process if the plan can have numbers attached to it. If we are thinking of a profit plan, then a number is automatically involved, and so are all the plans that involve revenues and costs. In some cases numbers are inappropriate: a journey plan will involve a destination; controlling the quality of a product or service may involve physical characteristics (glass bottles are visually checked for quality, no number is involved); and a newspaper editor controls the content of the paper by using some predetermined code of conduct and applying this to the stories being submitted. Again no numbers are involved, and could not be.

Actions

The actions have to be described in the same kind of way that the plans have been set. It is no use saying: 'Get this package to Mr X in Edinburgh quickly', and then complain because a plane was hired specially to carry out your instructions. So very often the actions of people have to be translated into some kind of common language which will enable the comparison to be made accurately between what happened and what ought to have happened.

All organisations keep records on the money side of their affairs, from the biggest firms in the world down to the smallest village Scout troop. It is, however, a mistake to believe that because records have been made, the requirements of good control have been met. Sometimes the records are not kept in sufficient detail to enable proper comparisons to be made. For instance, in the example we used earlier about controlling the movement of lorries, control would be ineffective if nobody kept a record of the amount of fuel issued to each lorry separately – to have the fuel consumption in total is useless. Sometimes records are kept in the wrong way. Many small independent shops suffer from this problem. The accounts show all items of expenditure on overheads in great detail (rent, rates, post, telephones, etc.), but ignore the fact that the shop may be selling hundreds of different products. All that appears is one number for sales, and one number for the cost of those sales. It will not solve the problems of a firm going downhill to know precisely what the telephone bill is, if it does not know what products are selling well – and which ones make the most money.

Compare plans and actual

Earlier the question of frequency was mentioned – how often do you make the comparison? The answer depends on two things: first, the cost of making the comparison and, second, the length of time that can be allowed to elapse before a difference begins to cost an unacceptable amount (either directly in money or in some other factor like time or effort).

With food products the quality, appearance and weight have all to be of a certain standard and continuous monitoring may well be needed. The costs of carrying out the comparison are not particularly high, whereas to check the specifications in fine detail of a washing machine, for example, would be very costly; in which case there will be a degree of 'sampling' – selecting one every so often for a detailed check-up.

It will be apparent that the closer the monitoring, the less the chance of serious loss. To take the opposite view, the less frequent the comparison, the greater the chance of serious loss. But the decision has to be made, How far are you prepared to risk the possibility of a serious loss?

OK or not?

Earlier, it was suggested that the important thing to work out in answering this question was whether the difference was big enough to worry about. It was referred to as the 'significant variation' and is quite a simple idea. The problem for the manager is to decide what actually is a significant variation.

Self-check

Suppose you want to control electricity use in an organisation (and this example could be almost anything from the corner shop to the pub, or the local laundry or even a big firm). You read the meter at the end of each day and compare the number of kilowatt hours actually used against a predetermined average for that time of the year. Your estimate is 500 kwh. What would be a significant variance?

Actual reading
- 505 kwh (= +1%).
- 525 kwh (= +5%).
- 550 (= +10%).
- More than 550 kwh.
- Between 505 (+1%) and 550 (+10%).
- Impossible to say.

(Ten minutes.)

You may well have decided that it is impossible to state how much a significant variance is in electricity consumption, partly because you have to allow for freak conditions which increase the use suddenly, but, even more significant, there is the question, How important is the cost of electricity in relation to the total business? If 30 per cent of your costs are electricity then an increase in the usage by 1 per cent has a significant impact on the overall costs of the organisation. On the other hand, if electricity costs are only

5 per cent of your total costs, then an increase in the consumption of electricity by anything less than 4 or 5 per cent could really be classed as insignificant.

Good news

When things are going according to plan, it is worth informing the people responsible of the good news. This does three things: it stops them worrying, it helps them resist the temptation to meddle and they feel good.

What to do

When things go adrift it was noted that only three alternative courses of action are possible: do nothing, change the plan or adjust operations. The decision depends on what caused the variation, and while it is often relatively easy to tell that something has gone adrift, it is, however, considerably more difficult to identify the real reason why things went adrift.

Activity

Suppose you are the manager of a poultry packing plant. Turkeys are packed into big boxes and chickens are packed into small boxes. The weekly cost of boxes is usually around £5,000, and nobody worries so long as the cost turns out close to this. However, one day you are told that the cost of boxes for the previous week was £5,850.
  List the three main possible causes of the excessive cost of boxes.

(Ten minutes.)

An increase in the cost of packaging over what is the 'norm' or usual amount can be the result of several completely different things:

- The price of the boxes may have gone up.
- The boxes may be made of more expensive materials than before.
- During the week more turkey boxes and less chicken boxes were used – sales of turkeys having gone up and chicken sales having fallen.
- During the week more boxes in total were used because sales rose.
- A lot of boxes were broken or damaged.
- A lot of boxes were stolen.

The importance of getting the right answer to the question Why is there a variance? can be seen if we ask two further questions about the possible answers identified above. These are:

- Who is responsible for the problem?
- What is going to be done?

Table 14.2   The poiultry-packing control problem: responsibility and actions

Cause	Person responsible	Action
1 Price increase	Buyer	Increase estimate to £5,850 or adjust operations by finding new supplier
2 More expensive materials	Buyer or Marketing	Adjust operations – reorder. (Deliberate policy.) Increase estimate
3 'Sales mix' change	Sales	Do nothing if exceptional or increase estimate
4 Sales rise	Sales	Increase estimate
5 Breakages	Production	Adjust operations
6 Loss	Production Stores	Adjust operations Adjust operations

Activity

Alongside the six alternative possible causes listed above, identify the people you think would be responsible in the poultry packing plant. Then state which of these three things you would do for each cause:

- Nothing.
- Increase the weekly estimate to £5,850.
- Investigate and adjust the way things are done.
  (Note: you may have either/or answers.)

It can be seen from Table 14.2 that it would be pointless blaming the buyer for an increase in packing costs if the reason was an increase in sales, for which the sales department must take credit. Unless the real reason for the variance is clearly established, then tensions are created unnecessarily or the wrong course of action is or may be taken.

14.2 Information: The Life and Death of Control

It will be plain to see that control depends on a good flow of information to the person responsible for whatever activity is being controlled. Figure 14.1 showed various lines joining the boxes and these indicate that messages are being passed on. The lines that lead back up to the 'planning' and 'actual' boxes are called 'feedback loops' because they feed information back. This flow of information is the lifeblood of good control – without it there is no control. However, because affairs are complicated there is a tendency for information to get complicated too. For instance, ten sales reps report to a sales manager. Each sells fifteen products, each incurs expenses and is paid a commission on top of the basic salary. Close control of the sales team requires the manager to look at seventeen bits of information for each rep at least; 170 in total and a further 170 representing plans or estimates. If there's a weekly reporting system then the manager has to look at 17,680 bits of information over the year, excluding totals and cumulative figures. On top of all this there will be various statistical reports, written reports and verbal reports, all of which adds up to a huge quantity of effort and time. Yet normally only one small proportion of the activities will demand some attention. The danger for every manager is that of being swamped with information which may be interesting and may be relevant, but which is largely no cause for concern. Managers can be strangled by too much control information, and organisations with highly developed control systems are sometimes like the mad yachtsman we mentioned earlier.

To get round this problem, there is the technique known as 'management by exception'. With this technique, the manager simply determines what makes a significant variance, and asks to be informed of significant variances only; everything else is assumed to be OK. To be able to say 'Only tell me about the exceptional things' requires a considerable effort of will because in doing so you are trusting that people will tell you when something exceptional happens. Moreover it appears you are deliberately keeping yourself in the dark. Of course, this is not so; you are working on the principle 'no news is good news', that is, there is a plan and things are going according to plan unless you hear something.

'Management by exception' can work only if there are detailed, agreed plans. It also helps if the whole system works automatically.

Automatic controls

A good example of automatic control is in a modern home central-heating system. The thermostat is set by the home owner to a desired temperature, and from then on the system is self-regulating. If the temperature falls below the desired level then the thermostat tells the boiler to pump more heat. At the desired temperature the thermostat tells the boiler to stop pumping.

Similarly in organisations it is possible to set up ways of working where the manager need not be involved once 'the thermostat is set'. For instance, many companies and tradesmen sell their products and services on a credit basis. In other words, at the time of sale no cash changes hands. An automatic system for collecting the money from these customers would be to instruct staff as follows:

1 Send a bill to the customer seven days after delivery of the goods.
2 After a further twenty-one days if the money has not been received send a reminder.
3 If no money is received after seven more days send a 'final reminder' (or maybe telephone the customer if his business is important).
4 Seven days later send a letter to the customer warning him of possible legal action, and send a copy to the responsible manager.

This example considerably oversimplifies how to control debtors since in reality it is often necessary to exercise discretion and be diplomatic towards one's customers. The important thing is that a way of dealing with the problem has been set which frees the manager so that there is no need to get involved unless exceptional events take place; corrective action is taken automatically.

This self-correcting or self-regulating system can be built into machinery or into jobs which people do without the aid of equipment. At one extreme there are many factories where control equipment is as important and as expensive as the machinery needed to make the product itself. This is particularly true where the product is of very high value, or where its formula has to be exactly right, e.g. some chemical which could be dangerous. At the other extreme there are many control systems which are carried out entirely by people.

The computer has revolutionised the whole area of control, mainly because of its ability to deal with huge amounts of information very quickly. For instance, to have effective control over the costs in a manufacturing firm of any reasonable size and complexity requires the services of quite a few people simply to record and process quickly the information needed. The faster the information is needed, the more people have to be employed. Computers avoid this problem and are particularly useful when it comes to control by exception since the machine usually can sift faster than people.

Levels and scope of control

Just as objectives and plans can be set and made at various levels within the organisation, so too control systems are established at different levels. There has to be overall control of the organisation, to make sure that overall objectives are being met. At this level information is likely to be very different from the information a first-line manager receives, although the first-line manager has to keep affairs under control within the area of activity for which he is responsible.

Similarly controls can be devised to operate on everything in an organisation: money, materials, equipment and even people. With impersonal things like money and materials the question is to decide how much control is needed to avoid significant loss. With people, an additional element is involved; it is not uncommon to have controls that identify if an individual is operating up to some expected standard – for instance, clocking in and out to make sure the hours worked are up to contract. But some systems go far beyond this, seeking to control every minute of the day. The extreme human control system was the Roman galley with its slave oarsmen. Each slave was watched over by the galley-master, and any small deviation in speed was rewarded with a lash from the whip. 'Good news' was indicated by fewer lashes.

Most managers find that they have to exercise some control over the activities of their staff; the difficulty is deciding how much control, not just over things that could result in monetary loss, but in other matters – especially how they spend their time. As we have seen, too much control leads to a feeling of not being trusted and loss of motivation. Too little control invites abuse from the idler. This problem is clearly illustrated in the 'great sales force question':

Self-check

You are a sales manager with ten sales reps reporting to you. The salesmen cover a wide area of the country and you see them only on Friday afternoon when they come in to collect their expenses, receive any special instructions for the following week and review the week just past with you. Their job is to get two new customers each week. More than this and they receive a commission.

Basically, you do not know during the week what the reps are doing.

- Is this adequate control?
- Do you want them to phone in every day and tell you what they are doing? If so, how often each day?
- How far do the answers to the above questions depend on the kind of people your sales people are?

(Ten minutes.)

If you wanted total control over your sales force, you would have them phoning in every hour from nine till five telling you where they were and what they were doing. They would do little work; you would do no work. It would be a zero-sum game – a game which nobody wins. Even then you could not be entirely sure they were not sleeping or drinking between phone calls.

The extent to which control is exercised really depends on the extent to which the manager trusts his staff. If no trust exists, then control is tight; if there is a good deal of trust then controls are easier. It's worth asking the question, If there is no trust, is it a good basis to run an organisation or department?

All this is not to suggest that salespeople should not phone the office regularly. It is a feature of many companies that they phone in each afternoon. The purpose is not (or should not be) control, but simply as part of an operating system – the only way to find out which customers need visiting the next day. As far as what your reps do all day there has to be some trust – although if they are handling cash, trust should not enter into it. It is dangerous to allow much trust as far as cash and other valuables are concerned; it is asking for losses to occur.

15 Control in Practice: Examples In and Out of Business

This chapter is a natural continuation of the last chapter. By the end of it you should be able to recognise some of the ways in which controls are used in practice, especially budgetary control, and identify their major advantages and disadvantages.

On page 224 we noted that controls can be devised to operate on everything in an organisation: money, materials, equipment and people. The general principles that were discussed apply to all control systems, namely:

- Make a plan.
- Compare plan and actual.
- Compare frequently.
- Report significant variance.
- Report variances fast.
- Take appropriate action.
- Make sure it is cost effective.

With these principles in mind some of the major control systems that are commonly in use will be discussed. Most of them are applicable to organisations in the public sector as well as in business.

15.1 **Budgetary Control**

What is a budget?

A budget is a statement which expresses somebody's plans in quantitative, usually money, terms. A sales manager may say, 'Next year I am going to put ten reps on the road and they are going to bring in a lot of money.' That is the plan, but a budget will go further than that and actually identify the following things:

- How much money are the reps going to bring in?
- When will the sales actually be made?
- How much will they cost in terms of salaries, commission, travelling expenses, entertaining customers, etc?

Properly set up, the purposes of the budget itself are to give the managers the chance to determine precisely how the part of the organisation will fare that is their responsibility. It will also give one's own boss the opportunity to make sure that the kind of intentions that are being produced are in line with the overall corporate, strategic plan. Finally a budget is useful for the financial people within the organisation so that they can plan how much money to invest, or how much to borrow, at different times of the year. A very important financial budget is called the 'Cash-flow forecast'. This is a detailed calculation of how much money is expected to flow into the organisation over the following few weeks or months, with a correspondingly detailed calculation of how the money is to be used. Cash-flow forecasting is essential for controlling money. Individual departmental budgets form the basis, therefore, by which total operating and financial plans can be made as well as providing individual managers with measures of their own future performance.

Budgets are to be found in most organisations, both in the public and commercial sector, except the very small and the very inefficient. Indeed, many individuals create budgets themselves for their own private affairs by estimating income and expenditure: balancing expenditure month by month so that the amount of money in the bank never falls beyond a certain point (which may not necessarily be zero!).

Self-check

Do you keep a personal budget? If not, how do you know if you can afford to buy that little luxury item next month?

A budget, therefore, is the plan turned into numbers.

'Budgetary control' is the name given to the control system which uses budgets as the basis for monitoring actual performance. A very simple example of this was given on page 221 with the little problem about the poultry packing plant.

The manager of the packing plant probably had made a statement to the effect that the weekly cost of boxes was going to be about £5,000. Strictly speaking this was not a budget at all, but a passive forecast based on experience. However, the kind of reasoning which might have taken place in the packing plant manager's mind could have proceeded like this:

1 The current weekly cost of boxes is £5,000.
2 This is based on the following formula:

$$20,000 \text{ turkey boxes at } 10p = £2,000$$
$$50,000 \text{ chicken boxes at } 6p = \underline{£3,000}$$
$$£5,000$$

3 For the foreseeable future the number of boxes we are likely to use each week will be much the same as at present.
4 The buyer informs me that no price changes are in the pipeline.
5 We have no plans to change the specification of the boxes.

On these assumptions and facts he would have created his budget.

Read the poultry packing plant case again, and also the discussion that followed it (pages 221–2). The case did not mention how the manager obtained the information that the actual cost had gone up from £5,000 to £5,850; it was assumed that the information would be available. In reality, of course, the provision of this kind of data is the responsibility of the accounting function, normally via a management accountant or budgeting manager, and it should not be taken for granted that the required information is automatically available. Unless a manager states precisely what is needed and when it is needed, the accounts department has to make assumptions about the manager's requirements. They can make a good guess, but they are not clairvoyant.

If the budgetary control function knows precisely what is required then it can set up the appropriate system to capture the figures and present them in the most appropriate way.

Similarly the system will not automatically come up with the basic reason for the adverse variation; it has to be deliberately built to give the information. In this case six possible reasons for the increase in cost were given. They can be classified as in Figure 15.1.

It may look simple to be able to analyse the cause of a variance in this way and in a small, relatively uncomplicated organisation it may be so. However, in large organisations, where there are many possible reasons for variances and where the sums of money involved are large, the process of diagnosis can be exceedingly complex. A good budgetary control system is one which can identify major reasons for variances *automatically* without incurring disproportionately high costs.

Other problems of budgetary control systems

Identifying the responsible manager
In the poultry packing case we discovered that of the six possible reasons for the adverse variance, only one of them could be attributed to the packing manager; all the other causes were other people's responsibility.

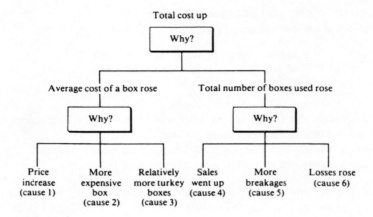

Fig 15.1   Variance analysis flow-chart

The difficulty which this example is highlighting is that various managers are responsible for particular aspects of the operation; each has to control a part. There is, however, a co-ordinating function as well and this is the role of the production manager in this example who must know the overall cost and the overall variance, because only he can decide how to overcome the problem (if it is a problem). Ultimately, in every organisation, the chief officer receives the overall variance on the budgeted profit and loss, or income and expenditure, account. Not every detail is seen, nor is the chief officer personally accountable for every penny of variation. But the overall result has to be accounted for and the subordinates have to account, in turn, for their own spheres of responsibility. It is simply effective delegation.

Is an adverse variance always bad? The adverse variance described in the poultry packing example could have been caused by undesirable happenings – price increases, more expensive materials, breakages or pilfering. These obviously are situations that need to be corrected or compensated for. On the other hand if the cost of packing had been due to an increase in sales or an increase in sales of large boxes (as opposed to small boxes) then these events would have been regarded as highly desirable. A poorly developed budgetary control system might have produced a report that looked like this:

BUDGET REPORT
W/ending 3 October

	Actual	*Budget*	*Adverse variance*
Cost of boxes	£5,850	£500	£850 = +17%

– and the production manager would have been criticised if no other information had been provided. 'Go on like this and you will have us bankrupt' is the kind of statement that could result. Contrast that simple report with a similar one developed to account for the major variances. The second report shows clearly:

- what happened; and
- precisely where the variances occurred.

Unless this kind of reporting is carried out, difficulties will appear and wrong decisions will be taken. Now no criticism can be levelled at the production manager, although he will have to discuss the results with the buyers to get at the underlying reasons for the price increases, so that appropriate action can be taken.

False budgets for added protection
If a manager is asked to prepare a budget it is possible to start with a blank piece of paper and calculate what is needed for all duties to be performed satisfactorily (sometimes known as 'zero base budgeting').

Or previous years' figures can be used as a basis, adding a percentage to cover inflation and growth in the volume of work to be done.

If, however, the budget is an expenses-only budget and taken in isolation by a vetting committee, it may well be decided to add on an extra 20 per cent to the total cost because previous experience indicates that the committee will prune the budget anyway.

This kind of activity is not uncommon and gives budgetary control a bad name. It is found most frequently in organisations which do not really understand the nature of the technique, where the committee is more concerned to make sure that budgets add up to a reasonable looking figure, rather than representing real plans in realistic monetary terms.

The activity is also to be found where overall expenditure limits have been set and the sum of individuals' budgets exceed the total. This occurs frequently in government departments and local authorities when it is felt that taxes and rates cannot be raised high enough to meet spending departments' demands. Similarly in commercial organisations capital expenditure is sometimes 'rationed' if insufficient finance is available to satisfy all needs.

A completely different reason for 'padding' budgets occurs when managers know that their performance will be judged by the size of the difference between the budgeted expenditure of the department and the actual amount spent. If the budget is artificially raised and the manager gets away with it then the results will almost automatically show a favourable variance and will also hide any relatively minor inefficiencies. It is clearly an undesirable system, but one which is not uncommon, occurring wherever budgetary control is imperfectly understood.

The imposed budget
Another way of setting budgets is if someone other than the person responsible does it; so instead of saying to the manager, 'What are your

intentions as regards spending next year?' the question becomes a statement: 'This is what you are entitled to spend next year.' If the manager is lucky more is approved than needed, but if less than needed cuts may be imposed that will spoil the department's efficiency or effectiveness.

Inflexible budgetary control

Activity

Consider the following statements:

- 'These figures bear no relationship to the budget because of the fire that burned down the warehouse earlier in the year.'
- 'Sorry, you cannot buy that piece of equipment, even though it will save money. You will have to wait till next year because it is not in this year's budget.'

What do you think about these two statements? Do you think they are helpful to anyone? Which elements of a good control system (see pages 214–16) have been missed out in both cases? (Ten to fifteen minutes.)

You probably thought that these two statements are not very helpful. The first is saying 'the information here is useless', and the second is saying 'you can't have it'. The reason why both situations have reached the point of uselessness is that in the first case the plan should have been changed, as it could not be achieved. In the second case the plan was possibly correctly set, but is now not appropriate. In both instances, therefore, inflexibility is creating problems.

In large organisations it is not uncommon to hear people say, 'We cannot go to the lavatory unless it is in the budget', and 'The system is so tight it is strangling initiative.' Budgetary control can be a very effective system. It must, however, have flexibility, otherwise initiative is lost. Eventually the system runs the organisation and that can be fatal. In fact the more volatile and changeable the organisation and its environment, the greater the amount of flexibility required.

Uses of budgetary control

Since budgetary control is the way plans and actions are translated into money terms (mainly) it can be readily appreciated that this kind of system can be applied wherever the expenditure of money is involved.

The process of setting up the system can be complicated and time-consuming and the reader is referred to the many textbooks on management accounting to follow this aspect of the question. Suffice it to say that the system must:

- have the support of top management;
- be in tune with long-term objectives and strategies;

- be prepared early;
- involve every level of responsibility;
- be flexible;
- be understood and appreciated by all users; and
- each part must correspond with the responsibility of each manager.

This last point in effect means that all first-line managers (who have discretion regarding expenditure) will create a budget and have a control system for it, which covers their area of responsibility. Sometimes these may be referred to as 'cost centres', which technically are defined as 'a location, function or items of equipment in respect of which costs may be ascertained and related to cost units for control purposes' (*Management Accounting – Official Terminology*, Institute of Cost and Management Accountants, 1991).

In addition, however, a budgetary control system can be devised to cover different sources of income, asset utilisation, cash and various financial activities. In fact, wherever money is involved budgetary control can be useful.

Capital budgeting

One important type of budget relates to expenditure on fixed assets or other investments. Capital budgeting uses very special techniques developed by financial people to help operational managers decide whether an investment is worthwhile, bearing in mind that the investment may take several years to come 'on-stream' and may generate income for many years thereafter. (See also page 289.)

15.2 Standard Costing

Standard costing is a technique which is similar to budgetary control in that it is concerned with providing control information about the costs of products or activities. It does, however, start from a different point; whereas budgetary control compares total figures, standard costing looks at the cost of a single unit.

The system is used particularly to identify variances in the buying price of materials or in the usage of materials (it is an excellent way of identifying quickly an unacceptable level of wastage). It is also in use for controlling labour costs where there are predetermined standards of labour time and money for jobs. The vehicle costing example we looked at in the last chapter is also a type of standard costing.

15.3 Quality Control

Quality has become a keyword in management literature in the last decade. Indeed more often than not, the talk is more of 'Total Quality Management'

(TQM) rather than of quality control itself. The best form of quality control is to make sure that in any kind of process, whether it be a physical production system or an office procedure, the quality of output should be up to a predetermined standard of quality. Moreover, some organisations are finding that they have to have formally recognised quality certification – such as British Standard (BS) 5750, or the international equivalent ISO 9000, so that their customers will continue to trade with them.

Quality standards fail to be achieved for many different reasons:

- The product may be underweight.
- It may be misformed or wrongly coloured.
- It may not be up to the correct specifications or formula.
- It may contain (in food and drink) a 'foreign body'.
- It may be damaged.
- It may smell incorrect.

Quality can go wrong in many different places. The commonest are:

- at the point of delivery (recall Spring Clamps);
- in storage (e.g. due to deterioration);
- throughout the production process;
- in packing;
- in transit to the customer.

Each potential location of a quality defect and each potential type of defect have to be the concern of the quality control staff. In some instances the adage that prevention is better than cure is appropriate. Hence the use of screens to keep out flies in food factories. A good quality control system will be one which draws up its specifications, plans and procedures carefully so that the risk of defective products is reduced.

A 100 per cent guarantee of no defects cannot be made, but as we indicated earlier if the product is medical or for consumption, or is high-technology or potentially dangerous, then quality controls will be much more stringent than in low-value, harmless products. Also quality controls will be tougher where a product has a quality image.

Self-check

How would you try to avoid the following in a batch of 10,000 bags of castor sugar at the time of manufacture?

- An underweight bag.
- A split bag.
- A bag with a drawing pin in it.
- A bag containing granulated sugar.

(Ten minutes.)

Underweight products can quickly be identified by machinery which automatically check-weighs each one at the end of the production process.

If a product is badly packed, it would be obvious very quickly in the case of sugar. To avoid the possibility often someone is placed at the end of the production line, visually checking for such defects.

Metal detectors are standard equipment in food and drink companies; they automatically sense metal and even remove the product that contains the offending article.

It is impossible to open every bag to make sure that it contains what the label says. Apart from the obvious precautionary step of double-checking that contents and packing correspond before the start of the run, normally samples would be taken off the end of the line at intervals and checked chemically, as well as for appearance.

Random spot-checking

Random spot-checks are used if there is a limited amount of money available for quality control. Before such a system is introduced, however, everyone involved must be made aware of what is going to happen. Nothing is more likely to cause trouble than a sudden visit from a quality control inspector unannounced, unexpected and for the first time. It is better still if groups are made responsible for their own quality control.

A quality control problem

It is useful to bear in mind with the quality control of finished products that testing and inspection can take as long as actual production – or longer with sophisticated electronics. Until a product is given that final OK it is not ready for sale but is still work-in-progress and a drain on the resources of the business, locking up expensive capital. When there is a possibility of this occurring, the inspection and testing function has to be given high priority in the allocation of human and equipment resources.

15.4 Stock Control

Some of the problems associated with control of stocks have been mentioned in Chapter 8 in relation to rules about buying. With stock control the problems can be identified as:

- Running out of space.
- Having items in the wrong place.
- Running short of key items.
- Having an excess of useless items.
- Losing items (through pilferage, animal pests or deterioration).

All the problems can relate to raw materials, components, packaging, sub-assemblies and finished goods, but whichever problem occurs, money is lost. Stock control systems have to minimise the loss.

Effective stock control can be achieved if it is built into a standard costing system, if it is related to control of the buying function (prevention of speculative buying is important here) and also related to quality control.

The importance of an effective stock control system is that every organisation has only a limited amount of money. If it is being spent on materials and in production at a faster rate than it is coming in from sales, sooner or later there is a cash crisis. This is known as the working capital problem, or the cash flow crisis, and often arises because of over-enthusiastic buying ('fantastic bargain') or piling up finished goods ('there's a boom time just around the corner').

15.5 Computer-Based Systems

The advent of computers resulted in a very fast growth of control systems using all the advantages of rapid processing and storage of data. Much of this growth occurred in larger organisations which felt that the costs could be justified in terms of the potential savings that could result.

Nowadays, with the coming of microcomputers and the widespread use of computer service bureaux, there is the real opportunity for even the smallest organisation to have control systems that would have been impossibly expensive in 1960, or even 1970. Computer-based information or control systems can provide effective answers to many of the problems facing the small firm, but it has to be kept clearly in mind that their use is only successful if the plans which are being controlled are good.

15.6 Overall Control

Overall control of an organisation takes place in the same way that different parts of an organisation are controlled. This is achieved by comparing overall performance with plans, usually via such reports as the trading accounts, profit and loss accounts and balance sheets as far as companies are concerned; and income and expenditure statements for public service organisations, societies and clubs. These traditional accounting statements do not of themselves monitor progress, but if they are related to corporate budgets, variances in total performance can be quickly identified.

Every organisation needs good control systems – not so that employees can be rewarded or punished (a common mistake) but so that the chances of going on the rocks are reduced to a minimum.

15.7 **A Final Word on Controls**

Controls, therefore, can help an organisation achieve its objectives, but too much emphasis on control can stifle initiative and lead to lack of motivation, and too much control can cost more than it saves. A good system of control needs a lot of different features to make it work properly, but in the end the best control system in the world is no good if plans being controlled are no good.

Beware the silly system

Finally on control, one thing to guard against is the 'silly system'. This is a system designed to do a job which becomes a monster – helping nobody and irritating everyone. A crazy example is the company that decided to control its salesforce by limiting the petrol put into their car tanks.

Every morning all reps completed a form (four parts) on which they had to state the number of miles they intended to travel. This was countersigned by the boss and then taken to the controller's office who would check it and approve it. The reps would then take the form with the car to the petrol pump and have the appropriate gallons put into the tank (according to the number of miles that had been forecast). At the end of the day the mileage was checked and the petrol in the tank was also checked by means of a dipstick. The form was then completed and the various parts distributed (together with various statistical analyses) at the end of the week to all concerned.

Crazy? Silly? Maybe – but every organisation has got a system somewhere inside it that is not far off being as silly as this.

Thought for the chapter
Just because you can control your cooker, that doesn't make you a good cook!

Part VI

Improving the Manager's Own Performance

Things go wrong inside organisations often not through poor planning, or lack of control, or because the systems are weak or staff are not motivated, but because of a misunderstanding or a hasty decision caused by pressure of events. If managers can improve their own efficiency, they will have a better chance of improving their organisation's efficiency too.

16 Using Time Wisely

This chapter has the specific objective of helping you to manage your own time. By the end of it you should know what needs to be done to make more time available for the really important things.

C. Northcote Parkinson, in his famous *Parkinson's Law*, tells the story of the old lady who has to write a postcard to her niece:

> An elderly lady of leisure can spend the entire day in writing and dispatching a postcard to her niece at Bognor Regis. An hour will be spent in finding the postcard, another in hunting for spectacles, half an hour in a search for the address, an hour and a quarter in composition, and twenty minutes in deciding whether or not to take an umbrella when going to the pillar box in the next street. The total effort that would occupy a busy man for three minutes all told may in this fashion leave another person prostrate after a day of doubt, anxiety and toil.

Parkinson's thesis was that the more time you have available to do a job, the longer it will take. 'Work expands,' he said, 'to fill the time available.'

Unfortunately many managers reading this tend to reply: 'That may be a correct analysis for old ladies of leisure, but it certainly does not apply to me. I work damned hard, I cut corners, things do not get done, yet there still aren't enough hours in the day.'

Self-check

When did you last say, or hear someone else say, 'I don't have enough time'?

It is quite likely that you have heard that expression, or one similar, within the last few days. It is in regular use whether as an excuse for failing to do something or as a way of getting out of doing something altogether. There are busy people whose day seems to be action-packed; who never rest, whose workload seems over-full and who often say, 'Sorry, I just have not had the time to deal with it.'

Yet there are other busy people who have action-packed days, who never rest and whose workload seems over-full. But these people always do things on time and even have spare time to deal with extra emergency jobs.

Self-check

Do you know of anyone who has more time than yourself?

The truth is that time is the only factor that a manager can do absolutely nothing to increase. Skills and knowledge can be increased; experience grows with the passage of time; he can foster and develop his personal relationships. But he cannot increase the amount of time he has; it is strictly limited. Admittedly there are a few people who need only a little sleep and who actually have an extra hour or two each day to do things, but for most people there is no difference at all in the time available. Some people achieve more each day than others; a few because they have more energy than the rest, and some because they have more to do, but most of all because they manage their workloads more efficiently within the time available.

Instead, therefore, of wasting time complaining about the lack of it, it is worth spending some time trying to organise things so that there is enough time available.

Activity

What three things waste your time most? (Five minutes.)

There are, of course, many answers to this question. Among the most common generally, many people rank television as a major time-consumer. However, in a work environment many people answer that it is their boss who is the greatest time-waster. Others consider that meetings are the main culprit, and others are convinced that the abolition of the telephone would solve all their problems. Unfortunately answers like these may well be missing the point: why worry about time spent over which one has no control? What has to be discovered is where time can be saved by a conscious effort on the part of the manager himself. The easiest way of doing this is to look at the major supposed causes of wasted time to see what scope exists for spending less time on them. (Meetings will be looked at separately in Chapter 17.)

16.1 **Travelling**

Sales personnel are the most travelled people in most organisations, and the biggest complaint of most sales managers is that they spend too much time travelling. Certainly a very high percentage of their time is spent on the road, presumably visiting clients who cannot be handled by the ordinary sales rep, or calling on individual sales personnel in their own territory. Leaving aside the argument that many people prefer to be out and about rather than sitting at a desk in the office, the main reason for travelling is to carry out some discussion which cannot be conducted by telephone. Among such discussions are:

* training subordinates if they are located in different places;
* where it is necessary to discuss complicated documents with others (e.g. discussing architect's drawings on the phone is a tricky and even dangerous activity);
* where a face-to-face discussion is more appropriate and has to be on the client's home ground.

The difficulty here is to decide what is appropriate. If, for instance, a customer has a complaint it may be handled by telephone, but the sales manager may feel that a face-to-face discussion will clear the air more effectively. Similarly within an organisation that has a number of locations some individuals spend a good deal of time visiting all the 'outposts of the empire'. These visits may simply be a public relations activity to make the branch or depot feel part of a planning or control process.

Travelling is, therefore, an essential ingredient in many managers' workload. The question that has to be asked is, Is it possible to reduce the amount of time spent in transit over the year? In order to answer it, the following supplementary questions can be asked:

* Is my journey really necessary? What would happen if I did not go because, for instance, I was ill?
* Why would a telephone conversation be insufficient?
* Is it possible to combine two or more visits and make one long trip? (This needs just a little more planning.)
* Why can a subordinate not make the journey instead of me? Many visits are made because an assistant is not considered to have sufficient expertise to successfully handle the discussion. The answer here is to make sure that one's assistants are trained to take this kind of responsibility. Again the question can be asked, What happens if I fall ill?
* Am I taking the quickest route and mode of transport?

And finally, on a completely different level:

* Am I based in the best place to minimise overall travelling time?

The above discussion has been related to travelling away from the place of work, but it also applies to a lesser extent within the place of work, especially if it is a large organisation. An enormous amount of time can be wasted walking from office to office, especially if there is a danger of many social meetings in the corridors. The six questions posed above are as relevant for journeys within the place of work as for journeys outside.

Activity

Keep a record of the amount of time you spend in transit during the day, excluding the journey to work from home and back again. (If you work at home, try to calculate how much time you spend on the move just the same.) Keep the record for a week, then calculate how much time you would save in a year if you were on the move for 10 per cent less time.

Here is a sly way of calculating the answer: multiply the minutes spent in transit during the week by 8 and divide by 100. This will give the hours saved in a 48-hour working year.

For example, if you average 60 minutes on the move each day (i.e. 300 minutes a week) and you cut this by 10 per cent you will save 24 hours over a year.

16.2 Doing Other People's Work

Very few people admit to doing work which does not strictly concern them and which should be done by someone else; yet it happens all the time. In Chapter 12 on decision-making and problem-solving, one question that was posed very early on was to ask, Is this really my problem, or is it just someone passing the buck? Too often a manager gets involved in something of no direct concern; becoming a vacuum-cleaner sucking in all sorts of jobs, all kinds of work much of which he should have nothing to do with at all. There are three main ways in which this can crop up.

First, there is the request for help from a colleague. Normally a manager has a particular expertise which is available to other managers as part of the everyday business of running the organisation. There is obviously no suggestion that managers should abrogate their responsibilities and deny colleagues technical assistance, but there are times when the request is not for technical help, merely for moral support. 'Have a look at this, George, and tell me what you think of it' is not entirely unknown, and George, if he is not careful, finds himself reading reports that do not really concern him, over which he has no influence and no control.

Second, a subordinate may come to the boss with a problem. If the subordinate is smart the problem can be passed to the boss without the boss having recognised it at all. It is often achieved by the use of some subtle flattery: 'You solved it last time so well. How did you do it?' It is often easier to do it yourself than coach subordinates to do it for themselves, and so the job changes hands.

The third way of acquiring more work than you need is by failing to pass it on to the person who should deal with it. In other words, not delegating work. There are several reasons why managers fail to delegate:

- The subordinate is not competent or trustworthy.
- The subordinate says 'I am too busy'.
- The subordinate will kick up a fuss.
- The manager enjoys doing that particular job ('We have to visit these ten organisations; you take the ones in London, Glasgow, Birmingham and Manchester. I suppose I had better visit the one in Paris').

Self-check

Which of the four reasons given for not delegating is justifiable? (Five minutes.)

Occasionally a manager may find that any of the first three are valid reasons for delegating; but part of the job is to make sure that the subordinates are ready, willing and able to take on work.

The important thing about delegation is that it is a sign of strength in a manager, not a weakness. To be effective it embraces four particular aspects:

1 Passing out the job to the subordinate.
2 Giving the subordinate the authority to do everything needed to complete the job.
3 Making him responsible for the successful completion of the job.
4 Rewarding him adequately.

In addition, the manager must make sure that the job to be done is properly understood by the subordinate.

As far as doing the things he enjoys doing is concerned, it is occasionally fair enough to take on something particularly enjoyable or interesting. However, too much of it demotivates subordinates, especially if the reasons for doing so are not entirely honest.

Delegation means passing out good things as well as not-so-good things.

16.3 The Ditherer

One of the most difficult time-wasters to pin down is the manager who is indecisive. He can often be recognised because he is the one who is either continually asking for more information on a problem, or who goes over the same ground several times. To be dependent on such people for a decision is exceedingly frustrating and is best countered by a fairly unequivocal statement to the effect that 'I would like a decision by Friday, otherwise I shall go ahead and paint it yellow.' You can be sure of provoking a response within the time limit.

16.4 The Chatterer

Chatting is a part of every manager's job; part of the process of getting on with the job, and an important part of developing good relationships. However, too much of it wastes time and it is a particularly difficult thing to cope with. Sometimes it has to be tolerated – like travelling – but if the chat is occasional, then a stop has to be put to it after a reasonable time. If it is a face-to-face chat, then have an excuse ready, for example that a meeting or a phone call is imminent. If it is a chatterer on the phone, then an excuse like 'The boss has just walked in' or even 'My desk has just caught fire' is a way of getting out of the difficulty.

16.5 The Meddler

The meddler is someone who will not let subordinates get on with the job, but who will continually interfere. Benign meddlers are those who like to help 'to speed things up', but who are really slowing things down. There is also the suspicious meddler, whose idea of control is to breathe down people's necks, watching every move. These kind of people often have to be tolerated, but they may, occasionally and politely, be asked to go away.

16.6 Doing It Yourself

A good way of wasting time is to try to do everything yourself, rather than to call in experts. This is important in relation to problem-solving where a manager may spend a good deal of time and effort trying to work out the solution when all he needs to do is to make a quick telephone call to an expert and get the answer in seconds.

16.7 The Elegant Solution

There are some people who will go to extraordinary lengths to solve a problem when only a quick, simple answer is required. To this kind of person the interest is not in the solution, but in the problem itself. Examples of this are to be found in all organisations: the fifty-page report containing complicated diagrams and charts to explain why the cost of fuel went up by 10 per cent; the expensive piece of equipment to solve a simple problem (e.g. the electronic fly swat). This kind of approach has its place, and such people are valuable in those circumstances that need a high degree of precision and care. It is up to the manager of such people to make sure that they understand precisely the level of detail required and their efforts should be focused on problems that need painstaking skill. If a problem can be solved by a quick calculation on the back of an envelope, ask someone who is good at that kind of thing.

Activity

The people described in the previous four paragraphs are all people who are wasting *your* time. Do you never waste the time of others in these ways? Be honest!

16.8 Paper, Paper Everywhere

Most managers have to deal with quite a lot of paperwork. If the documents are the result of a request by the manager make sure that they are all as brief as possible. This point was made in Chapter 14 concerning the amount of information a sales manager would need to control a sales force of ten closely. If a manager is in a position to state how much information is to be received, then it must be made known and should normally err on the side of brevity. This will be looked at in more detail in Chapter 18 on communications.

Just as long reports are time-wasters, so too is a large proportion of the unsolicited paper that a manager receives. If it is not dealt with fairly quickly, it can soon build up into monster piles under which the manager finally gets buried. There are only three things that can be done with paper:

- Throw it away.
- File it.
- Do something with it.

The decision rules on which category to classify paper are fairly simple – see Figure 16.1.

Self-check

There is a saying: 'A cluttered desk is a sign of genius'. True or false? If it is false, what *is* such a state a sign of?

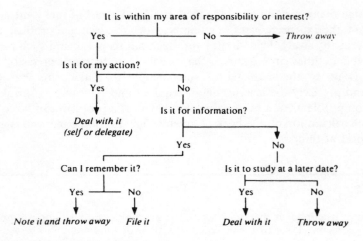

Fig 16.1   How to handle paper

16.9 Some Ideas on Saving Time

Handling the boss

In addition to the points already noted about boss/subordinate relationships there are just four extra things to note about handling the boss (assuming that he is aware of the subordinate's competence). Ask:

- What is wanted, precisely?
- When is it wanted?
- In what form does the boss want it?

Then state whether it can be done or not. Just occasionally it may be necessary to say 'no' or 'later' to a boss if there is a valid reason for doing so.

Using a secretary/assistant

A good secretary or personal assistant can save a lot of time if used as a secretary and not just as a shorthand-typist. For example, in Chapter 12 you will recall the problem of the spring clamps. One of the apparent difficulties seemed to be that the young secretary failed to contact Fred Smith at Spring Clamps. If she had been given an explanation of the problem, it is possible she would have been more persistent in her efforts. A good secretary would have got either the right person or an acceptable substitute.

Among the other useful secretarial functions which save time are:

- Blocking unwanted telephone, or personal, callers (especially if a meeting is in progress).

- Planning timetables for travelling and meetings.
- Keeping filing in order.
- Acting as an information researcher and source.

Where is not possible to have a secretary or an assistant many of these things have to be carried out by the individual. In these circumstances it is useful to be on good terms with whoever does typing work (e.g. the typing pool), also with the telephone switchboard operators, and be able to operate a voice mail system.

Discussion and interview control

A very high proportion of most managers' time is spent talking to people inside and outside of meetings. Discussions, interviews or telephone conversations are usually on a one-to-one basis, or with just two or three people at most. To save time on these occasions:

- Decide how long is needed to discuss the issue.
- Tell the people involved how long.
- Make sure there will be no interruptions (if possible).
- Decide and inform what the purpose of the interview, etc., will be.
- Give adequate notice to all concerned.

Crisis avoidance

A crisis is an unplanned event which disrupts or threatens to disrupt normal operations. When a crisis occurs it wastes a colossal amount of time, as we saw with the Spring Clamps case. Obviously crises will occur even in the best-managed organisations, but too often crisis management becomes a way of life rather than an exception. An organisation which is likely to have completely unpredictable, big crises may create a permanent standing committee consisting of a cross-section of senior managers, who are called together in the event of a storm. Generally, though, a crisis is overcome by hard work and effort on the part of the individual managers who get involved.

Crisis avoidance is a preferable way of running an organisation, and the purpose of control systems is to ensure that if things start to get out of hand steps can be taken quickly to avoid the problem spreading. You will recall that one of the keys to successful control is the speed with which the system operates. Since the responsible manager is at the centre of the system he or she must get the information, decide and act quickly to stop the crisis. If the manager is disorganised and not managing time properly, then the crisis gets out of hand.

Workload planning

The most effective managers are those who manage their time in such a way that the important things get priority. This needs thinking through, and therefore a certain amount of time has to be invested at the outset. The key steps in this particular activity are:

1 Decide how you should spend your time over a normal week. Establish priorities; give most time to the most important things. Bear in mind that at least 15 per cent of working time is wasted for natural reasons. This is called the 'relaxation factor' by work study experts.
2 Find out how you actually spend your time by keeping a fairly detailed log over a four-week period.
3 Look for obvious time-wasters and resolve to eliminate them.
4 Set aside regular times for carrying out regular tasks like correspondence and reading any journals or magazines you should read.
5 Allow adequate time for the unexpected.
6 Give yourself some 'thinking time', especially before an interview or meeting.
7 Maintain your time-log and use it as a basis for a personal time-control system.

Questions to ask continually from your time-log

- Am I doing anything that need not be done at all?
- Am I doing anything that should (or could) be done by someone else?
- Am I doing anything that wastes other people's time?
- Did I understand properly what I should do?
- Do other people understand properly what I need?
- How many time-wasting crises were my fault? How can I avoid a recurrence?
- Are the operating control systems efficient?

Review

During the last seven days, have you at any time

- Wondered where a day went to?   *yes/no*
- Achieved half of what you wanted to achieve?   *yes/no*
- Spent more than twenty minutes on one telephone call?   *yes/no*
- Worked on something you enjoyed and left alone something more important but less pleasant?   *yes/no*
- Said, 'I must read that', and have not?   *yes/no*
- Passed out a vague instruction?   *yes/no*
- Had a meeting, interview or discussion lasting more than three hours?   *yes/no*

- Walked the same ground twice within half an hour because you forgot something the first time?   *yes/no*
- Seen the size of your 'things to be done' list grow?   *yes/no*
- Worked hard?   *yes/no*

SCORING

If you scored 'yes'

0–3 times only: you are exceptionally well organised.

4–7 times: you are well organised.

8–10 times: you are just like the rest of us.

A case to consider

One of the most accomplished time managers I ever met was the president of a big bank. I saw him once a month for two years. My appointment was always for an hour and a half, and there was never more than one item on the agenda. When I had been with him for an hour and twenty minutes the president would turn to me and say, 'Mr Drucker, I believe you'd better sum up now and outline what we should do next.' And an hour and thirty minutes after I had been ushered into his office, he was at the door saying goodbye to me. I finally asked him why the conference always took an hour and a half. He answered, 'That's easy. I have found that my attention span is about an hour and a half. If I work on any one topic longer than this, I begin to repeat myself. But I have also found that nothing of importance can really be tackled in much less time.'

While I was in his office the telephone never rang and his secretary never stuck her head through the doorway to announce that an important man wanted to see him urgently. One day I asked him about this. He said: 'My secretary has strict instructions not to put anyone through except the President of the United States and my wife. The President very rarely calls and my wife knows better. When we have finished our conference, I take half an hour to return every call. I have yet to come across a crisis which could not wait ninety minutes'. But even this disciplined man had to resign himself to having at least half his working time taken up by things of minor importance and dubious value.

(From *The Effective Executive* by Peter Drucker)

17 Meetings: Using Time to Save Time

This chapter should help you to appreciate that a meeting can waste time better than anything else. It can also save time and effort and lead to more effective management – but only if it is managed properly.

Nearly everyone has some horror story to relate about a meeting that achieved nothing except a great deal of wasted time; it seems to happen all the time, yet nobody seems prepared to do anything about it. Suppose, however, that every meeting had to produce benefits greater than the costs incurred during the meeting; the number of hours spent in meetings would drop to one-tenth of their present level. For instance, a meeting of six managers, each earning £30,000, costs £150 an hour (assuming a 33 per cent wages oncost for pension fund contributions, etc., and a 48-week year).

So why do meetings exist and what can be done to improve their effectiveness?

17.1 The Purpose of Meetings

Statutory

Many meeting are legally necessary, according to the constitution of the company, society or club concerned, and they usually fall into two (or three) subdivisions.

The annual general meeting (AGM)

This is the meeting of the members of the organisation (shareholders in the case of a limited company). Normally these are fairly well-managed affairs because the rules under which they operate are clearly set out in the organisation's constitution. One of the most useful things to note about an AGM is that members have to be given plenty of advance notice that it is going to occur and have to be provided with adequate information about matters that are going to be discussed.

Self-check

Have you ever been to a meeting where you spent the first twenty minutes reading the information in the papers you were given on arrival?
Why is it a bad thing to arrive at a meeting unprepared?

Meetings of officers

Also often written into constitutions of organisations are rules concerning the frequency of meetings of the elected or appointed officers of the organisation – whether the body is called the board of directors, the board of management, the council, or meeting of governors.

Since this kind of committee meeting is the senior one in any organisation there is usually a lot of business to get through. Only by efficient management can they be completed in time; once again it is useful if the committee members have adequate warning of meetings and have a good idea of the topics that will be discussed. In commercial undertakings it is usual for the members of the board of directors to have a meeting monthly at which the accounting results for the previous month are discussed. For a director to do the job well information is needed several days in advance, especially if there is an expectation of a contribution by way of an explanation or some help and advice. How can a director be helpful if the nature of the problem is unknown?

Meeting of executive officers

Some organisations have written into their constitutions provision for regular meetings of the senior executives of the larger management committee. This may be an inner circle consisting of the chairman, secretary, treasurer (or other most senior financial manager) and the managing director (if a separate individual to the chairman). These three or four should, whether legally obliged to or not, have regular meetings to decide matters that do not need full committee approval, and also to make sure that full committee meetings are as efficient as possible.

In addition, if these executive officers are conscientious and fully devoted to the aims and values of the organisation they are serving, then the meetings should be used to develop a shared understanding of the prospects and problems for the organisation: very much a think-tank or ideas laboratory at a very high level.

Meetings for information dissemination

A completely different kind of meeting is the kind called to spread information. This is best achieved by a meeting if:

● there are many people to be informed;
● an element of persuasion is needed;

- something has to be shown or seen;
- the information is confidential;
- many questions are likely to be asked.

A good example of this is where a large company wants to tell its sales force about a new range of products. By calling them together a much more effective way of spreading knowledge – and raising spirits – is achieved.

It must be noted that meetings like this do not just happen; they take a great deal of planning and management if they are to be successful. Managers wishing to put on a large information-giving meeting of the kind just described have to be absolutely sure they can afford to devote a great deal of time to it. If not, professional conference organisers should be appointed to handle the whole affair.

Smaller information-giving meetings need adequate planning too, and three essential points must be remembered:

1 Tell people the subject-matter of the meeting (as well as time, duration and place).
2 Prepare materials that people can see, clearly understand and take away with them.
3 Have a programme, tell everyone what it is and stick to it.

Problem-solving meetings

This kind of meeting is very common and comes up because one individual does not have all the knowledge and information to solve the problem on his own. Other people are called in either because they have some specialist knowledge or because the outcome of the meeting will affect their own operations in some way. There is a temptation, however, to invite to such meetings too many people who have only a marginal contribution to make. It is better either to ask such people beforehand to stand by in case they are needed, or ask for their opinion in advance. Too much time is wasted sitting in meetings waiting to be asked to make a contribution that is only minor.

The other problem that crops up with over-inviting is that the meeting takes longer. Remember Graicunas' theory of relationships in Chapter 6 (page 94): the more people there are in a meeting, the more the number of conversations that can be held. What four people could solve in twenty minutes would take six people two hours, and eight people would take five hours. Clearly, however, in the interests of democracy and participation extra people have to be invited.

Activity

Can democracy and efficiency go together? Or must one be sacrificed for the other? (Good for an hour or two's debate with your friends.)

Once again, it is important to plan meetings like this adequately:

- Give people as much notice as possible.
- Tell them as precisely as possible what the problem is.
- Inform them of what might be expected of them.
- Let them know who else will be there.
- Tell them how long the meeting will be.
- Give them any helpful documents and an agenda.
- Make it clear that the decision will be yours alone and not a collective one.

Collective-decision meetings

Often meetings are used to get a collective decision from the members attending. If one individual does not have the power or authority to take the decision on his own then a meeting will have to be called to make the decision. Sometimes it is laid down in the organisation's constitution precisely what has to be decided by committee. In limited companies the auditors have to be appointed by the AGM of the company, for example. Decisions about high finance – borrowing or raising new share capital – are often taken by boards of directors or by AGMs on the recommendation of the directors.

The use of committees to make decisions is widespread, partly because it is felt that the decision is better if several people make it, and partly because of the fear of delegating too much power and authority to any one individual.

Often many decisions are actually taken by the senior executive officer but put to the full committee for ratification. This is a difficult path to tread, depending for its success on the degree of trust that the officer has built up with the committee.

There are occasions, however, when any manager feels that to take a decision on something would be quite beyond his or her own authority, even though they may be absolutely convinced in their own minds what should be done.

Self-check

You have been buying coffee for your organisation for years. You have always bought Brazilian coffee – everyone liked it and the quality was always high. One day you hear that, because of frosts and a poor harvest, the price will be going up by 80 per cent. You know that you can get an adequate supply of Kenya coffee at only 20 per cent more than the original price. This is what you want to do. What would you do?

- Go out and buy, then tell everyone?
- Tell everyone and then go out and buy?

- Tell everyone; wait a bit; then buy if nobody complained?
- Call a meeting of everyone concerned and get a collective decision?
- Do something else?

(Five minutes.)

With a problem like this there are a number of factors that may affect the decision: How quickly does the decision have to be taken? How will my colleagues react? People naturally feel aggrieved if, without their knowledge, decisions are taken which affect them. What is worse is the situation where a decision only comes to the manager's notice via the informal communication system in the organisation.

Taking these points into consideration, the course of action you take may, in the end, depends on how you view decision-making. The first course of action is the fastest, but the least consultative; the fourth is the most consultative but the slowest; the second and third are compromise positions which are not unacceptable provided that there is enough time.

Finally, a meeting is sometimes called for a collective decision to be made where the manager is not able to make up his own mind (even though he should). This is tantamount to an abdication of his responsibilities – he is saying, 'I am not capable of taking the decision.' This is perfectly acceptable occasionally, as long as it is done openly; but it can become a habit.

Creative-thinking meetings

Sometimes meetings are called for the purpose of creativity: to try to come up with some new ideas. Creative thinking uses the idea of 'social facilitation'. This is another way of describing what happens when a group of people get together and stimulate each other's thinking.

There are many different ways of tackling this kind of meeting. One such technique is known as 'brainstorming' and was developed by Alex Osborn in the early 1950s to help come up with new ideas in advertising, e.g. a new brand name for a product. In these sessions the problem is not actually stated before the session but stated clearly at the start. People are encouraged to produce many ideas out of which the best can be selected for further evaluation. Criticism of ideas is not allowed; the important thing is the development of lots of ideas.

Another creative thinking technique is called the 'Gordon technique' after its originator, William Gordon. The rules of this technique are that only the leader knows the problem, and the subject for discussion is chosen with great care, usually a key word or phrase. However, the success of such meetings depends largely on having an expert leader.

General tips for good creative-thinking meetings
Have a mixed-knowledge group; male and female, if consumer goods are being considered. Six to nine participants is ideal. Use a secretary or tape recorder. A blackboard or flip-chart is handy for posting up key words.

Brainstorming needs up to half an hour to be effective, but no more than one hour.

The Gordon technique needs two or three hours.

Participants must know beforehand what kind of a meeting they will be attending and what will be expected of them.

Activity

Creative-thinking sessions need not be at work. People are generally very glad to come up with ideas about such things as what to do with the garden; home decorating and décor; where to go for your holidays and so on. So try it out on your friends for a change.

Other miscellaneous meetings

There are many other kinds of meetings: meetings to select new members of an organisation; one-off meetings of neighbours to fight a proposed new building, or of managers to fight an unwelcome change.

There are also psychological group activities such as T-groups and role-playing exercises which have specific behavioural objectives.

17.2 Making the Most of Meetings

Planning

Sufficient has already been said about planning not to have to stress the general importance of this. As far as meetings are concerned the following need to be considered:

- Allow plenty of time.
- Decide why the meeting is needed (if at all).
- Decide when and where to hold it – the more notice that can be given the better.
- Build an agenda.
- Put financial statements (if any) first, because the state of financial health may determine the outcome of other matters up for discussion.
- Put the most serious or urgent matters next.
- Make a timetable for the meeting.

- Clearly state what each item on the agenda means. If it is an issue where there will be argument and it is to finish with a vote, then it is better to put the item in the form of a proposal or motion. For instance: *Item 4*. To consider and vote on the following resolution: That this meeting agrees to move the company's operations to the Bahamas. This is a more suitable form than: *Item 4*: The move to the Bahamas.
- Obtain any reading matter and assemble it with the agenda.
- Decide who needs to attend, inform them well ahead and send them the full agenda with background papers.
- Tell the attenders what they will be expected to do at the meeting (e.g. make a speech, present some information).

Activity

- When trade unions have their AGMs there are often many resolutions to discuss. Look out for them and see how they are phrased.
- Study any limited company's annual accounts, which usually these days also contain the Notice of the AGM and the agenda. You will see how their resolutions are put.

During the meeting

If you are the chairman see how others do it first. It is worth watching a really good chairman in action – the most easily available meeting to attend is a meeting of the local council – although you cannot guarantee high-quality chairmanship, unfortunately. However, good clues will be found on such occasions as to the effective conduct of meetings. The following points need to be remembered:

- Start on time.
- Stick to the timetable.
- Be fair.
- Give everyone a chance.
- Be prepared to shut someone up if they get over-talkative or repetitive.
- Make sure people stick to the subject under discussion and that their remarks are relevant.
- State clearly which item is to be discussed.
- If a vote is needed be sure that everyone is clear what they are voting for.
- Allow only one person to talk at once. (If you expect a noisy meeting, get a hammer and a block of wood. Hitting the block may not stop the noise, but it relieves frustration.)
- If action is needed as a result of a discussion make sure it is clear who carries out the task and by when.

- Make sure that decisions and significant statements are all fully recorded.
- Do not let the meeting drag on. (People in meetings tend to get tired after $1\frac{1}{2}$ to 2 hours. After that, mental agility falls rapidly. This is especially true of evening meetings. It is better to stop the meeting and arrange to continue at another time.)

If you are a participant at a meeting you should:

- Arrive on time.
- Come prepared.
- Listen.
- Avoid rambling discourses and repetition.
- If you have a strong view on something, then make sure the meeting understands your view and why you hold it.

After the meeting

Make sure that minutes are prepared quickly and sent out to all who need to receive them. The minutes should state:

- what was decided;
- who would take action.

It is helpful that any people whose names appear in the minutes should have their attention drawn to the fact, so that they know they have to act.

Self-check

Which of these two alternative ways of presenting a minute is best?

- '*Item 4.* It was decided to move to the Bahamas. John Smith is to arrange it.'
- '*Item 4*. It was decided to move to the Bahamas before the end of the tax year. John Smith will prepare a timetable and draw up a list of names of those who will form the moving subcommittee. These will be circulated before the next meeting.'

The second alternative way of presenting the decisions of the meeting is fuller and more precise. It tells everyone exactly what is going to happen, when, and who will be managing it. One extra useful bit of information is to add a note at the top of the minutes stating: 'Your attention is drawn to item X, for your action.' This makes doubly certain that the individual concerned knows exactly what is supposed to be done.

The position of secretary

The special responsibilities of the inner circle of officers was mentioned on page 253. The secretary has many duties of an administrative and legal nature, but in addition he or she has to do much of the preplanning that comes before the rest of the inner circle get involved. In particular it is the secretary who advises the chairman on how to handle the agenda, and who should also make sure that the chairman is fully briefed on the meeting. To this end the preparation of the 'chairman's briefing paper' is invaluable, and the secretary should make sure that the chairman actually reads (and understands) it.

The contents of a briefing paper vary but will include information about newcomers, meanings of technical terms that may be used, the legal position on things that may come up, and also notes on any hostile attitudes that may appear.

A thoughtful secretary can save much time in meetings without having to do anything during the meeting to speed up the proceedings. After the meeting he or she can speed up the implementation of decisions by making sure that things are happening – and helping to make them happen if there are problems.

17.3 Disadvantages of Meetings

Apart from the obvious disadvantages that meetings can cost money and may waste time, there are two main dangers that have to be guarded against:

Meetings may lead to unsatisfactory compromise

It has been said that there are some things you can compromise over, and other things you should not. It is possible, for example, in an argument over which two small boys should eat the apple to compromise nicely by cutting the apple in two. Compromise would not work if those two small boys were squabbling over a white rabbit. Meetings may end up doing something like cutting the white rabbit in half, simply because they do not want to upset one of their members.

Meetings may be indecisive

It has also been said that if you do not want to have to take a decision, appoint a committee to inquire into the problem. Inevitably, that committee will spawn a couple of subcommittees and another special committee will be created to co-ordinate the work of the other two. A great number of meetings results, everybody grows to appreciate and love the problem; in fact it becomes the *raison d'être* for some, their jobs depend on it and no conclusion is ever reached.

Fig 17.1 Two-layered board structure

17.4 The Board of Directors: Executive or Not

Boards of directors of companies limited under the Companies Acts have legal responsibilities and powers, but in addition their meetings may cover many other aspects of the company's affairs. There has been a trend over the last forty years which is worth noting.

The board is appointed by the shareholders, and traditionally only one or two directors were executive officers of the company, usually the managing director and the deputy managing director. The chairman of the board and most of the directors had no job inside the organisation. Many organisation structures had a two-layer appearance – see Figure 17.1. The board of directors met to consider broad strategy, policy and legal matters; the senior management committee met to consider everything else. In recent years this division has become less and less pronounced and indeed in many companies the board of directors consists mainly of full-time executives. The distinction between responsibilities is no longer seen; it is now understood that senior management are better placed to formulate strategy and policy as well as ensure its execution.

There is, however, still a very important role for the non-executive director. As well as being shareholders' representatives, these people are objective and impartial. Often they have many other business interests, which enables them to appraise proposals more keenly than the manager who lives with them day to day.

Individuals v. committees

Review

On the next page several managerial activities are listed. Each could be handled by an individual or by a committee. Indicate which you think is the most appropriate way of dealing with each activity by placing a tick in the relevant column.

(Twenty minutes.)

	Better handled by committee	Individual action better	Does not matter
1 Setting objectives			
2 Planning			
3 Getting things organised			
4 Control			
5 Decision-making			
6 Leadership			
7 Communications			
8 Innovation			
9 Settling disputes			
10 Evaluating environmental changes			

If you put all your ticks in the first column (better handled by a committee) – do you like meetings?

If all the ticks went into the second column (individual handling better) – do you hate meetings?

If you put all the ticks in the third column, get a second opinion from someone who has to work in meetings frequently.

Research into executives' preference has come up with the following suggestions. *Committee action* is better for setting objectives (**1**), settling disputes (**9**), evaluating environmental changes (**10**). *Individual action* is thought to be better for all the other items except possibly innovation (**8**) – where it does not seem to matter. Quite definitely, leadership (**6**) and getting things organised (**3**) are the two activities where there is hardly any support for them to be carried out in committee.

It should be stressed that these are only opinions and there is often room for the alternative approach. However, the consensus indicates clearly that individual action is more effective than group action.

If a meeting is suggested, ask:

- Is it really necessary?
- How can it be used to save time, money and effort?
- How can it be managed so as not to waste time?

A quote to remember
Parkinson's Law of Triviality states: '. . . the time spent on any item of the agenda will be in inverse proportion to the sum involved'.

18 Effective Communications

In this chapter our concern is with the questions of why it is important to be able to communicate effectively and how it can be achieved.

By the end of the chapter you should be able to appreciate the importance of good communications, identify the main barriers that prevent effective communication and be aware of how to go about improving your own skills in communicating.

Activity

Imagine that you are standing in the carpark of a busy airport, but you cannot find the way into the terminal building. You see a man standing by a car, so you go up to him and ask him to direct you to the terminal. He does not reply, but merely stares at you.

List three reasons why you might not have got a response.

(Five minutes.)

There are many possible reasons why the question you put directly was not answered. They include:

- A plane took off at that moment and drowned your words.
- He could have been deaf.
- You could have been speaking in a foreign language (or had a strange accent) which he did not understand.
- You could have used a form of address that insulted or irritated him (e.g. 'Ere, you, where's the way in?').
- You may have been wearing a funny hat or strange clothing or been carrying something which distracted his attention from the words you were speaking.

What went wrong?

In effect, what happened was that you (who were the sender of the message, the transmitter) failed to communicate with the receiver of the message. The failure to communicate could have been caused by a number of factors, singularly or in combination. It could have been:

- an interruption (the aircraft);
- a physical barrier (deafness);
- the wrong language;
- the wrong tone of voice;
- a distraction (funny hat).

Suppose that the message does get across and the man hears you. He may decide that he is not interested in your problem (he has some of his own), so he walks away. Or he may point you in a certain direction only for you to find yourself in the aircraft maintenance hangar, instead of the terminal building. If this happens, there are only three possible causes:

1 He misled you (deliberately or not).
2 He misunderstood you.
3 You misunderstood him (or failed to follow his instructions).

In the situation we have described we have to make sure that all the conditions are right, so that our chances of getting the message across are high. Moreover it is not just a question of making sure that the receiver hears, but that he understands what he is hearing, and also that he is prepared to respond positively to what he hears.

In that scene at the airport we identified nine possible problem areas that could have caused you to fail to get what you wanted. Some of the problems were connected with hearing the message, some with understanding it and others with responding positively to it. It was a simple communication issue with nothing very important at stake, so the failure did not result in great loss. But suppose that the communication had been a transatlantic telephone call in connection with a multimillion-pound sale of aero-engines. If there had been a failure of communications on such a conversation, someone could have lost a great deal of money – or finished up with a lot more engines than he needed.

There can be no doubt that not only is there a growing need to communicate more, there is also a much greater need to ensure that communications are much more effective than they have been in the past. There is evidence that many organisational problems have been caused, or aggravated, by inadequate communications; and managerial responsibility in this cannot be avoided.

18.1 The Importance of Effective Communications

Communications is all about passing on information. It is either a request for information – 'Please send me your price list' – or it is actually giving out information – 'Here is our price list.' There are many reasons why people give out (or ask for) information and therein lies the importance of being effective with it. Information is needed for all the aspects of organisational life that have been looked at in this book: to help in planning, for better decision-making and problem-solving, for creating understanding between people and for effective control. It is also needed for more persuasive ends than just understanding: advertising is information communicated to potential customers to persuade them to buy; public relations is information to the world to persuade it that the organisation is beneficial.

It can be said that there are communications made for reasons of operational effectiveness, and there are communications for political reasons, using the word 'politics' in its widest sense.

Most of the organisation's communications effort is directed within the organisation itself and is never seen outside. There is, however, a fairly large proportion that concerns groups that are external to the organisation and it is useful to consider these two aspects separately, looking at each from the viewpoint of the various receivers.

18.2 Internal Communications

Inside an organisation a manager has to communicate with several different types of people: his boss, his colleagues and his subordinates being the commonest. In addition, if his organisation is unionised he may have to devote a considerable amount of time communicating with the union representatives. In all cases by far the greater proportion of the communicating will be of the operational type – concerned with planning, doing the job and with control; but every manager has some political communications needs too – persuading the boss to decide an issue in a certain way, trying to introduce change to an old-established workforce, negotiating for additional equipment with the accounts department. All these are political reasons for communicating, and the successful manager cultivates his talents in this direction, as well as his operational communicative skills.

The manager and his boss

Activity

A question to consider. Have you ever heard this complaint: 'If only my boss would listen'? It is a fairly common complaint, and looking at the reasons why communications fail, on pages 263–4, what is the most likely cause of this manager's complaint? (Ten minutes.)

On the assumption that there are no obvious physical barriers to communicating with the boss (the two causes on page 264), it must be the case that he is hearing, but either not understanding or not responding for some other reason.

A lack of understanding can be caused by the wrong language (even though it may technically be the same) or the wrong tone. So ask, Does he understand what I am saying? If the answer is, Yes, but still will not do anything, then the reason for the lack of response has to be found. It could be that the boss's own problems are more pressing. Or it could be a lack of interest, or that the problem can be solved without interference.

It is part of the job of every manager to learn to manage the boss. Being able to communicate is part of this, and the first step therefore is to identify the cause of the problem. This, as we saw with problem-solving, can lead straight to the solution.

The manager and his subordinates

Every good manager must make sure that subordinates have the opportunity to communicate regularly, not only by having an open-door policy – 'Come in and see me any time' – but by taking the trouble actually to be in their place of work frequently. To do it irregularly is considerably less effective because it is only with constant appearances that a level of familiarity is built up, so that people are willing to talk freely with their manager. It is not uncommon for young office workers to literally tremble at the thought of being spoken to by a senior manager whom they rarely see.

To establish a degree of goodwill and trust with subordinates enables the good manager to find out more about attitudes and atmosphere than a shelf of statistical reports, and it enables him also to approach the change process on a more relaxed, participatory basis.

In return for a flow of information upwards, staff expect information to be passed downwards too. The expression 'the information filters down' is not a good commendation for an organisation's skill at communicating. One of the causes of concern felt by trade unions these days is the issue of disclosure of information. It is felt that the ordinary working individual, particularly in a large organisation, is being kept in the dark over too many issues, particularly those at the corporate strategy and policy level.

Research has indicated that a few companies have deliberate policies to restrict the amount of information given out to employees, but many avoid disclosing information only where it is 'sensitive', in other words potentially harmful to the organisation if a competitor heard too soon. Possibly the majority of organisations simply do not consider the question to be important. However, there is a growing trend for the increased dissemination of information and this is noticeable among the more progressive companies. The staff newspaper or magazine has long been a feature of corporate attempts at communication. Nowadays specially designed reports are being prepared alongside annual reports and accounts, in order to explain the significance of the firm's profit and loss account and balance sheet information.

All these efforts do not mean that the individual manager can give up worrying about the question. On the contrary, his responsibility is to explain the significance of these formal communications and also to inform his staff about development and changes that are taking place in his own department.

The manager and the trade union

Apart from the regular communications that take place between managers and trade-union representatives, many managers find that a good deal of time and effort needs to be spent (whether in or out of meetings) in negotiating and bargaining with the union representatives. It has been said that the existence of strong works councils in such countries as Germany, Sweden and Norway is a major factor in accounting for their low industrial dispute statistics. The purpose of the works council is seen as an effective vehicle for good communications – both of information (to create understanding) and of persuasion (to avoid conflict).

Self-check

Do you think that people who meet frequently will generally communicate more efficiently with each other than people who meet rarely?

The manager and his colleagues

It appears that managers generally spend as much time with their colleagues as with their subordinates or bosses. This partly reflects the nature of the problems that managers face and partly it reflects the trend towards delegated responsibility, as we saw in the matrix organisation. Good communications with one's peers is important where problems need to be solved together, where each is facing a similar problem or where the formal channels of communication (i.e. up and down the line) are slow, inefficient or politically inappropriate.

For example if a factory manager finds that there is a danger of running out of a particular component, a good position to be in to avoid a crisis is if the appropriate purchasing manager can be phoned for more. If they do not know, or have never met each other, then there may be a communications barrier which will cause trouble in an emergency.

18.3 External Communications

An organisation and its managers have to be in constant communication with many different groups of people. Some managers have considerable responsibility in this respect, whereas the contact that other managers have with the outside world is limited.

Many communications activities are strictly commercial, such as selling and buying; others are purely financial or legal. All these are handled by experts in the appropriate skills and professions, and their ability to communicate effectively is closely related to their professional skills. The skilled sales rep. communicates with prospective customers better than the company's doctor (at least one hopes so) because his training and experience have taught him how to be effective. Similarly the accountant's skill at communicating with the tax authorities is a result of his training.

However, there are other very important aspects of external communications which need to be mentioned.

Political role
Some communications take place between an organisation and its environment which are designed to show a group, or groups, of people that the organisation is an acceptable, creditable institution in society. This is the political role of the organisation and is an important part of the work of managing directors and other senior managers. To ignore this activity is possibly to fail to build bridges of confidence with various power groups in society as a whole.

Information
Every organisation must receive information from the environment, other than from its obvious commercial sources (like its customers and suppliers). This is the information that is needed for assessing threats and opportunities, as we saw in Chapter 4. To have an effective radar system an organisation must have good listeners and watchers. Too often, unfortunately, this kind of activity is left to chance and casual encounter.

In all communications situations (both internally and externally) the individual who is intending to send a message must always ask these three things if he wants a positive response:

1 With whom do I wish to communicate (*the audience*)?
2 What do I wish to communicate (*the message*)?
3 How do I communicate (*the method*)?

18.4 The Audience

Determining precisely who is the audience may sound easy and certainly often it is. If I wish to speak to the bus-conductor I know precisely who my audience will be. But suppose I want to advertise soap – who is my audience then? (A little brainstorming here will produce some amusing answers.)

A second question to ask is, Is there anything about my audience that could prevent them from hearing or understanding what I am about to say? Just as with the man at the airport, several potential blockages can be in the way and it is important to be able to identify these and avoid or overcome them. So the answer to this question will actually determine what we say and how we say it.

18.5 The Message

In a casual conversation people adjust their language to suit their audience quite spontaneously and without thinking about it. In a working environment, however, a conscious effort has to be made to choose the words and phrases carefully to make sure that the message is received and understood. There are three main ways in which a poor choice of words can cause a communications problem:

Corporate jargon

All organisations develop their own jargon, sometimes to such an extent that it sounds almost like another language. People are referred to by their initials, documents are referred to by their code numbers, and departments' names are abbreviated. It may be nice and handy for the initiated, but to an outsider it is totally meaningless. It also makes life exceedingly difficult for the newcomer in the organisation. Indeed a useful addition to an induction programme would be a corporate language dictionary.

Professional and technical jargon

A similar specialised use of words is to be found wherever experts in a particular area get together. These special languages are incomprehensible to outsiders, but are common; doctors have one, accountants have one and so do motor mechanics, plumbers and stockbrokers. If you know and use a technical language great care has to be taken to ensure that the person you are addressing is a member of your jargon club.

Multiple meanings

A great deal of misunderstanding occurs in oral communications because a word that is used by one person in one meaning is taken by someone else to mean something different. Consider the following:

Self-check

How many different meanings can you think up for the word 'stock' in two minutes?

The dictionary lists quite a few meanings including:

Flower	Share in a company
Store	Breeding source
Contents of store	Soup
Part of a rifle	Fill up

If we take the plural 'stocks' we can add many more meanings. The problem would be compounded if a British business manager and an American business manager were in conversation, because stock to the American would be the shares in a company, whereas common British business usage has stock to mean the contents of the stores or warehouse.

So as far as the message is concerned, choose words that the receiver will not confuse with others and which will be understood. Use his or her language, not yours.

18.6 **The Method**

Self-check

How would you tell a group of sales reps about a new product they will have to sell next month?

- By letter to each one individually?
- By telephone to each one individually?
- Call a meeting of all of them?
- Interview each one separately?

(Five minutes.)

To call a meeting of all the sales reps is the most efficient way of getting the message across and has these points in its favour:

- The sales reps will both hear about the product and see it.
- There will be opportunity to ask and answer questions.
- It is less time-consuming than an individual approach.
- You can guarantee that everyone who should get the message actually receives it.
- It gives the sales reps a chance to meet each other and discuss common problems, and helps to improve motivation.

It must be noted that the other ways of communicating are not necessarily wrong; it is just that the sales conference is probably the best way of getting the message across in this case – even though it may well be more expensive than a letter or series of individual interviews.

There are many different ways of answering the question, How do I get the message across? Messages can be spoken or written; in pictures, in sound or in signs. They can be directed at the receiver's eyes, ears or even the other senses. They may be conducted by an individual using his own skills alone or they may involve the use of technology such as radio and electronic systems. The choice has to be made with care, always keeping the thought in mind, Which has the best chance of success? Some of the main communicating methods need to be looked at in terms of their overall suitability, limitations and dangers to avoid.

Face-to-face communications

It is recognised that the most powerful way of communicating can be the face-to-face method, where the target sees and hears the sender of the message. This can range from a simple interview between a manager and the boss to the company management conference where the managing director may be addressing several hundred managers. Unfortunately many people are not good at communicating via speech, and the potential power of the method is lost (possibly even having the opposite effect of that desired).

Activity

Next time you hear a boring speech, try to determine why it is boring; and when you hear an interesting speech – why is that? The best sources of both types of speech are to be found at the annual conferences of political parties and trade unions.

Some ways of being boring
- Speak about a boring subject.
- Talk at length.
- Use long words and sentences, with a lot of technical jargon.
- Speak in a monotone.
- Speak in the first person: 'I did this, I did that.'
- Avoid humour.
- Try to be pompous.

In addition, if you want to get your audience a bit hostile, tell them that they are wrong, you are right; they know nothing and you know everything.

Some ways of arousing interest and getting support

- Very carefully plan what you intend to do.
- Stand up; speak up; shut up.
- Do the opposite of the things we listed in the how-to-be-boring section.
- Use visual aids if appropriate: pictures, models, a list of key words on a screen, a display of the key numbers.
- Practise.

Activity

Study carefully how the news on television is presented. Time each news item and see just how briefly each subject is handled. Also notice how the technique changes frequently from a picture of the newsreader to a film about the event using a different voice. Diagrams, maps and charts come into use frequently, and numbers quoted are always shown on the screen.

Also listen to the kind of language used (in contrast to the way people being interviewed speak).

Try to learn from the professional communicators.

Written reports

Written reports are valuable where face-to-face contact is impossible, or where the information needs to be studied and given a lot of thought. A poor report, however, quickly becomes a dust-gathering pile of waste paper.

In the last chapter we noted that a great deal of time can be wasted if reports are exceedingly long. Moreover many reports are badly written and the problem of wasted time is therefore compounded, because effort has to be spent translating into a language that can be understood.

A report may simply be an account of what has been going on inside a part of an organisation. It may be a document describing a piece of research – a fact-finding survey for example. Or it may be the result of a problem-solving team, e.g. 'Recommendations for changing the system of bonus payments'.

Brevity is always welcome, especially for narrative reports that simply relate that everything has gone according to plan. Keep these as brief as possible.

With all reports busy managers want to see the conclusions. Make sure they can be found easily and are easily understood. In writing a report, and for that matter a simple memo, be sure to answer the following questions at the outset:

- Who wants it?
- What precisely do they want?
- Why do they want it?

If the answers to these questions are not clear, then no further work should be carried out until they have been answered properly. Thereafter the job is largely one of gathering the facts – background data, specific information on the matter in question, case histories if necessary, interviews and so on. All this information has to be sifted and sorted, leaving out everything irrelevant. The reader should have all the information needed, and no information that is unnecessary.

Having done this the next stage is to design the report itself. Here it is worth bearing in mind the contents of this note which Winston Churchill sent to government departments when he was Prime Minister:

To do our work, we all have to read a mass of papers. Nearly all of them are far too long. This wastes time, while energy has to be spent in looking for the essential points.

I ask my colleagues and their staffs to see to it that their reports are shorter.

i   The aim should be reports which set out the main points in a series of short, crisp paragraphs.

ii If a report relies on detailed analysis of some complicated factors, or statistics, these should be set out in an appendix.

iii Often the occasion is best met by submitting not a full-dress report, but an *aide mémoire* consisting of headings only, which can be expanded orally if needed.

iv Let us have an end of such phrases as these: 'It is also of importance to bear in mind the following considerations...', or 'Consideration should be given to the possibility of carrying into effect...' Most of these woolly phrases are mere padding, which can be left out altogether, or replaced by a single word. Let us not shrink from using the short expressive phrase, even if it is conversational.

Reports drawn up on the lines I propose may at first seem rough as compared with the flat surface of officialese jargon, but the saving in time will be great, while the discipline of setting out the real points concisely will prove an aid to clearer thinking.

W.S.C.
10 Downing Street

Other points on report writing

- Each section should be numbered (see any official government report).
- Break up a long report with simple charts and diagrams.
- Avoid slang or foreign expressions.
- State the precise source of quotations.
- Avoid generalisations unless supported by facts (e.g. 'All multi-nationals are immoral' is not a valid statement. 'Multinationals can wield considerable financial power' *is* valid).
- Watch the 'fog index'. The fog index is a measure of how obscure a piece of writing can be. It is calculated in the following way:

1 Work out the number of sentences in a piece of writing 100 words long.
2 Divide the number of sentences into 100 to get the average number of words per sentence.
3 Count the number of words with more than two syllables.
4 Add the results of 2 and 3 together.
5 Multiply that result by 0.4 to get the fog index.

The lower the index, the clearer the communication. To achieve a rating of 12 would be considered a good, clearly written piece of communication.

Activity

Take two pieces of writing – one from a newspaper and the other from a textbook or technical journal. Calculate the 'fog index' of each and then ask yourself why one is foggier than the other.

Signs and signals

Signs and signals are much more common than may be thought at first. There are signals that people make to each other: deliberate ones such a nudge or a wink, and unconscious ones, body language, whereby our gestures signify things our speech may be hiding.

Most signs, though, are written or painted and created to inform us of something. They are to be found everywhere and sometimes they fail because the receiver has not been given the translation. Every day you will see signs you do not recognise, because the creator has failed to inform what the sign represents. When, however, we do tell people the meaning we have a powerful communications device at our disposal. See, for instance, Figure 18.1 below.

In organisations, signs and symbols are frequently used as an integral part of a control system, to draw the attention of key people to those things that need attention. This may range from a piece of information being underlined or circled to a series of flashing lights on the control panel of a machine.

Fig 18.1   A symbol, coupled with its meaning, makes a powerful message

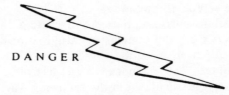

DANGER

Pictures and diagrams

Pictures and diagrams when they look good are a great help in making good communications; poor pictures are a waste of time, money and effort. To be effective they should be:

- clear
- simple
- relevant
- well made

Numbers

In the next chapter the use of numbers will be looked at in more detail, but the general rules mentioned already should be noted: keep them simple, and few. If details have to be shown put these in appendices or supporting papers.

Technological help

Technology can help the communications process in many ways. These days it is common to bundle everything into the phrase 'Information Technology' (IT) and to talk about 'Information Management', being the process of making the technology work in a useful way.

At work, the telephone and the computer are the primary items of technology and nowadays it is increasingly common to find the two linked together in interesting and novel ways to improve communications, both within the organisation and externally.

The telephone's main purpose is to communicate with people who are too far away to be called personally, and the advent of mobile phones theoretically means that soon nobody need ever be out of reach; you will always be able to get in touch with anyone. Moreover, the ability now to leave messages on an answering machine or, when connected to a computer, through 'voice-mail', together with the transmission of written material via facsimile (Fax) equipment, all should help to speed up the transfer of information.

The disadvantages of telephones are that they can make people lazy (phoning next door, for example) and actually waste time and money by unnecessary or over-lengthy calls. The golden rule, at work especially, is *think before you speak*.

The ways in which computers are used these days was hardly dreamed of forty years ago. At first it was believed that the total world-wide market for these machines would run into the thousands, not the millions we have today. Originally, their function was to make a great number of calculations with speed and accuracy – 'electronic data processing'. While this is still an important function, just as important now are their use in word-processing, and in designing anything from buildings and bridges, to kitchens, motorcars and cartoons (Computer-Aided Design: CAD).

Linking computers together and creating networks enables data to be transferred from person to person fast and without the tedium of typing, proof-reading, correcting, copying and physical despatch. Amendments to text are easy, answers to complex questions are more easily handled and such techniques as 'electronic mail' (E-mail) enable messages to be left in a safe way until the recipient can deal with them. We have already seen how the use of networks by supermarkets can enable suppliers to get closer to the consumer, bringing nearer to reality the marketeer's dream.

One extra advantage of networked computers is that access can be gained to large stores of data (databases), theoretically enabling users with the proper authority to obtain the answers to literally any question they may have on any topic.

With access to all this information, two major hazards are apparent:

- If the technology fails, valuable data could be lost.
- Unauthorised access may cause loss or damage ('hackers' and 'bugs', especially).

Technology will therefore continue to:

- speed communications;
- save time;
- avoid the need to travel;
- provide more and better information, very fast.

But its success will depend on the skill of the sender of the information in the first place (or the individual's ability to ask the right question) and also on how the data is interpreted. Undoubtedly by the turn of the century, information technology will have transformed the way we live and work. The manager who wants to be a really effective communicator must know about and be able to use these techniques — and those on the horizon.

Activity

How up-to-date are you on information management and technology? You should know something about the following (if not, see Further Reading):

Information superhighway (or 'Infobahn')
Virtual reality
Expert systems
Artificial intelligence
Neural networks
Internet

18.7 Listening

Most of this chapter has been concerned with the sending side of communications, but it is important never to forget that listening is just as important. Without effective listening there can be no effective communication.

It has been discovered that people forget most of what they have heard within a couple of days. This can be improved by better messages, repeated messages and also by helping the receiver to learn to be a better listener. Among the many ideas for better listening are:

- Concentrate on what is being said, not who is saying it.
- If you do not understand, ask for a repeat if you can.
- Try to concentrate on the meaning of the message (ignore distractions; avoid daydreaming).
- Do not get emotionally involved (it is very easy to be roused to anger or another emotion and miss a key point).
- Remember that thoughts are quicker than words and you can evaluate what is being said without missing anything.
- Do not take many notes – just the key points – and (if important) write them out fully after the speaker has finished.

Review

Look at this memorandum; its 'fog index' is very high and it is an extremely pompous memo, so turn it into a sentence with a very low fog index.

It would be greatly appreciated if a prompt response could be initiated in relation to the requisition dated the 9th inst. regarding the stationery sundries, namely two boxes of small sized paper clips, and that the aforementioned could be dispatched to the undersigned as efficaciously as expedient, since it is becoming increasingly difficult to operate efficiently without the necessary supportive materials.

Do you think there is another better way of communicating the request? (Five minutes.)

A quote to remember

A successful American businessman went to India for three weeks to share with an Indian organisation his experience in a particularly difficult technical area; and his wife accompanied him.

On the way out to the airport at the end of the three weeks he remarked to a friend: 'We didn't bother about television in the hotel, and do you know for the first time in twenty-three years me and the missus actually communicated with each other? What's more I've discovered that she's quite intelligent.'

19 Managing with Numbers: Help or Hindrance?

In this chapter you will learn how to handle numbers more easily and see some of the ways numbers can be used for better management.

You will remember that one of the decisions my Uncle James had to take each week in the shoe shop (see Chapter 1) was the quantity of each type of shoe to order from the warehouse.

Self-check

On the assumption that Uncle James was a fairly successful (and responsible) manager, how do you think he decided on the quantity of each shoe to order?

- Take a guess.
- Stick a pin in a list of numbers.
- Order the same as last week's order.
- Order the same number as were sold last week.
- Look at the trend of sales over a few weeks and order more or less than last week accordingly.

(Five minutes.)

It is most likely that Uncle James would have used the last method to decide on the number of pairs of shoes to order. He would want to see if the demand for each type was rising or falling; if demand was going up he would probably order more than he had ordered the week before. If demand had been falling he would estimate the number of shoes that would be sold and place an order to cover likely demand, bearing in mind the number of shoes already in stock.

Consider Table 19.1, which shows the sales of a particular style of shoe over a five-week period, and also the number of pairs of shoes ordered:

Table 19.1   A re-ordering problem

Week number	1	2	3	4	5	6
Number of pairs of shoes in stock at beginning of the week	0	3	4	3	3	3
Number of pairs of shoes delivered on Monday mornings	10	10	10	13	15	
Number of pairs of shoes sold each week	7	9	11	13	15	
Number of pairs of shoes left on Saturday night	3	4	3	3	3	

Activity

How many shoes should he order for week 6? (Assume that it will be an ordinary week.) (Five minutes.)

The decision, How many shoes to order? depends on the answer to the question, How many shoes will be sold? Looking at the trend, it is easy to see that over the five weeks the number of shoes has risen by two pairs each week. Therefore if fifteen pairs were sold last week, we might expect seventeen pairs to be sold this week.

We cannot of course be certain about this, but the trend suggests seventeen, so if we begin with this number, the next steps are easy:

● we have in the stores three pairs;
● we will sell about seventeen pairs; therefore
● we need to order fourteen pairs for delivery on Monday morning.

If all this happens, at the end of the week we have no shoes of this type left on the shelves. To be safe, though, in case customers come flooding in we ought to have a few pairs up our sleeve and in that case we need to order some extra. How many more than fourteen pairs? There is a fair chance of selling fifteen pairs in total; some chance of selling sixteen; a small possibility of selling seventeen. So order seventeen pairs; after all, if they are not sold, next week's order can be reduced.

This is a simple example of the use of numbers in planning and decision-making. Of course in reality Uncle James would have had many more statistics to help him arrive at his decision, but (if he had been less concerned) he might have used the line of least resistance and said, 'Same as last week.'

Unfortunately many small businesses fail to make the most of their opportunities because they do not spend enough time studying the numbers. Many do not even collect enough numbers to help them get better decisions and control more effectively; they simply collect the minimum.

In the next few pages some of the ways of coming to terms with numbers are explained, so that they can be handled confidently. In addition some techniques are introduced that can help managers be more effective.

19.1 How to Handle Big numbers

In the example above, the numbers that were being used were very small and probably cause no problem, but suppose that the numbers we had been using had been much bigger? Would it have been any more difficult to have arrived at a decision if we had been discussing barrels of beer to a pub? Or gallons of oil to a petrol station? Or gallons of petrol to refine in the oil refineries?

Self-check

What is the difference between a small number and a big number? Everyone knows that numbers 1 to 9 are small, but count up – when do you arrive at a big number?

There is an organisation that had sales in 1993 amounting to £63,350 (net of VAT, etc.). Was this total small? Another firm's sales were £633,500. Was this small? Yet another's were £6,335,000 – obviously considerably larger. Finally there is the sales of Shell, which in 1993 amounted to £63,350 million or (including all the 0s) £63,350,000,000. This is very big indeed compared with nearly every other commercial organisation in the world – but even this is smaller than the sales of General Motors, the biggest of them all.

The fact is that numbers are all relative in size. To speak about big or small alone is irrelevant; what is important is the relative size of the number, and that signifies the need to make some kind of comparison. This point was fully discussed in Chapter 3, in looking at the question of how to analyse the strengths and weaknesses of an organisation (pages 38–44).

So the first rule in handling numbers is:

● Do not be put off if the number seems particularly large.

Many people eliminate all but the three or four digits from the left to make it easy to add up and compare: so that Shell's turnover becomes about £63 billion, the distance from London to Chicago is about 4,000 miles, and the population of Great Britain is about 56 million. This is known as rounding off and means it is only necessary to count to the last penny if you are a banker, an accountant or a cashier actually handling cash. In planning, decision-making and often in control it is unnecessary to go into the finest detail.

The second rule about numbers is:

● Do not look at numbers in isolation; compare them with others.

As we saw in Chapter 3, only by comparing can you begin to draw any conclusions about a number, and often it helps if the numbers can be converted into ratios and percentages.

19.2 The Numbers Game Reviewed

In Chapter 14 there was a chart illustrating how a control system works (Figure 14.1, page 218). That chart might be summarised into three stages, and at each point numbers are used extensively – see Figure 19.1.

Numbers in planning

● To collect information about trends in the environment. This involves the technique of forecasting – looking ahead to see what you think is going to happen.
● To assess the present position of the organisation and its strengths and weaknesses. This involves the technique of appraisal.
● To calculate where the organisation will be if the present strategies, policies and activities continue; another forecasting requirement.
● To help evaluate proposed alternative courses of action. This is the stage in planning where a number of strategies or options are available. Numbers can sometimes help to eliminate the poor alternatives – and even point to the best. Moreover some questions have to use numbers: how much to raise prices (or taxes or rates); whether to invest in certain projects; how much to borrow and so on.

Fig 19.1   The three key managerial tasks

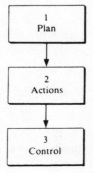

- To quantify the organisation's plans – the creation of budgets and standards, after the decisions have been made as a result of the previous point above.

Numbers related to actions

Every action inside an organisation creates a number. Many of these numbers have to be recorded properly, in particular numbers involving money. There is, for limited companies, the legal need to keep records. In addition tax people and the VAT inspectors need to see properly kept books of account as they are termed (if these are unavailable it is easy to pay too much tax).

Traditionally, keeping proper records of transactions involving money was for four purposes:

- to prevent fraud;
- to detect fraud (if it happened);
- to work out the amount of profit on a deal;
- to decide how to share out profits

All these are still valid reasons for keeping proper records, but in addition nowadays many records are kept that are purely for the benefit of the managers – information to help them manage more effectively. Some of it is related to money and profits but some of it is purely statistical: details of volumes and quantities made or sold; hours worked; employees hired; numbers of lorries and cars, and so on.

Most of the numbers are needed by managers, but there is a danger, especially with computer-based information systems, of producing too much information and drowning the poor manager in a flood of numbers.

Numbers for control

We have seen how control systems work in Chapters 14 and 15; they are the joining together of planned numbers and actual numbers. The joining process produces variances, and you will remember that the really important thing about information in this area is the need to identify significant variations, and associated with this was the idea of reporting the exceptional variances only. Therefore, the third rule in handling numbers is:

- Wherever possible simplify, by reducing the numbers of figures shown to those that are really important.

The principles that were set out in the last chapter are important here. If detailed statistics are likely to be needed show these in an appendix or in supplementary papers.

19.3 **How to Handle a Complicated Page of Numbers**

- Ask if it really is anything to do with you, i.e. how does it help?
- Ask someone (preferably the creator) to explain it.
- Identify key words, especially 'total', 'forecast', 'actual', 'estimate'.
- Underline, in bright colours if you can, key numbers, especially totals and significant variances. (Circle adverse variances in red, favourable ones in green.)
- Transfer the important data on to another piece of paper, simplifying as you go (getting rid of the pennies and rounding off).
- If the table is a list of numbers, a good idea is to look at the middle numbers (this is usually called the 'median'), and the ones a quarter the way down (from the top) and a quarter the way up (from the bottom). These are known as the upper and lower quartiles respectively.

To calculate the extremes in a range of results ignore the top and the bottom result – they could be exceptional for many reasons. Use instead the results two, three or four away from the extreme ends (depending on the size of the list). For example, listing all the numbers from 1 to 23: 12 is the median; the quartiles are 6 and 18; and 2 and 22 represent the range.

Activity

Here is a list of the times taken by different trains to cover the journey from London to Preston. This list has been arranged in order of speed. What is the median time? What are the quartiles and the range of results (excluding the extremes)? (Ten minutes.)

(*Hours and minutes*)			
2.31	2.39	3.01	4.02
2.32	2.47	3.03	
2.38	2.50	3.05	
2.39	2.58	3.16	
2.39	3.00	3.18	
2.39	3.00	3.49	

It will be noticed that the list of numbers shown above has been split up into groups of three. This is simply a device for making reading and calculating easier. The median time works out at 2 hours 58 minutes, and if we ignore the two fastest times and the two slow times the range of times varies from 2 hours 38 minutes to 3 hours 18 minutes.

The quartiles are (approximately) 2 hours 39 minutes and 3 hours 5 minutes.

19.4 **What is Average?**

Most people, if asked to calculate the average journey time from London to Preston, would do it like this:

- Add together all the journey times in the list (to save time it adds up to 3,386 minutes for the nineteen journeys).
- Divide the total figure of 3,386 minutes by the total number of journeys. This gives a figure of 178 minutes per journey or 2 hours 58 minutes per journey.

This, we would say, is the average journey time. Technically it is known as the 'arithmetic mean' and is very useful for making comparisons between activities – from bowling and batting at cricket, to the efficiency of different salesmen, to the amount of money spent on books by different education authorities.

The arithmetic mean is not the only way of calculating an average, the other common one (there are several others) being the 'median', which we used earlier to find the middle of the range. These two measures of average are usually fairly close together; the choice depends on what you want to do with the average.

19.5 **Using Numbers in Forecasting**

The point has already been made that since the future is uncertain, forecasts are purely estimates and cannot be guaranteed. However, as we saw with Uncle James in his shoe shop, some attention to the numbers helps to produce a more likely forecast than if he had merely stuck a pin in a list of numbers.

Activity

If you do not believe this last statement, try out this little exercise. Make a note of the temperature that is reported in your newspaper for a particular city or town and keep your record going over a three-week period. At the end of this period look over the numbers you have collected and then make a forecast for the next day. At the same time pick a number at random from a list of all the possible temperatures (say 28°F to 75°F for somewhere in the British Isles). To do the random picking properly, all the numbers should be put in a hat or a box, or by some similar method.

Once you have the actual result, make the comparison. Unless you are very unlucky, your estimate should be fairly close to the actual temperature, and the random number will be far away (if the random number is exactly correct you are exceedingly lucky).

A similar exercise can be done forecasting a cricket or rugby team's score, using from 1 to 400 for the cricket score range and 3 to 80 for the rugby score range.

At one end of the forecasting scale, therefore, there is the 'shot in the dark' approach and at the other there are a number of very sophisticated techniques using computers that have been shown to produce much better forecasts. Between them is the technique called 'extrapolation', which is what Uncle James was doing in his shoe shop.

Extrapolation involves looking at a trend and trying to calculate what will happen next. Estimates made by extrapolation can be obtained in several ways; drawing graphs is one of the simplest and using various mathematical formulae another. Extrapolation is widely used and can produce good forecasts.

The technique which is proving even more useful these days is 'regression analysis': an excellent example of modern scientific management at work, and particularly useful in sales and profit forecasting.

Regression is a mathematical exercise. It involves relating a number of factors to whatever it is we are trying to forecast. A simple regression is where there is only one factor affecting the item being forecasted. For example if we say that sales of ice-cream are dependent on the temperature, we can calculate historically how closely the two move together. If there is more than one variable affecting sales, the term used is 'multiple regression'.

The problem with multiple regressions is that the greater the number of variables, the further back into history you have to go to get enough information to be able to test whether the variables really are relevant. The more information you have, the more involved the sums; to do the job properly a computer is needed.

Moreover it is necessary to get estimates of the variables that have been found to affect sales, costs or whatever it is we are forecasting. Often these are economic estimates, and various organisations specialise in making them, as we have seen.

Regression has to be used with care because it depends on the knowledge and understanding of the manager to identify the important factors that affect his operations. No amount of sophisticated computer analysis can generate good forecasts if understanding of the environment is poor.

19.6 Using Numbers for Making Decisions

Many decisions, especially in business, relate ultimately to money. They are concerned with costs, revenue or profit, or all three. Sometimes it is possible to calculate with certainty the alternatives, so that for instance if we buy coffee in one shop it will cost us £1.99; if we buy it in another it will cost us £2.08. The numbers give us the answer and the decision is easy.

Unfortunately many decisions are taken under conditions of great doubt, where the outcome is uncertain.

Activity

Turn back to the problem about Len's Launderette on pages 150–1 and refresh your memory on his dilemma.

Len had three courses of action:

- Do nothing.
- Borrow and buy the second launderette.
- Invite the brother-in-law in and buy the second launderette.

Unfortunately the amount of profit that could be made might have been anything, and different courses of action would produce different amounts of profit at different times. Len was dealing in probabilities – and in such circumstances the technique that can help is called 'decision analysis'.

The steps of decision analysis are as follows:

Step 1. List all the possible courses of action.
Step 2. List all the possible results (usually known as outcomes).

To take a simple example, Walter Bottle had £100,000 in the bank, earning 8 per cent interest. One day he saw for sale a small country inn costing exactly £100,000 and which would produce a profit of 10 per cent; guaranteed.

Self-check

Which would you have done: left your money in the bank or bought the inn (assuming you liked the idea)?

Obviously on purely financial grounds you would be better off buying the inn. But suppose the result was guaranteed only if there was no competition: if someone built another inn nearby Walter calculated that the profit would be nearer 5 per cent.

Self-check

Which course of action would you take now?

This question is not as easy to answer as the previous one. The reason is that there is a possibility of being worse off by investing in the project. So,

Step 3. Set out all the alternatives:

Events	Do nothing	Invest in the project
No competition	8% = £8K*	20% = £20K
Competition	8% = £8K	5% = £5K

* K is shorthand for a thousand.

This is sometimes called a 'payoff table', because it shows all the possible alternative results.

At this point either a decision can be made or more information and calculations can be carried out. Therefore,

Step 4(a). Make a decision now, by choosing an action based on what you think is the most likely outcome, e.g. I think there will be no competition, therefore the best course of action is to invest in the project.

Another way of making the decision now would be to select the course of action which gives you the 'best-worst' outcome. This means that if the money is left in the bank, the worst possible outcome is 8 per cent. Alternatively if the money is invested in the project the worst possible outcome is 5 per cent. The best-worst outcome is 8 per cent, so the decision is: leave the money in the bank.

This method tries to avoid the worst possible results, but since it concentrates on the worst possible in all cases, it ignores the great potential that exists.

Step 4(b). Assess probabilities.

This is where personal judgement and skill enter into the picture, and the way of approaching this step is to follow these three rules:

• Each possible outcome should be given a probability number of a scale of 0 to 1.0.
• If it is impossible (if you think it cannot happen) give it a probability rating of 0.
• All the possible outcomes must add up to 1.0 (by definition, one outcome must happen, and after the event all the other possible outcomes are 0).

For example in horse-racing the odds are another way of assessing the probability of a horse winning. If there are four horses we could have a list like this:

Horse	Probability of winning	
A	0.3	
B	0.1	
		Total probabilities = 1.0
C	0.4	
D	0.2	

A dead-cert theoretically would have a probability of 1.0 and all the others 0.0!

In the country-inn investment decision example Walter decided that the probability of competition was 0.2. Therefore the chances of no competition were 0.8.

Step 5. Calculate the *expected value* (EV) of each outcome.

This simply means multiplying the probabilities by the appropriate outcomes in each case. Our payoff table can be expanded to show how this looks:

	Do nothing	*Invest in project*	*Probability*
No competition	£8K	£20K	0.8
Competition	£8K	£ 5K	0.2

The calculations to get the expected values are:

1 *Do nothing*

		Outcome		Probability		
No competition	=	£8,000	×	0.8	=	£6,400
Competition	=	£8,000	×	0.2	=	£1,600
Expected value (EV)						= £8,000

2 Invest in project

		Outcome		Probability		
No competition	=	£20,000	×	0.8	=	£16,000
Competition	=	£ 5,000	×	0.2	=	£ 1,000
Expected value (EV)						= £17,000

The size of the expected values gives the clue as to which course of action to take. The figures are not guaranteed, however, and Walter realised:

- that the expected values were only as good as his probability estimates; and
- he could still get the worst outcome. (He has to ask himself if he is willing to accept the risk – could he afford the worst outcome?)

These two points have to be remembered in all investment decision exercises.

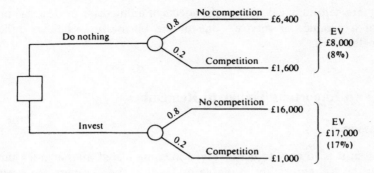

Fig 19.2   Example of a decision-tree

Decision trees

A common way of presenting decision analysis is by way of a diagram. Using the example that has just been discussed, the diagram known as a 'decision tree' is illustrated in Figure 19.2.

19.7 Other Decision-Making Aids

A whole range of techniques similar to the ones that have been described are available to help managers make better decisions. What they have in common is that they adopt mathematical techniques to help solve problems, but none of them can take the decision; that remains the manager's job.

Techniques such as linear programming, critical path analysis, and others in what is sometimes called 'operational research', are all part of the weapons that can be used nowadays. Their use is made considerably easier with computers – indeed many are impossible without.

Linear programming is particularly useful in production planning where there are many products that can be made on many different machines with different costs and rates of production.

Critical path analysis is used on projects like buildings and ships where a hold-up, such as waiting for a component or for a job to be finished, can cost a great deal of money.

In the financial world the technique called 'discounted cash flow' (DCF) is recognised to be an invaluable method for capital budgeting, i.e. for assessing the likely profitability of an investment over the life of that investment (see page 233).

'Break-even analysis' is another useful financial technique that helps managers appreciate just what level of business has to be achieved before the firm makes any profit at all. This and the related technique FO 'marginal costing' are helpful in calculating the effects of an increase or decrease in the price of a product or service – one of the businessman's most difficult, regular decisions.

19.8 Two Important Things to Remember

Keep it simple

Very often it is so easy to get involved in complicated mathematics simply because the techniques are available or because the numbers are given in detail. Sometimes a few quick simple calculations will give the answer, rounding off wherever possible. For example, a few years ago, I filled up my car with petrol in Italy. The cost was 53,808 lire which seemed an awful lot of money. The other facts about the situation were: the price of petrol was 1,121 lire per litre; at the time there were 2,462 lire to £1; there are 4.546 litres per gallon and I had travelled 294 miles since the last fill-up.

Self-check

In situations like this it is easy to panic; was there any cause for panic in this case? (five minutes.)

With the aid of a calculator, the problem is not hard to solve, but if you only have a scrap of paper and a pencil it is vital to keep it simple:

1 *Decide what you want to find out. Namely*
   (a) The total bill in £s
   (b) The price per gallon in £s
   (c) How many miles per gallon?

2 *Take each calculation separately.*
   (a) The cost was roughly 55 thousand lire and there were roughly 2,500 lire to the £. So the cost of the petrol was about £22.
   (b) Petrol costs L1,100 a litre. As there about 4.5 litres to a gallon, the price of fuel works out at about L5,000 or £2 a gallon.
   (c) Since the fuel cost me £22 and a gallon cost £2, my car had used eleven gallons of petrol since the last fill-up, some three hundred miles before. This works out at almost 28 mpg.

These rough answers were near enough in the circumstances. If I had tried to do all these sums in detail by hand, I would still be doing them now and the chances of making a mistake are very high.

Do not let the system take over: a case with a moral

Once there was a firm which sold sheds. It was called Gardenomes Ltd. Somebody worked out that the overheads of the firm (rent, rates, advertising, etc.) were going to be £52,000 in the following year, or £1,000 a week. Usually they sold 1,000 sheds a week, so they added £10 to the cost of each shed to pay for the overheads and another £10 for profit. At the end of the first ten weeks, they discovered that they had sold only 800 sheds instead of 1,000. In an attempt to get more money to pay for the 'lost' overheads and profit, they decided to put the price up by £4 a shed. Unfortunately in the next ten weeks they sold only 700 sheds, so they put the price up again in an attempt to recover the 'lost' money.

Self-check

- Can you see what went wrong?
- Can you guess what they did next?

The only thing that went wrong was that the price increase caused a drop in sales.

At this point the system started to run the business. The alternatives were only two (as far as they could see): cut overheads, or raise prices again just a little to compensate for the drop in volume.

The effect of raising prices even more would be to cut volume further. Trimming overhead costs may occasionally be a useful exercise if it gets rid of waste, but it is dangerous if it starts to affect essential services.

The point is that the firm, by sticking to a rigid system, became locked into a vicious circle; the system had taken over. The danger for all organisations is to adopt techniques which become a normal part of operating practice and then to regard them as unchangeable. All systems must be reviewed constantly to ensure that their function is still useful.

19.9 Scientific Management

We introduced the idea of scientific management in Chapter 1 (page 12) with the work of F. W. Taylor. Taylor was concerned with efficiency and with improving the way things were done. His conviction that there is a best way of doing things has become the basis of scientific management. Today the widespread availability of computers and calculators means that more and more information can be collected, stored and processed. This has helped to produce one of the great steps forward in management, namely the technique of model-building.

In the natural sciences, experiments are common. They are often carried out to discover what happens if certain acts occur. If we pour water on a lighted match the light goes out; if we pour petrol on it we have an explosion. In management, like many social sciences such as psychology, the scope for experiment is limited. It is not possible for a company to change its prices every day until it finds the best price, partly because it is practically impossible, partly because of the huge range of prices that could be established and partly because the economic conditions outside and inside the firm change too fast for comparable measurement.

To overcome this, model-building is now growing in importance. Sometimes these may be physical models such as tiny bridges, ships or aircraft, but often they are built entirely of numbers or in code. In the same way, chess (and every other boardgame) can be played without a board and pieces, just using a specially built code.

Models try to help the manager understand better what is going on in the environment of the organisation and what will happen if, inside it, he takes certain courses of action. A decision to drill for oil in the North Sea is such a problem – wisely not done on the back of an envelope, but requiring a lengthy and painstaking analysis of many variables.

A quote to remember
In a large-volume mass production industry a variance of one half per cent in selling price can make a difference of a million or more pounds profit per year. We will pay a very high salary indeed to any economist who can measure the elasticity of demand for a particular motorcar within these limits.

(S. J. Elliott, former finance director, Ford Motor Co; quoted at the BIM Conference, 1960)

Part VII
Management of Tomorrow

Tomorrow's world looks like being an even more complex place than it is today, and it looks like change is going to take place at an even faster rate. Our times have been referred to as turbulent – an age of uncertainty and discontinuity. For the manager, what skills are needed to cope with all this? The same skills as always but more of them and more refined? Or are some new ones needed too?

20 The Package of Skills for Tomorrow's Manager

This final chapter draws together some of the ideas that have already been presented about the nature of the managerial task, and presents some further thoughts. It discusses what different authorities have said, and are saying, about the particular characteristics that managers need in order to be successful themselves and help develop successful organisations.

The first chapter opened up the world of the manager, and it could be seen that there are many, many elements in it. Towards the end of the chapter (page 15) a list was made of all the different activities that a successful manager has to get involved in, and many of these general managerial skills have been discussed. Armed with this knowledge, therefore, it is now time to look at the attributes or competences required of a successful manager in a little more detail, to find out what is important today and to try to assess what will be important in the future.

Many lists of attributes have been drawn up in an attempt to describe the perfect manager. One such list of attributes is set out below:

Knowledge of
- their own area of specialisation
- the organisation
- the sector of the economy (or society)
- the environment of the organisation
- management techniques and principles
- other areas of specialisation that are relevant

Ability to
- solve problems ⎫
- take decisions ⎬ analytical skills
- relate to people ⎭
- build team spirit ⎫
- communicate ⎪
- persuade and negotiate ⎬ social skills
- delegate ⎪
- lead ⎭

Have personal qualities of
- emotional resilience (to cope with stress)
- creativity (some good ideas)
- mental agility
- positive thinking

Self-check

The eighteen attributes of successful managers that have been listed above are not a comprehensive list, but intended more as a way of getting you thinking about what makes a successful manager. You may therefore want to add some more to the list. Try the following experiment:

- Alongside each attribute place a number between 0 and 5 according to how important you think the attribute is; 0 meaning totally unimportant, and 5 signifying vital.
- Add up the score (the maximum is 90).
- Alongside each attribute place a number between 0 and 5 signifying how you yourself score; 0 meaning that you have no knowledge or skill in that area and 5 meaning that you are an expert in it.
- Total your own score.

SCORING

If your personal score exceeded the first total, then you need not read any more of this book.

If you scored more than 50 then you could classify yourself as a relatively successful manager.

A score of less than 50 is normal, and of course a school-leaver is not likely to score more than a manager of ten years' experience. The longer people have been managers, the higher should be their scores.

One attribute which was left out of this list and which should not be forgotten is that relating to learning. The fact that every individual's score in this little game is lower than the maximum indicates that some learning is needed. The view is that no manager must stop making a conscious effort to learn, partly because no one's skills and knowledge can ever be complete, even in a world that is standing still, partly because of the way knowledge is growing so fast and partly because of the speed of change.

The problem can be viewed from the angle of a manager who wants to recruit someone to take over a top management job. This could be in a school, a hospital, a bank or in a manufacturing concern; the problem is the same: namely, the attributes needed to run the organisation today are identifiable, but will they be the same thirty years from now? To answer this, we need to refer to some famous people in management and to see what they have said about the features of a successful manager – in the past, now and tomorrow.

20.1 **Henri Fayol Again**

The five functions of management have been adequately discussed, but there are two other aspects of management that Fayol mentioned that must be looked at separately. They are his 'principles of management' and his ideas on the qualities and training of managers.

Activity

For each principle, and each quality, ask yourself how far you think each is applicable (and how important), both in your own situation and generally these days.

Fayol identified fourteen principles, or guidelines, and he emphasised that these are not rigid but have to be adapted to suit the particular needs of the situation.

- Division of work – the need to specialise.
- Authority and responsibility – the manager's official status and his personal authority.
- Discipline – firm but fair.
- Unity of command – one boss to give the orders.
- Unit of direction – everyone pulling the same way.
- Subordination of individual interest to general interest – the group's needs come first.
- Remuneration – pay must be fair.
- Centralisation – the extent to which authority is delegated.
- Chain of authority – must be maintained (unless it would cause harm).
- Order – 'a place for everything and everything in its place', e.g. the organisation chart and statements of areas of responsibility.
- Equity – kindliness and justice by managers help to produce loyalty from staff.
- Stability of tenure of staff – job security.
- Initiative – thinking out and action on ideas, 'one of the keenest satisfactions of man'. Let subordinates exercise it.
- *Esprit de corps* – teamwork builds up the strength of an organisation or a group.

Qualities needed in a manager

- physical: healthy, vigorous;
- mental: ability to understand and learn, judgement, mental vigour, adaptability;
- moral: firmness, acceptance of responsibility, initiative, loyalty, tact;

- general education: good general knowledge;
- special knowledge: for the work;
- experience.

Activity

Have you come across many people with all these qualities?

Fayol also stressed the importance of managerial training, 'steady, methodical training of all employees and at all levels', and made the point that a manager should not ignore his responsibility for his own training.

Interestingly F. W. Taylor had something to say about training too:

It becomes the duty of those on the management side to deliberately study the character, nature and performance of each workman...The scientific selection of the workman and his development is not a single act; it goes on from year to year and is the subject of continual study on the part of management.

20.2 F. W. Taylor

F. W. Taylor's book *The Principles of Scientific Management*, published in 1911, was written for the following reasons:

First, to point out...the great loss which the country is suffering through inefficiency in almost all our daily acts.
Second, to try to convince the reader that the remedy for this inefficiency lies in systematic management, rather than in searching for some unusual and extraordinary man.
Third, to prove that the best management is a true science, resting upon clearly defined laws, rules and principles, as a foundation...and to convince the reader that whenever these principles are correctly applied, results must follow which are truly astounding.

20.3 Blake's Grid

Blake's grid is a common name for a technique called 'the managerial grid' which was developed by Dr Robert Blake and Dr Jane Mouton in the early 1960s. The grid's function is concerned with the development of organisations through the development of individual managers and it is based on the idea that management has two concerns: the concern for people and the concern for production (although the word 'production' should not be taken literally, but signifies the job to be done). The grid itself is a simple chart, marked off in squares – see Figure 20.1.

The numbers signify the extent of a manager's concern. A very low concern is signified by number 1, and a very high level of concern by number 9.

All managers can be placed on the grid somewhere and five distinct basic styles can be identified from it:

1,1. Signifies a style where minimum effort is put into getting the work done, and just enough to keep the organisation going.

9,1. Here the emphasis is on getting the job done, and not paying much attention to human factors.

1,9. Here the primary concern is people, creating a good atmosphere and good conditions.

5,5. This is a balancing point – some concern for both factors.

9,9. In this extreme situation not only is the organisation geared to satisfying the needs of people, but at the same time the job gets done. The

Fig 20.1   Blake's grid

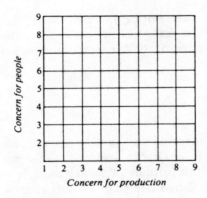

Concern for production

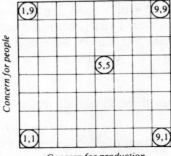

Concern for production

aims and objectives of individuals and the organisation are very similar or, as the jargon puts it, there is a high degree of goal congruence (which means the same thing!).

Activity

Where do you put yourself on the grid? Where do you place some other people you know well?

20.4 Chester Barnard

One of the things that Chester Barnard said was that management needs a high degree of intelligence. He said that to deal with all the many complications of business, considerable ability in logical reasoning and analysis is vital. He also said that the really effective manager is one who is continually asking the question: what can I contribute to help the effectiveness of the organisation I work for?

Remember, Barnard was writing in 1938. Since then complexity of organisations has grown as fast as (if not faster than) the growth in their size. If it was a true statement in 1938, how much more important will it be in 1998?

20.5 Peter Drucker

No evaluation of the managerial task would be complete without reference to the contribution that Peter Drucker has made to the practice of management. In 1964 at the British Institute of Management he made a speech to which we have already referred (see page 26). His address was called 'The Effective Executive' and in it he made the following remarks:

> It is amazing how great the differences are between one man in an executive position and another. There is not much difference in ability or intelligence, but one man gets things done and another never gets anything done... I believe that effectiveness is neither an ability nor a talent. It is a habit, a practice.

Drucker went on to discuss three things all effective managers have in common:

- They understand the importance of managing time, especially in relation to decision-making.

- They accept responsibility for their own contribution, and for acquiring adequate knowledge, training and education in management, and 'whatever else one needs to know in the major disciplines and in their approaches to the job of building and running that terribly complicated institution, that terribly complicated structure, a modern business or any modern organisation'.
- Effective people look for strength in others and build on it. Everybody has weaknesses and the manager's job is to neutralise them. The key question is, What can a man do?

More recently Drucker has commented that the manager of tomorrow will have to do much the same things as today, but will have to tackle them with more knowledge and more thought. But in addition there will be some changes, especially in the public service (hospitals, schools, government agencies, etc.), where a more systematic approach to management will take place.

Two areas of change will be in industrial relations and in the social responsibility of organisations; in both these, managers will have to take the lead and show much more concern.

20.6 **The Systems Manager**

The use of the word 'systematic' in the last but one paragraph is important because it is referring to a way of managing organisations that is becoming increasingly important, namely the systems approach. The word 'system' has been used a number of times in this book, especially in relation to control and information.

The most appropriate way of explaining what is meant by 'systems' is to consider the way in which the parts of a living body can be described; such terms as the nervous system, the digestive system and the circulatory system are all familiar. They are the names given to essential functions of the body; the body being the total system. In the same way, organisations can be described as systems and contain many subsystems on which the success of the whole depends.

However, unlike the human body, an organisation's systems can be of any shape, size or form, and can work in many different ways. Some are better developed than others; control systems are well understood and there is general agreement as to their essentials. However, many other systems are less well developed and completely absent in some cases. For example it is believed that many organisations do not have any regular system for evaluating the environment – or even analysing their own internal strengths and weaknesses.

The role of management can be described as being to make sure that there are sufficient systems within the organisation to make it work, and that the systems are efficient so that the corporate body stays healthy.

Essential ingredients in the development of good systems are good communications channels and information systems because, as in the human body, all the subsystems are linked to each other. If they do not know what is going on in other parts, the whole body falls ill. Already in many organisations, managers are using computer-based systems as a normal part of their day-to-day work. In the near future we shall see the advent of so-called 'expert systems' which will be of enormous help to managers, especially for decision-making. These systems will provide the manager with all the information needed in his area of expertise at the touch of a button.

Some of the dangers of systems have already been highlighted: the silly system that helps nobody and hinders everyone; and the organisation that is run for the benefit of the system. There is, however, one other problem that needs to be emphasised, namely that of inflexibility, and this is a problem that will grow as the rate of change accelerates. A great deal of effort is put into designing a major system within an organisation, and the temptation is always there to preserve it even though it may have outlived its usefulness. Flexibility in the design of systems is likely to be of considerable importance in the future, and to this end the coming of desktop computers and similar devices is timely.

Activity

Consider the ways in which you do the following things, and the alternative systems. Have you changed any of them in the last twelve months, and if so why?

- The system you use to pay your bills.
- Your system of shopping.
- How you get to your place of work/study/leisure activity.
- Your way of working/studying.

(Twenty minutes.)

The answers to these questions should give you practice in identifying systems. Changes were made because circumstances changed and as an individual you found it more convenient to do something differently. The alternative ways of paying gas and electricity bills provide excellent examples of flexible systems: there are six ways of paying each and you choose the best at the time.

Activity

Something to think about: Are the systems in the organisation you know best as flexible as those you have just been considering?

20.7 **The Futuristic Manager**

The following quotation comes from the book *The Management of Change* by Basil and Cook (McGraw-Hill, 1974, page 131), which has already been quoted:

> The ratio of managers to workers will increase to handle the shift in the management orientation from the routine manipulation of material objects to the creation of ideas and the motivation of individuals to implement such ideas. Reflection and diagnosis will replace action as the prime activity of the manager.

The authors go on to state their belief that the successful manager of the future will have to encourage dissent, tolerate conflict and be willing to accept new ideas and new ways of working. Moreover they consider that the team will have a much more important role in solving problems than it does today. In his most recent book, Alvin Toffler (*The Adaptive Corporation*, Pan Books, 1985, page 97) considers that organisations of the future will require people who can learn very fast – to be able to understand novel situations and problems – and have imagination – to be able to invent new solutions.

These views echo many of the ideas, theories and beliefs that have been quoted in this book. Some of them are debatable and indeed are being debated at length.

Activity

Join in the debate: A great deal is being said and written about tomorrow's managers and their job. You have now to make up your mind how far you think these views will solve the long-term problems of the organisations you know.

Recently Sir Peter Parker, former Chairman of British Rail, writing in *Management Today* (March 1994) on 'The Shape of Leaders to Come', asserts:

> So what are some of the elements that will be going into the magic-mix of leadership as we turn the century? How the elements mix will depend on circumstances. There are good attacking generals and good retreating generals but generals with a two-way stretch – Field Marshall Alexander from world war two for instance – are exceptional. But whatever the circumstances, I see that the star of any managerial leader rising in the future will be five-pointed. He or she will be:
>
> • a risk-taking professional, recognisable perhaps by a business degree, certainly by experience;

- an educator and team builder, an exponent of 'the learning organisation';
- an internationalist in the global markets. A man or woman of the world;
- a political animal – interested in the efficiency of government, as any efficient government high-tech society should be interested in business;
- a citizen, sharing with other citizens at work the concerns of the community as a whole – the social priorities of the environment and unemployment.

...A leader better listen.

Contrast those comments with the remarks of Lord Weinstock, managing director of GEC, writing about British industry (*The Guardian*, 19 November 1980):

the proper duty of industrial managers is to improve the efficiency of their own businesses for the benefit of customers, shareholders and employees, and ultimately the whole community...We must discourage the false belief that there is a single magic formula which, once imposed, would produce a stunning improvement in British industry...we have had plenty of these *vade mecums* [handbooks or books of rules] – nationalization, incomes policy, no tax, more (or fewer) non-executive directors, more (or fewer) engineers on boards, two-tier boards, co-operative ownership, inflation accounting – you name it, someone has recommended it.

But none of them lifts from industrial managers their responsibility to make and sell enough products acceptable to customers at proper margins which allow them to maintain and improve the prospects of their companies.

Lord Weinstock goes on to discuss the importance of raising productivity and generating adequate returns on capital, and he continues:

The effort to improve communications within companies...must continue for many years before it will have the chance to generate the necessary extension of understanding by the different specialists in the business of the needs of the business as a whole – whether the specialists be shop floor workers, design engineers, accountants or salesmen...

In the field of job training, it is in this country the largest companies who shoulder the main burden of responsibility. They are going to have to respond more efficiently to the quicker obsolescence of individual skills if the advancing parts of industry are not to be strangled by constant shortages of properly trained people for particular jobs.

Activity

Something to think about: How far do you consider Lord Weinstock's remarks are just as applicable to management outside industry?

Finally, an article appeared in 1980 in the *Financial Times*, on the management page, entitled 'The Manager as a Paragon of All Virtues' (26 September 1980). The article reported the results of an exercise carried out by a team of leading European and American businessmen and academics to investigate 'management and management education in a world of changing expectations', under the joint auspices of the European Foundation for Management Development and the American Assembly of Collegiate Schools of Business. The picture that emerges of the manager of the future is that he will be a diplomat, a 'Renaissance-man', a decision-maker, a negotiator, a persuader, a consensus-builder, a co-ordinator, and a strategic planner. These virtues will all be necessary because: 'While there will still be concern for the economic and technological factors, there will be much greater concern than in the past for the political, social and psychological impact of the organisation.' The report also comments:

> Ten years ago chief executives were mainly concerned with internal problems, spending 1–15 per cent of their time on external activities; today some were spending 50–75 per cent of their time on external activities... The manager has traditionally been thought of as sitting at the centre of a circle, directing all the various activities of the organisation from within it; today he sits on the periphery, on its edge, dealing with the outside world while trying to keep an eye on what goes on inside the circle.

Activity

Something to think about: Do you think that all this is true of the managers, invented and real, mentioned in this book? Such characters as Uncle James in his shoe shop, Len with the launderette, Bert and his buses, the owner of Daisy Cycles, John Brown and Spring Clamps; and of course such top managers as Lord Weinstock as well as all the other thousands of managers in business and in the public service?

Further Reading

Most of these books are easily available in bookshops or through local libraries.

Chapter 1

Peter F. Drucker, *Management* (Pan Books, 1979): A book that ranges far and wide, containing further thoughts and ideas on most of the topics covered in this book.

Chapters 2 to 5

John Argenti, *Systematic Corporate Planning* (Allen & Unwin, 1971) contains a very readable section on objectives and planning generally.

Igor H. Ansoff, *Corporate Strategy* (Penguin, 1968) goes into the same subject in greater depth.

John Sizer, *An Insight into Management Accounting* (Penguin, 1991) is useful if you want to find out more about profit and profitability.

Chapter 6

To go deeper into organisations and their development, you have to look to some very serious books. One such (but stimulating and becoming a classic) is Alfred D. Chandler, *Strategy and Structure* (MIT Press, 1962).

Two books by Charles Handy should be referred to:

Understanding Organisations (Penguin Books, 1976) and *The Gods of Management* (Souvenir Press, 1991).

A British view about managing strategic change will be found in *Successful Change Strategies* by Bernard Taylor (Director Books, 1994).

Chapters 7 to 10

A good starter on marketing is Martin Christopher, Malcolm McDonald and Gordon Wills, *Introducing Marketing* (Pan Books, 1980).

Basic reading on production and operations would include R. Wild, *Production – Principles and Techniques* (Holt, Rinehard & Winston, 1979).

On personnel and industrial relations, two helpful books are P. Hackett, *Success in Management: Personnel* (John Murray, second edition 1985) and Christopher Brewster, *Understanding Industrial Relations* (Pan Books, 1984).

A recent addition to managing the human resource is M. Armstrong, *Strategies for Human Resource Management* (Kogan Page, 1992).

On the finance side, see John Sizer's book mentioned above. Also, Roger Oldcorn, *Accounting for Managers* (Routledge, 1993).

The Boston Consulting Group technique was reviewed in detail in the *Financial Times*, 11, 13 and 16 November 1981.

Chapter 11

There are masses of books on motivation. If you want to pursue this topic, try Victor Vroom and Edward L. Deci (eds), *Management and Motivation* (Penguin, 1979).

Leadership is well-covered by John Adair, with several titles.

Chapter 12

A nice book on decision-making and problem-solving is John Adair, *Effective Decision Making* (Pan Books, 1985).

Chapter 13

If you have to manage change, a useful aid is D. C. Basil and I. Cook, *The Management of Change* (McGraw-Hill, 1974). Sadly, now out of print!

Chapters 14 and 15

More information on control will be found in the book by John Sizer mentioned above, particularly budgetary control. Similarly most texts on operations and production management contain sections on control.

Chapters 16 and 17

Managing time is discussed in greater detail in Peter F. Drucker, *The Effective Executive* (Pan Books, new edition 1979). See also Rosemary Stewart, *Managers and their Jobs* (Macmillan, new edition 1988).

Chapter 18

A useful, practical book on communicating is Barry T. Turner, *Effective Technical Writing and Speaking* (Business Books, 1974). See also C. Northcote Parkinson and Nigel Row, *Communicate: Parkinson's Formula for Business Survival* (Pan Books, 1979).

For a clear book on information management try D. J. Silk, *Planning IT* (Heinemann, 1992)

Chapter 19

On statistics there is D. Croft, *Applied Statistics for Management Studies* (Macdonald & Evans, 1983).

308   *Further Reading*

Chapter 20

One of the latest efforts to find formulae for success is the book *In Search of Excellence* by Thomas J. Peters and Robert H. Waterman (Harper & Row, 1982). But also read the 'sequels': *A Passion for Excellence* by Tom Peters and Nancy Austin (Macmillan, 1985) and *Thriving on Chaos* by Tom Peters (Macmillan, 1988).

Each of the above books contains references and suggestions for further reading if you are really keen to pursue any of the ideas you have been reading about. Also, do not forget the other books which have been mentioned in the text.

To find out about the way the Japanese go about business, read Kenichi Ohmae, *The Mind of the Strategist* (Penguin Books, 1983).

A thought-provoking text which exhorts managers to be revolutionary is *Managing on the Edge* by Richard Pascale (Viking, 1990).

Matters strategic are well-covered by the book *Writers on Strategy and Strategic Management* by J. I. Moore (Penguin, 1992).

Finally, for a different view of tomorrow's world read Charles Handy's book *The Empty Raincoat* (Hutchinson, 1994).

If you want to keep up to date, the best way is to get hold of such journals as *Management Today*, the monthly magazine of the Institute of Management, or the *Harvard Business Review*, the prestigious American journal in which many new ideas and theories first see the light of day.

Index